Bernard Bosanquet, Francis Herbert Bradley

# Knowledge and Reality

Bernard Bosanquet, Francis Herbert Bradley

**Knowledge and Reality**

ISBN/EAN: 9783337217426

Printed in Europe, USA, Canada, Australia, Japan

Cover: Foto ©Thomas Meinert / pixelio.de

More available books at **www.hansebooks.com**

# KNOWLEDGE AND REALITY

# KNOWLEDGE AND REALITY

BY

BERNARD BOSANQUET, M.A., Hon. Ll D. (Glasg.)

LATE FELLOW AND TUTOR OF UNIVERSITY COLLEGE, OXFORD ; AUTHOR OF

*" A History of Aesthetic," " Logic, or the Morphology of Knowledge," "Essays and Addresses," etc., etc.*

LONDON

SWAN SONNENSCHEIN & CO.

PATERNOSTER SQUARE

1892

FIRST EDITION ... .. 1885
RE-ISSUED ... ... ... ... 1892

# PREFACE.

THE present volume consists of a series of logical studies, based for the most part upon ideas propounded in Mr. F. H. Bradley's recent work, "Principles of Logic." I have not attempted an exhaustive criticism of his views—a larger book than this might be devoted to the psychology alone—but have aimed at expounding a few definite aspects and results of his position, by means of free re-statement and illustration.

It may be convenient that I should explain in a few words my conception of the present philosophical situation, so far as it affects my attitude towards Mr. Bradley's speculations. It appears to me that English logic, under the influence of the idealism on which science inevitably rests, has almost outgrown the narrow traditions of its one-sided and, so to speak, pre-scientific schools ; and that there are signs of a philosophical

a 3

movement in this country which may assimilate what is really great in European philosophy, without forfeiting the distinctive merits of English thought. But with this forward tendency in England there coincides in time a philosophical reaction in Germany—a reaction partly determined by those very influences of English speculation, which we hope that the present generation has in some degree outgrown. In the country of Kant, Fichte, and Hegel, such a reaction ·will do much good, and can do little harm. It does not imply that their work is being undone, but only that the plan of the great masters is being handed over, to be carried out piecemeal by the journeymen.

In England, where constructive idealism has never yet had free play, the prospect is very different. It would be a misfortune if sympathy with the German reaction should restore the rule of traditions which we are just beginning to lay aside. Adherents of commonplace empiricism would in such a case simply imagine that their German neighbours had regained a sound mind, and had admitted idealism to be a blunder.

In such a state of the philosophical world Mr. Bradley's work has a twofold significance. In essentials, he belongs to the movement in advance, and is an effective pioneer of that English philosophy which we hope for—a philosophy distinct and national, not from sheer ignorance of foreign thought, but by the characteristic appropriation of the world's intellectual inheritance. But in some external matters, and in some which are more than mere externals, he attaches himself, to an extent which perplexes me, to the writers of the German reaction; who, in spite of their extraordinary good sense, knowledge, and industry, appear to me to be fatally deficient in philosophical thoroughness.

It is my object in the following pages to show how Mr. Bradley's essential and original conceptions might be disengaged from some peculiarities which he apparently shares with reactionary logic. Whether I may succeed in this attempt or not, I shall at least have done what I can to call attention to the leading ideas of a work which deserves to be epoch-making in English philosophy.

BERNARD BOSANQUET.

*April* 9, 1885.

# TABLE OF CONTENTS.

—◄►—

## CHAPTER I.



## CHAPTER II.

## CHAPTER VI.



## CONCLUSION.

# KNOWLEDGE AND REALITY.

## CHAPTER I.

### THE DISTINCTION BETWEEN THE CATEGORICAL AND THE HYPOTHETICAL JUDGMENT.

1. IF we ask for a mark by which we may distinguish judgment from other intellectual acts or states, the first that occurs to us is this ; that judgment, and judgment only, can be in the strict sense true or false. And if a Categorical judgment merely means the thought conveyed in any sentence which can be true or false, then the epithet "categorical" appears to be superfluous, as meaning no more than the Aristotelian term "apophantic" or "enunciative"—a term coextensive with assertion or judgment.

It is by contrast with the *hypothetical* judgment or *conditional* proposition that the term categorical has acquired a distinctive usage unknown to Aristotle, who did not recognize the hypothetical judgment as a species of enunciation. It would be interesting, if space and knowledge permitted, to trace the steps by which logicians became aware that the obvious distinction of form between the simple and the conditional proposition did not indicate an equally obvious distinction of meaning.

The term "simple" suggests that the sentences in question were primarily distinguished as containing respectively one proposition, and more than one. But the unity of the judgment embodied in the conditional proposition—the hypothetical judgment—was not hard to discover, and was insisted on by earlier logicians as by many in this century.

This being so, however, and it being clear that in both classes of judgments, the categorical and the hypothetical, a single direct assertion was made, it became necessary, if the distinction was to be maintained, to look more closely at the nature of this assertion. How questionable the distinction, as commonly conceived, really was, may be seen in the following quotation from so acute a logician as Sir W. Hamilton.[1] "In the proposition, B *is* A, the subject B is unconditionally thought to exist, and it thus constitutes a categorical proposition. But if we think the subject B existing only conditionally, and under this conditional existence enunciate the judgment, we shall have the hypothetical proposition—*If* B *is*, A *is* ; or, in a concrete example, *Rainy weather is wet weather*, is a categorical proposition. *If it rains, it will be wet*, is an hypothetical."

[1] "Lectures," vol. iii. p. 237.

Here, *judging from the instances*, we have a distinction without a difference. "Rainy weather is wet" certainly does not allege that the weather is rainy at the time of speaking ; and if it may be held to affirm that rainy weather exists *in rerum natura*, so perhaps, and to the same degree, does the hypothetical judgment, "If it rains, it is wet."

But apart from his instances, Hamilton's distinction is one not to be disregarded. "*Propositio conditionalis*," as his editor quotes from Weiss in a footnote, "*nihil ponit in esse.*"[1] The Hypothetical judgment expresses the relation of reason and consequent ; the Categorical that of subject and attribute. Krug, whom Hamilton[2] quotes at length, insists so emphatically on the essential difference between the two judgments, that I suspect him of having felt uneasy about this Kantian distinction. He had hit on an instance, however, which in those days would be generally held to fulfil the requirement that the subject should be unconditionally thought to exist, "A righteous God punishes the wicked." But there is no indication that he sees any peculiarity in this judgment relating to the existence of the subject, which should distinguish it from such an affirmation as that "All men are mortal." His distinction is probably right in the case he gives, but the case is not typical. He is comparing not an *abstract* or *universal* categorical judgment with a hypothetical, but a *singular* with a hypothetical

[1] "Lectures," vol. iii. p. 239.   [2] Ibid.

judgment made in appearance about the same subject. In becoming hypothetical the singular subject undergoes a change, becomes a type, a general idea; but in the so-called *universal* categorical, the subject is a general idea already.   In short, Krug, and Hamilton who relies on him, did not see the real problem.   They maintained that a Hypothetical judgment could not be converted into a Categorical ; it did not occur to them that a large class of Categorical judgments, namely, those with abstract subjects, might perhaps be converted into Hypotheticals.

We will keep clear for the present of peculiar instances, and consider merely the Universal affirmative judgments of ordinary Logic.   And it must then appear, as recent logicians have contended with overwhelming insistence, that these judgments must elect either to refer to known individual cases (which their natural significance, depending on intension, does not permit them genuinely to do), or to remain abstract, and without reference to particular instances, and so be classed as Hypothetical, and translated into propositions beginning with "if" and going on with " then."

These considerations have been variously applied by logicians.   My present purpose is to discuss the boundary between Categorical and Hypothetical judgments as recently laid down by Mr. Bradley, in his important work, " Principles of Logic."

2. The Universal judgment, if *bonâ fide* universal,

and in no sense singular or collective, cannot, so Mr. Bradley maintains, be Categorical. A Categorical judgment affirms the existence of its elements, and enunciates some matters, conveyed by an idea, as true directly of Reality. But a universal or abstract judgment does not affirm the existence of its elements, and may be true though none of them exist or are even possible in Reality. It does not, therefore, allege its elements as such to be true of Reality, which is the same as to affirm that they are real. Reality is indeed, as Mr. Bradley has excellently explained, always the *ultimate* subject in judgment. But in the singular judgment, or in the so-called collective, which is only, it is said, a summation of singulars, the meaning or content which is affirmed is referred directly to some aspect of reality—of that continuous existence and activity which we have present to us at every moment in perception : whereas in the Hypothetical or abstract judgment this seems impossible, for such a reference would affirm the actual existence of the elements spoken about in the judgment, and the judgment would in that case become false if—in one sense or another—they did not exist. Now the existence or non-existence in reality of its ideal content does not affect the truth of an abstract judgment.

The result drawn from these considerations is that universal judgments do not refer directly to reality, but only illustrate some quality of what actually exists—a quality that underlies and justifies the supposal whose consequence the hypothetical judgment affirms. "If you asked him he would refuse" does not *state*, it is contended, a real and actual fact about the man, but merely *illustrates* or reveals a quality in him, *e.g.* the quality that he is churlish. And all judgments whose subjects are not individual realities are affirmed to be reducible to this type.

Before passing on, it is important to make as clear as we can the exact limits of this distinction, to which I shall have to recur.

Individual judgments, as I gather from Mr. Bradley's account of them, are taken by him to be of three main classes.[1] There are, (i.) Judgments which merely analyze what is given in present perception. In these the subject is always the whole or some part of what is present to our perception. These judgments Mr. Bradley calls analytic judgments of sense, a title which I presume that he adopts from Sigwart. Instances are such as, "It is cold," "I have a toothache," "That bough is broken." (ii.) Judgments which go beyond present perception, stating either a fact of space or time, or some quality of what is present, which is not given in perception. Such judgments are, "It rained yesterday," "This road goes to London." (iii.) Judgments which affirm about a subject which is not an event. Such are judgments dealing with the history of man or a nation, that is of an individual related to some given period of time, or

---

[1] "Principles of Logic," p. 48, *cf.* p. 79 and p. 107.

again judgments about such subjects as the Universe, God, the self, which are related to no time in particular.[1]

In all these singular judgments, and in these only, "truth expresses fact, there is here no mere adjective and no hypothesis." The antithesis between Categorical and Hypothetical judgment is thus identified with that between Singular and Universal, or between Individual and Abstract Judgments.

3. The view thus propounded is of grave importance in the theory of knowledge. A change of the name by which a *whole* region of phenomena is designated is seldom a serious matter. To say that all judgments are hypothetical, or again, that all judgments are categorical—and, in different senses, Mr. Bradley upholds both these theses—may indicate an advance in the analysis of judgments as such, but need involve no change of principle affecting their *relative* values. It is thus that a consistent materialist and a thorough idealist hold positions which are distinguishable only in name. But to leave a category standing, and yet to transfer the greater part of its contents to some other place in a system, is a disturbance of the *status quo* that must always demand the most careful scrutiny.

The distinction before us has, I think, paradoxical results. This is no reason for condemning it, but a good reason for considering exactly where it leads us. We have seen that a judgment whose subject is a

---

[1] *Cf.* "Principles of Logic," p. 79.

person, or a nation, and also a judgment whose subject is not in time, as God, the universe, or the soul, counts under the distinction as an individual judgment. Disregarding for the moment the latter sub-class, we may compare judgments whose subjects are limited in time with some which would be, I presume, classed as abstract and hypothetical. It seems that an identity which is related only to a portion of the temporal or spatial series is the subject of a singular or individual judgment; while one which we take as an essential factor in the totality which we are always building up out of these series, one, therefore, of which we indicate no particular limitation to any portion of them, forfeits thereby its claim to be fact, ceases to be a subject of categorical judgment, and becomes only a more or less arbitrary illustration of a latent quality of the real. The names of nations indicate subjects of categorical judgment; the names of permanent races of men, or of their characteristic states, "Aryan," "Mongolian," "savages," "civilized men," are abstract and adjectival, in as far as permanent, but I presume should rank as singular and individual, if considered with reference to their limitations as identities extending over a portion only of the history of our globe. Or again, if we turn to the second sub-class, "Phenomena" [1] (as such) are affirmed

---

[1] I am aware that the subject whose real existence is affirmed is not necessarily taken to be the grammatical subject. But (i.) it is natural to suppose that an author's own instances are couched in a form which exactly represents the underlying judgment, and (ii.) judgments analogous

to exist, when, by a judgment, we pronounce upon their nature; I really do not know whether space and time have the same good fortune, of which they appear to me no less worthy. It is clear, I think, that the majority of judgments which compose the classificatory sciences of organic life, might claim to be categorical, for no species endure for ever. And if we appeal to usage, I do not doubt that when I say, " The *Primula Scotica* is a survival of a very cold period," I am understood to assert its existence, not indeed now in the mere moment of my speaking, but in the age or epoch to which the content of my judgment necessarily refers. But such an affirmation as " Gold is an element," supposing that we take the sixty-four elements to be permanent features of our universe, will become, I suppose, abstract and hypothetical, merely because the subject's existence is not affirmed *as specially related to any time in particular.* Now this is the very reason for which a judgment, *e.g.* about the Universe, is pronounced to be categorical.[1]

I will discuss two objections which seem to me likely to be made against the above comparisons. It may be said that I confuse an organic individual unity with a mere community of attributes, and that I propose

in type might be expected to be capable of analogous transformations, revealing ultimate subjects of the same class.

[1] " Principles of Logic," p. 79. It may be said, and ought in strictness to be said, that the distinction I have drawn is idle, for no element or characteristic of the sensible world can thus belong to all time alike ; our globe is related to some limited time. But if so, then *à fortiori* all the judgments in dispute must be categorical.

to accept completeness *in* the infinite series, which is unattainable, as the equivalent of a non-phenomenal character, the character of an object which does not enter into that sensible series. In fact, the two objections resolve themselves into one, which is this; that I take an abstract identity distributed through space and time, whether partially or impartially, for a true concrete individual complete in itself.

I shall not be sorry if any error of mine leads to an elucidation of this point. A species, my critic might I suppose continue, is not an identity in the same sense as a nation. The actual relations between its members, as parts of a whole, are wanting. It is not, therefore, one in acting and suffering as a nation is, and cannot be treated as concrete and singular. It remains abstract whether related to a portion of the series of time, or, what we can never really know and must rather assume to be false, impartially related to the series in its whole extent.

To rebut this objection, which is not without force, I can only say that I do not know where to draw the line. No nation has its individuality completely realized ; it is not easy to say what is a nation and what is merely a nationality or a race ; and from race to species, in the logical sense of distinct and relatively permanent type, is no great step. Every species has, of course, in many respects, an absolute identity, of which predication may be made as of an individual. We are speaking, indeed, it may be said, of the distinction between a whole in reality and a whole for knowledge.  But is Mr. Bradley, with his fundamental view that fact is *for us* an ideal construction, prepared to treat this as an ultimate and self-explaining demarcation ?  One might, perhaps, distinguish between judgments bearing on the history of a species as such, and judgments which affirm about indefinite individuals through the specific attributes. But this distinction would be evanescent, though in spirit it would, I incline to think, solve the crux before us.  I might compare such a judgment as " The British Constitution is the growth of eight hundred years " with " This genus (*Ursus cultridens*) is one of considerable antiquity in the tertiary formations of Europe " (Lyell). I think that the latter is concrete and individual if the former is so.  The zoological characters, again, of such a genus are predicable of the several individuals in a sense in which the above fact is not, for it is only the genus, and not *all* the individuals, that reaches back to the *greatest* antiquity.  But I suppose the genus as a whole is also qualified by its zoological character, so that the demarcation could not be absolute.  It might not be true to say " The genus *Ursus cultridens* as a whole has very broad teeth," but we could hardly be prevented, even if it were reckoned an equivocation, from saying " The genus *Ursus cultridens* is characterized by the fact that its members have," etc.

Then to take what is really the same objection in its

deeper and ultimate form.  "Gold," it will be said, "is in the first place not an individual even if it were limited in the time during which it exists.  But in the second place, it cannot be taken as a permanent and absolute feature of the Universe, for that presupposes the completion of the infinite series of its appearances in space and time, which is absurd."  I ought not, that is, to say that gold is "not related to any time in particular," because there is no time to which it may not be related, or because it is related impartially to all times.  For we can never have this relation to all time completed for our knowledge;  and therefore the phrase in question, when applied to God or to the soul, means something quite different from this, something which *can* be known, because not dependent on the impossible completion of a series ; it means that in their nature these eternal subjects are not called upon to enter into the sensible series at all.

I may observe in considering this, the ultimate form of the objection, first, that in speaking of the soul as a non-phenomenal subject, Mr. Bradley adds the reservation, " If we take the soul to be eternal."  This expression seems to me to point to infinite duration, not to something different in kind ; if so, I think it is a mistake.

And secondly, I may observe that though reality appears to us in the series of phenomena, I did not think we were to look for it as completed in that series. " But *you are* looking for it there."  This is a familiar and difficult type of puzzle. I say that I am not looking for it there, because I think that in looking for it rightly, in the organic relations of knowledge, we escape from the series. My supposed critic says, that I am looking for it there, because he identifies with the series what I allege to be outside the series. Each of us accuses the other of *the same* mistake.

I am not concerned at present to make out a view, but only to display a *primâ facie* paradox in the results of Mr. Bradley's distinction between the categorical or individual and the hypothetical or abstract judgment. I will now embody the paradox in instances.

*a.* First, I should like to compare with Mr. Bradley's "Synthetic Judgments," and with those individual judgments which deal with the history of a man or a nation, some judgments drawn from the classificatory or anthropological sciences, whose subjects are obviously and definitely taken as limited in time.

As admitted individual judgments, then, I take (*a*) "Synthetic," "It rained yesterday"; "This road leads to London"; "To-morrow there will be full moon"; and (*b*) I take also as Individual judgments, but of the third class and first sub-class (history of man or nation), "Athens was extinct as a political power after the fourth century B.C."; "The Hellenic colonies were founded chiefly in the three centuries preceding 500 B.C."; "The Hellenic race approached without attaining a complete national unity."

Compare with the first set (*a*), "Bronze and not iron was generally in use when Hesiod wrote"; "The mounds of shells, etc., in Massachusetts, were left by the North American Indians"; "Next century the Danish shell-mounds will be still further from the sea."

It will be said, "Why, these are collective judgments, *i.e.* collections of singular judgments." I persist that they are *not*, and that to force them into this category depends on an unnatural assumption. The subjects are thought *generally*, through abstract characteristics, and are not individually known. Nevertheless, they are fact. They are *universal fact*, and to say this is impossible seems to me a flat denial of the commonest experience. Now for the second set (*b*): "Greek art was worthless after the fourth century B.C."; "The Aryan race originated in Europe"; "During the stone age of North Europe the edible oyster flourished in the Baltic"; "The oyster is now dependent on artificial cultivation"; "The Scotch Primula is the same plant that grows in the Engadine, and is sporadic in Britain, having retired into the hills with the change of climate"; "The fuchsia belongs to the same natural order as the common willow-herb"; "Organic life is of unknown antiquity, but for physical reasons may be pronounced far from coeval with the earth."

I presume, to speak quite candidly, that we pass into abstraction and hypothesis in these judgments where we begin to speak *of* individuals *through* the specific attributes, and not of the *bonâ fide* history of the species or genus as a whole. But I absolutely do not know whether Mr. Bradley would take the last judgment, " Organic life," etc., to be categorical (*qua* individual) or not. Its subject is limited in time, and causally and essentially related to one part of the temporal series more than to another.

*b.* I pass to the second sub-class of individual judgments belonging to Mr. Bradley's third type. His instances are, " God is a spirit " ; " The soul is a substance " ; " The self is real " ; " Phenomena are nothing beyond the appearance of spirit to spirit." Judgments about the soul are only in point, Mr. Bradley warns us, if we take the soul to be eternal.

Compare with these—" Gold is an element " ; " Gases have a spectrum consisting of lines " ; " Heat is a mode of motion." These judgments seem to be impartially related to the time series ; but of course our elements at least *may* not be coeval with the universe. Still, *in* and *for* our *knowledge*, the subjects are not related to any time in particular. Compare further, " Space is externality in co-existence " ; " Time is externality in succession " ; " The triangle has its angles equal to two right angles " ; " Phenomena are essentially of a nature which demands causal explanation." These judgments appear impartially essential to our conception of reality.

If the judgments mentioned under *a* pass for categorical it will be impossible to treat these as hypothetical merely because they have a more impartial relation to time. They clearly affirm the existence of their subjects as aspects of reality, though not necessarily at the time of predication. No judgment does affirm this, except *per accidens.* The difficulty which arises from a strict interpretation of the hypothetical form of sentence will be dealt with lower down. If this second set, *b*, are Categorical, I think we must admit the individual *of knowledge* as an individual for the purpose of the distinction between hypothetical and categorical judgments. But if so, the whole point of the new demarcation is blunted. I shall attempt, at the end of this chapter, to resolve the distinction into a matter of degree.

4. I proceed to give my reasons for thinking that Mr. Bradley's general views incline him to restrict the province of actual fact, and therefore of the categorical judgment, unduly, to the series of sensible phenomena. It is true that he is also disposed to speak of qualities and facts which are altogether latent and non-phenomenal. We have thus two extremes : a sensible but fugitive series, and a non-phenomenal but permanent unknown. But our knowledge of the nature, and I presume of the distribution,[1] of the things around us, is to

---

[1] Distribution would in some cases be fact, and in some not. " There is gold in California " would be fact, California being the real subject. But distribution, as science advances, tends to become *necessary*, its causes being ascertained, and thus it ceases to be fact. " Maize will only grow south of the 52nd parallel."

him, in the language of English philosophy, "phenomenal of the unknown."

Mr. Bradley believes, indeed, that everything, whether in space or in time, which we know without at the moment perceiving, is known to us solely as an ideal construction based on inference. This doctrine naturally leads up to some form of Monism, nor do I deny that a Monistic conception might prove to be the distant goal of his enquiries. But the most striking feature of these discussions is—I will not venture to say a confessed dualism, but—an angry scorn of a "cheap and easy Monism." It was well done, in my judgment, to invest Perception with the pre-eminent importance of being the one point in which we have direct contact with reality, and to give this contact with reality the decisive position in the activity of judgment. It is one thing, however, to recognize the actual differences of elements in a whole; another to establish two centres for the world of reality. You cannot at once treat reality as ideal construction, and demand from it characteristics approaching to those of presence in the sensible series.

It is my belief that dualistic feeling, aroused by reaction against the fatal facility of Monistic views, causes Mr. Bradley to adopt the attitude which I have thus described, and that this is the real secret of the distinction which casts all abstract knowledge into the class of the hypothetical judgment *as contrasted with the categorical.* This contrast is the essential point, for the

analysis which shows that a Universal affirmative judgment can always be treated as a Hypothetical, is in my
opinion irrefragable.

I propose to support the above criticism by adducing
evidence of Mr. Bradley's anti-monistic *attitude*, I would
almost say *bias*, and then to apply the criticism to the
case of the categorical judgment.

I find in " Principles of Logic " several antitheses,
some affecting mere matters of feeling and emphasis,
some concerning important logical conceptions, which
I cannot reconcile with a view of reality as " for us an
ideal construction." [1]

Scientific truth, for instance, is "mutilation," "a garbled
extract," "not the facts."   These expressions are mainly
ironical, as imputed to popular realism.   But I do not
think that they are wholly so.   The author has true and
just sympathy for the claims of feeling as contrasted
with intellect, or at least not identical with intellect, and
therefore cherishes a deep discontent with any effort to
resolve reality into an intellectual movement.   Only a
rich man may wear a bad coat, and only a philosopher
of Mr. Bradley's force could escape suspicions of a crude
dualistic realism when he writes as follows :— [2]

[1] p. 74.  " Events past and future, and all things not perceived, exist *for
us* only as ideal constructions connected, by an inference through identity
of quality, with the real that appears in perception."   This is a statement
which I take to express what all modern thinkers believe.   An antithesis,
however, to which I take exception lurks in the words, " all things not
perceived."   All perception draws largely on things past and remote.

[2] " Principles of Logic," p. 533.  This extract is fair as illustrating the

" It may come from a failure in my metaphysics, or from a weakness of the flesh that continues to blind me, but the notion that existence could be the same as understanding strikes as cold and ghost-like as the dreariest materialism. That the glory of this world in the end is appearance, leaves the world more glorious, if we feel it is a show of some fuller splendour; but the sensuous curtain is a deception and a cheat if it hides some colourless movement of atoms, some spectral woof of impalpable abstractions, or unearthly ballet of bloodless categories. Though dragged to such conclusions, we cannot embrace them. Our principles may be true, but they are not reality. They no more *make* that whole which commands our devotion than some shredded dissection of human tatters *is* that warm and breathing beauty of flesh which our hearts found delightful."

The dream of the intellectual world as a land of shadows, now below and now above, now more obscure and now more brilliant than reality, a dream which the unwisdom of ages has ascribed to Plato, seems never to lose its maleficent spell. There have been some who have hoped that the labour of centuries had in part overcome this baleful enchantment, and attained the lesson that reality alike for feeling and for intellect is

point which I am immediately discussing, that of unjustifiable antitheses. It is not fair as representing the author's entire position, to which the antitheses in question are not essential. I may observe in reference to his entire position that the distinction between reality and the discursive movement of the intellect appears to me to be for us a distinction *within the intellectual world.*

the world in which we live ; a world which is sustained
and transformed by the patient labour of the intellect
and will, but can only be maimed and degraded by the
impatience which splits it into a shadow on the one
hand, and on the other hand a substance more shadowy
still.    Surely the more glorious reality is that which
our vision and our will can make of the world in which
we are ; and the certain frustration of all such achievement is to relax the toilsome grasp which holds real and
ideal in one.    I direct these observations rather against
my own probable misunderstanding of Mr. Bradley than
against any view which I can believe him actually to
hold.    But I seem to trace in him a similar attitude on
purely logical questions.

Cause,[1] for instance, is not the sum of conditions, because to say that it is so is to say that a reality is a sum
of ideas.    (I do not defend the word " sum," but that is
not now in question.)    Now, on looking at the excellent
account of Causation near the close of the treatise, we
find that Cause is after all ideal ; given in reality no
doubt, but abstracted, isolated, and known as the
antecedent of a hypothetical judgment.    A condition
may be more ideal, as being more abstract ; but if cause
is real in the absence of effect (and often, if not always,
it is impossible for them to coexist in time), then a
condition may surely be real in the absence of the
elements which make up the totality known as cause.

---

[1] " Principles of Logic," p. 195.

The idea of this antithesis is, I suppose, that cause exists all at once in present perception, and condition does not, being completed by a relation to what is at the moment non-existent. But reality is continuous, and the atomic "now" and "here" always need and obtain completion from the non-existent, whether they are taken as cause or as condition.

Here is another case. To justify the inference by abstraction which lies at the root of the method of Difference (a method which as given Mr. Bradley takes to be fallacious) we need, if I read Mr. Bradley right, not merely ideal but actual isolation of the suspected cause or condition. But there is no such thing as actual isolation. All isolation is ideal, and consists of combinations which are believed to be neutral as regards the matter in hand. You can only escape from A B C by substituting A D E ; or if A were so concrete that you could appear to treat it independently, then the first step of analytic suspicion would be to break up the concrete A into a further A B C, and the isolation of A would again become in form, as it had been all along in fact, merely ideal. To contrast actual and ideal isolation is to forget that the value of perception is derived from knowledge.

Again, Mr. Bradley accepts Sigwart's position, that there must be unproved premises of proof. " All mediate certainty must stand in the end on immediate knowledge ; the ultimate premises of proof cannot be proved."

I shall examine this conception more fully at a later part of the present volume (see conclusion). Here I have only to say that it appears to demand a basis of fact at once definite and given. Such a basis cannot, indeed, be identical with Mr. Bradley's fact of sense, or even fact got by simple perception ;[1] if that is, as it appears to be, opposed to a judgment. But still less can it be identical with a fact which is an ideal construction. Whatever this basis of fact may mean, it can only be taken as immediate in virtue of a rigid dualism.

The distinction which Mr. Bradley adopts, I believe, from Sigwart, between analytic and synthetic judgments of sense, bears witness to the same intellectual attitude. The analytic judgment of sense is called so from keeping within the limits of perception, which it simply analyses, or resolves into parts. But no judgment ever kept within " present perception," unless present perception is taken as including all it owes to the past and the remote.

So, too, when Mr. Bradley distinguishes a collective from a true abstract judgment, he appears to treat a collection of *actual* cases [2] as a collection of cases existing at the time to which the judgment refers. Now, I do not mean to cut the knot of this question by simply affirming the actual existence of the past ; but there is no doubt on the other hand, and Mr. Bradley knows it well, that you cannot get down to an

---

[1] " Principles of Logic," p. 365.　　[2] " Principles of Logic," p. 82.

atomic reality in time by whittling the present thinner and thinner; and, as a matter of fact, no judgment, not even the purest collective or aggregation of singulars which language can embody, is thus limited, unless a certain time-relation is of the essence of the judgment. Present perception is a kind of limit, though less definite than it seems; and a set of known individual cases has a limit; but there is no tendency even in a merely plural or collective judgment, to affirm that its cases exist all at one time. "The two first kings of England after the Conquest were called William," is a judgment about individuals as truly as is "The present members of the House of Lords will outlive it"; though there was never a time at which both the kings were "existing" cases. Existing may indeed mean existing at the time in which the predicated content was true of the subject, in which case the term existing adds nothing to the phrase "individual cases." But as Mr. Bradley more than once raises the question whether a judgment becomes false if made when its subject is non-existent, I am inclined to believe that he considers all judgments which affirm existence to assert more especially existence *at the time of predication*, at least when the predication is in the present tense. It appears to me, however, that no judgment affirms the existence of its content *at the time of predication*, except *per accidens* through the predication of or about a content essentially bearing reference to present time, as in the above judgment, "The present members," etc. The affirmation of existence in the synthetic judgment of sense, for instance, is as often as not that of past existence. Here also, then, as it seems to me, Mr. Bradley gives an unreal pre-eminence to present time, *qua* present in the sensible series.

And even the conception of a present, or rather of a presentation, which does not exclude lapse of time, [1] though preferable to the " atomic now," appears to me to share the theoretical tendency which I deprecate. True, it dispels the fiction of a reality confined to the now and here, which must reduce itself under examination to a point without parts or magnitude. But it effects this at the cost of breaking the continuity between present and past, and forgetting that, though the existence of the past for us depends on the present, yet the interpretation of the present depends on the past. If we are in earnest with the doctrine of ideal construction, it is superfluous to assign duration to the present; while, by maintaining the duration of the present, we give rise to the suspicion that we should not be sorry to select a section of the series, and say, " This is given, and is the foundation ; it is not artificial, and is not construction."

One word more, before I return to the main subject of this chapter. It is plain that explicit Inference is distinguishable from direct Judgment ; from such a

---

[1] " Principles of Logic," pp. 50–53 ; *cf.* Lotze, " Metaphysik," sect. 150.

judgment, for instance, as that which expresses an un-ambiguous perception. It is less plain that Inference such as is involved in comparison, abstraction, or recognition, when the attributes on which it is founded are not brought into full light, or stated in definite shape, does not cover the whole region of judgment. When, therefore, I am told of [1] "arbitrary synthesis of suggestion with reality," of "mere judgment," founded *e.g.* on prominent sensuous suggestion, or on external testimony, I am obliged to doubt whether what we are discussing corresponds to actual fact. I will illustrate by the simple case of affirmation based on testimony. So far as I understand my own experience, it is not possible simply to re-think as true an allegation furnished *ab extra*. The endorsement by which one's own judgment ratifies it is not formal or empty ; it arises either out of a coherence in the alleged content with the existing content of our own world of reality, or in some external mark of credibility, also appealing to our prior knowledge, which applies not perhaps specifically to the content in question, but generally to the conditions under which it is brought before us. No judgment can be nearer to passive reception than that by which we re-affirm the death of a friend which we have learnt from the column of deaths in the *Times* newspaper. Yet even here we judge upon grounds. Besides the specific probabilities which are rarely absent in any

---

[1] " Principles of Logic," pp. 405, 406.

case that interests us, we have a definite ground for our confidence in these notices, viz. that they are not "news," but are specially inserted by those most intimately concerned. If we find similar intelligence in a "paragraph," we scrutinize its marks of authenticity with severity. Here again, then, in the mention of a "mere judgment," I find a value attached to the *given* which seems to me incompatible with an omnipresent activity of construction.

5. I now return to the question of the demarcation between the Categorical and the abstract or Hypothetical judgment. Mr. Bradley's favourite test of Categorical character seems to be the affirmation or non-affirmation by a judgment of the existence of its content. I have already pointed out that, if only for the sake of Mr. Bradley's synthetic judgments of sense, such as "It rained yesterday," the affirmation of existence must refer to the time *in* the predication, as essentially involved in the content, not to the time *of* the predication, *i.e.* the time at which the predication is made. Now, in a truly universal judgment there is not *in* the predication a reference to any particular time more than another, because the content is or claims to be essentially unaffected by time. And therefore, when, taking an accidental "now" in the time-series, the time of predication, we ask, "Does the judgment affirm the existence of its content *now?*" the answer is of course in the negative, and might conceivably be negative even in the

most categorical class of judgments which Mr. Bradley instances as categorical because individual. Suppose, as has been held, that the soul has intervals of non-existence;[1] then a judgment about the soul may be made without affirming the existence of its subject at the moment *of* predication. At all events, I can see no theoretical objection to this, unless continuity is held essential to Identity, and I think Mr. Bradley does not hold it to be so.[2] I have hinted above, that his condition, "If the soul is eternal," is *suspect* to me. I fear it may mean that, in order to be a subject of categorical judgment, the soul must exist at every moment so as to be existing in every present of predication.

*A fortiori*, then, when tried by this test, the hypothetical and disjunctive judgments fail to be categorical. The hypothetical or abstract judgment can no doubt be true though its content is non-existent at the time of predication. The disjunctive judgment affirms the existence of its subject, or of *a* subject in which its predication is realized; but the disjunctive predication itself is incapable of corresponding to fact. You cannot have "either—or" given as a fact. The true content, in respect of which the predication is categorical, is, in disjunctives and hypotheticals alike, a certain quality predicated absolutely of an existent subject. *This* subject must be existent, I take it, in the case of the hypothetical as well as in that of the disjunctive, and

---

[1] Lotze, "Metaphysik," sect. 307.    [2] "Principles of Logic," p. 269.

the two are therefore more on all-fours than Mr. Bradley makes plain. Clearly, too, a disjunctive judgment is also universal, and there is nothing to prevent it from being explicitly hypothetical. "Whatever is B, is either C or D."

Now, I do not see that the nature of reality demands that a content which is real should be existent in *every* present, or should be exempt from modification in time or in space. It seems to me that in the species of a genus we have an actual coexistent "either—or," and in a present which has duration (or is continuous with the past), we have a real presentation of a successive "either—or." It may be answered, "No, you must abide by one aspect; either you include in your reality a field of coexistence and an extended section of succession—and then you have *both* alternatives given as real—or you reduce reality to a point, and then you have only one."[1]

Now, it must be understood from the very beginning that time as a *pure* series, or extension as, so to speak, a *pure* coexistent series, cannot be represented in judgment, and whether as such they could exist is at least a doubtful question. In judging, it is impossible to avoid using the elements of continuity in both these series. "Then within our reality we shall have *both* alternatives, and *not* 'either—or.'" I must persist in denying this conclusion. The actual series reveals to us identities in

[1] *Cf.* Sigwart, "Logik," p. 253.

difference of various kinds, bearing various relations to their differences. I cannot see why in characterizing the reality we should be bound to omit an essential distinction in the relation of its elements. An identity in succession *is* a disjunction. The reciprocal exclusion of the successive terms is what tells us of the identity beneath them ; and *if* a succession can be real, a disjunction can correspond to fact. I am even inclined to surrender an opinion which I have held about the perplexity arising from the substitution of a universal for an individual as the subject of a disjunction. "This triangle," "a triangle," "the triangle," "every triangle," all introduce the same statement. It is not true that "the triangle can be both equilateral and scalene." We are speaking of a single identical content in relation to its modifications, not of different individual or particular subjects. You cannot make a universal judgment about a number of different subjects taken as different. The only difficulty is with "all triangles," which might mean that all triangles are scalene, or again all triangles are isosceles, or all equilateral, though we do not know which is true. This only brings out a character inherent also in the other form of expression ; the fact that they may stand, when thus abstractly stated, for a disjunction of ignorance, in which *an entire species is the subject to disjoined genera.* In this disjunction you guess that a species must be determined as belonging to one of two or more genera, but you cannot, I think, be really sure of this, for in order to be sure you want the actual determination, and with the actual determination the disjunction is destroyed. The disjunction of doubt is a spurious disjunction, and should never be expressed in strict categorical form, but always as problematic.

I maintain, then, that every judgment which predicates a quality crystallizes into an attribute, in doing so, an identity which in its manifestation for us is discontinuous, and also includes differences which are at least liable to exclude each other. To say that predication which is not falsified in case of discontinuity and disjunction cannot embody reality, and must actually be reduced to the predication of permanent though latent qualities, is a step that demands a good deal of justification.

The result of this assumption is the paradox which has been pointed out above. Judgments whose subjects have a more or less limited existence in time, are made categorical by this limitation, although *within* the epoch to which they belong discontinuity is admissible in their existence without falsifying the judgments that are made concerning them. Judgments just the same in every other respect, but not essentially limited to one part of the temporal process, lose their character of fact by the elimination of time from their content. And yet the non-existence of their elements which they permit without becoming false, is merely analogous to the non-existence which interrupts every discontinuous phenomenon, and which is not supposed to falsify the judgment that affirms its existence. Non-existence such as befalls a phenomenon outside the epoch to which it is related, if true of it within that epoch, *would* make a judgment dealing with it false. But of course it is not easy to find an analogy for *such* non-existence in the case of non-temporal judgments, which speak of no epoch in particular. We may find it, however, in judgments whose subjects are wholly non-existent ; non-existent, that is, in the sphere of being in which the predication requires them to move and act. "Material spheres of which the earth is the centre carry the heavenly bodies." "Disembodied spirits love to rap on tables." "Forces acting at a distance connect all matter." "A combination of light and darkness is the cause of colour." If we take the subjects of all these judgments as exploded fictions (I purposely employ some which are doubtful to give more reality to the illustration), then their non-existence, *i.e.* their existence merely as fictions, falsifies these judgments, and therefore, if the judgments are true, the subjects exist. Take, again, "Gravity is the chief attribute of matter." "The ether is the vehicle of luminous undulations." "Energy is the power of doing work." "The perihelion of comets is their period of greatest velocity." These judgments would all be falsified by the absolute non-existence of their subjects, although the last, in which the subject is discontinuous in its nature, is not falsified by there happening to be no comet in perihelion when it is made. Indeed no judgment, as we have seen, affirms primarily about the time of predication, unless by means of its content. The question is, as we shall see, when or how far *the predication requires the subject to exist.*

I think, then, that judgments of the above type, though abstract and therefore hypothetical, are judgments about reality and representing fact, and that, in the only sense in which any judgments need do so, they affirm the existence of their content—its existence as an aspect of reality, whose place and significance is in each case analyzed in the judgment.

I need not enlarge upon disjunctions, which in my opinion rank precisely with other universal judgments, every predication of an attribute being resolvable into the predication of the forms taken by that attribute under varying conditions.

How do we stand now? We have, claiming to be categorical, first, judgments whose contents have an existence essentially limited in time, and therefore necessarily falsified by the non-existence of those contents for the time to which they were related, in as far as their relation demands their existence. And in strictness it is hardly possible to say of any features of the sensible universe that they are not of this class. Who can assure us of the eternity of gravity?

Secondly, judgments whose contents have no essential

limitation to one part of the temporal series, and are therefore treated as existing in no special relation to any time in particular. We can hardly deny that there are judgments of this kind, even if we relegate the present laws of matter to the last-named category.

I do not think that the claim of these judgments can be set aside. Neither usage nor analysis appear to me to support such a course. Partial and abstract of course they are, and hypothetical, therefore, in the sense in which every judgment short of the whole truth is hypothetical. Still I cannot see my way to making a break between them and individual judgments, and, though not to be in time is different from being for all time, yet considering the nature which reality has for us as a construction which more and more emancipates us from space and time, I cannot but think that we must regard the subjects of these judgments as individual aspects of reality, and, as I have said, I do not know where Mr. Bradley himself would draw the line between his individual judgments and mere abstract ones.

I will restate my conclusions thus far.

i. A judgment, in order to represent fact, need not be true within an indivisible " now " or " here "; and in reality no judgment can be made under such a restriction. There is, therefore, nothing in the nature of fact to prevent its being embodied in hypothetical or disjunctive judgments, merely because their affirmation is not confined to a single point of time.

D

ii. Abstract universal judgments whose subjects are essentially limited in time, affirm the existence of these subjects within the region of time to which they are limited.   These are on all-fours with judgments about a man or a nation.

iii. Abstract universal judgments whose subjects are not for us essentially limited in time, nevertheless may affirm the existence of their subjects as far as required by the predicated content.   It is a paradox to say that simply because not limited to any portion of the series which manifests reality they are therefore not true of reality as a whole.

6. Of what use are such considerations as the above in face of Mr. Bradley's direct account of judgment based on supposal,[1] which is calculated to sweep away all distinctions within the region of abstract judgment?   His doctrine comes to this : Every abstract or universal judgment is hypothetical, in the sense that the elements of the judgment are not asserted to exist *at all.*   We may sometimes take their existence as implied ; but this is a mere fancy of our own, arising partly from the customary application of the same adjectives which we combine in such judgments to something existing, partly from our bad habit of beginning the judgment with "all," which leads us to waver between the collective and the true universal affirmation. But when we say "all" we mean "any," "whatever,"

---

[1] See especially " Principles of Logic," pp. 47 and 85.

" whenever," and these involve " if." The abstract judgment is thus hypothetical. Now a hypothetical judgment deals with a mere supposal (the positive side of *nihil ponit in esse ;* see sec. 1). The nature of supposal is illustrated by comparison with experiment, a comparison which I shall discuss in a later chapter.[1] An experiment consists, so I understand Mr. Bradley's comparison, in bringing some realities into contact for the purpose of observing what happens in consequence. A supposal or "ideal experiment" is the same process conducted in the mind. Indeed, I incline to object to the comparison on the ground that the distinction is doubtful. Manipulation of the external world is not of the essence of experiment, which simply consists in selection and the purpose to observe, usually implying and resulting in precise knowledge of conditions. However, for our present purpose the comparison holds good, depending simply on the fact that the selection of a content to observe commits us to nothing beyond the intention to observe it ; and therefore is, apart from unessential concomitants, free or arbitrary. It does not matter for this purpose whether the process is perceptive as in actual experiment, or reflective as in a judgment which is made on the basis of a supposal. We have here an intrusion of *choice*, which in science is chance, into the region of intelligible necessity, which ought only to be vitalized by a general *will to know*, not

---

[1] See chap. vi.

dominated by accidental interests. The beginnings of science are much at the mercy of chance; that is why they move so slowly. The guide of research is the body of existing knowledge, and it is this that endows the will to observe, which in ignorance must be the servant of caprice, with aims properly subordinated to the discovery of truth. I do not mean, therefore, that an experiment which we "choose" to make cannot be chosen for good scientific reasons, but I mean that it is none the less an experiment if our guide in making it is mere capricious curiosity. Thus the differentia of supposal which it shares with experiment as such, is the replacement of intellectual by arbitrary motive. This consideration should be borne in mind when we are asked to class all our scientific knowledge among judgments that deal with supposal.

In discussing the connection of supposal with the scientific judgment, I must begin with an admission which *formally* gives up the game. Supposal as such excludes the affirmation of what is supposed, in the sense that an act which is supposal is not, *qua* supposal, also affirmation. And the meaning of every abstract universal judgment can, according to usage, with more or less straining, be represented, as Mr. Bradley contends, by a proposition which says, "Given this, you will *then* have that," or "*If* A, *then* B."

7. I now proceed to palliate this admission; and shall end the present chapter by suggesting a compromise.

The question is, how far "truth can state fact." I am aware that all truths are incomplete, and that not only as abstract, but also as *wrongly* abstract, *i.e.* as charged with positive errors of connection, they are in varying degrees *false.* The only question between me and Mr. Bradley is whether our scientific principles are to be taken as explicit analyses of aspects of reality, or as mere hints and illustrations of latent qualities, whose real nature is, as I understand him, inaccessible to us.

i. I begin by calling to mind what I have already insisted on, that nothing in the nature of fact or reality is incompatible with their being embodied in the hypothetical or disjunctive form. Mr. Bradley evidently leans to thinking, that if all animal life could be suspended for an interval, the predication which affirms mortality of it would not thereby become false. I agree in this belief, but not in the explanation of what is believed. That the predication of mortality would in such a case remain true does not mean that existence of the content is not affirmed, but that it is affirmed independently of time. I do not therefore admit that "Animals as such are mortal" is on the same level with "Trespassers will be prosecuted," an instance given by Mr. Bradley, which I shall discuss directly.

ii. Supposal is more a psychological than a logical attitude. It excludes affirmation of the matter supposed only as any mental attitude excludes any other. It does not exclude ability and readiness to affirm. It can be applied to certainties no less than to possibilities. All that we have to bear in mind is that it does not *ipso facto* involve an affirmation that the matter attended to in the supposal is real. I am not disposed to acquiesce in deriving the main logical features of a very various region of knowledge from an attitude which often is obviously constrained, and which is always an attitude no less of the will than of the intellect. In criticising the quantitative forms of judgment recent logical analysis has taught us to go behind the external appearance of a proposition, and we may here apply the instruction. Take such a judgment as "Gold has a specific gravity of 19·362." It is undoubtedly a paradox to translate this into "Wherever there is gold, there is a specific gravity of," etc.; and then again into, "If there is gold, there is," etc. When the judgment is thus transformed, the content is no longer *given* but *taken*, and taken by supererogation, although it is given as a permanent feature of reality. Such an employment of the hypothetical judgment appears to me abusive, nor am I as a matter of fact perfectly sure whether Mr. Bradley would have recourse to it in instances of which the above is a type. The question is, as I have pointed out above, what constitutes an individual reality, and whether to be individually real can be a matter of degree. I will not reopen it here.

An employment of the hypothetical judgment which is natural and not abusive is in such a case as the above to specify the condition under which the predicate attaches. "If gold is compared with water in respect of its density, the ratio between the two densities is represented by 19·362." The propriety of the hypothetical judgment here arises from the content being artificial and not a given aspect of reality but an observation initiated by the will. The substantive and permanent result is naturally thrown into the form, "Gold and water have densities whose ratio is represented by 19·362." There is nothing in the adaptability of the content to the hypothetical form which unfits it to be a fact. But no doubt, when we envisage it in the hypothetical form, we insist on the connection between the elements as illustrated in a contact brought about at our pleasure, and neglect, though we cannot destroy, their aspect of fact. The assertiveness of an assertion, however, is, as I shall contend more fully below, in the content; and the intrusion of the selective will cannot deprive a content of its relation to reality.

iii. Supposal, I have conceded, does not involve affirmation that the content supposed is real. Nevertheless, it must involve some intellectual relation to the content assumed; and it is worth while to see what this is.

First, the connection assumed must be conceivable, or, as I do not want to profit by any connection between conceivability and possibility, I will say that it must be either conceivable or imaginable. Much may be imagined which cannot be conceived, if conception is taken as excluding wilful abstraction; but also much may be conceived which cannot be imagined, if imagined means presented before the mind's eye by help of quasi-sensuous images. This is a limitation on hypothesis, though not a very narrow one; it excludes, I presume, hypothetical contents which are actually self-contradictory within the limits of that which we select for attention; it does not exclude what is really or materially impossible.

Secondly, a more subtle question presents itself. On the basis of supposal, we judge; we affirm something, whatever it may be, to hold true of reality. In such judgment can we wholly disregard even considerations which are *not* within the limits of that which we immediately select for attention? Must we not take account of matter *ab extra*, which, though we may not desire to attend to it, yet claims a right to intrude and vitiate the judgment based upon our supposal? In other words, what is a *legitimate* supposal?

We constantly deprecate the use of supposal as fallacious. "I decline to entertain the supposal." "The hypothesis is too much at variance with fact for any conclusion to be drawn from it." The meaning of this is that we have tried to keep out, in framing the supposition, considerations which, even if we can conceive or imagine what we suppose, yet cannot be kept out when we come to affirm anything about reality. It will not always do to judge subject to the conditions to which the supposition is subject, for they may be such as will destroy the affirmation. Mr. Bradley, in criticising Mr. Venn,[1] recognizes a difference between mere abstractions and impossibilities, but holds that, even where antecedent and consequent are both impossible, a quality which is the basis of the hypothetical judgment may nevertheless be affirmed of reality. In a purely illustrative hypothesis this may be the case, and Mr. Bradley in fact reduces all suppositions to this type, only that we do not know what they illustrate. But sometimes I think the affirmation cannot be made, although the *mere* matter selected and supposed would justify it. Not even a latent quality is then asserted of Reality. I give some instances. " If the Duke of Wellington had run away at Waterloo, he would have been a coward." "If Christianity had never appeared, the world would have been better (or " worse ") than it is." " If there is space of four dimensions, you can tie a knot in a string whose ends are held." These are not cases in which the judgment is directly contradicted by any conditions neglected in the supposition. The difficulty is merely that the suppositions go so deep into reality, that we cannot tell what change they might actually involve. If the most potent factor in the world's history for eighteen centuries had been absent, who can tell what might have happened? All suppositions about any

---

[1] " Principles of Logic," p. 219.

other course of historical events than the actual one, are purely illustrative, their consequences being neither verifiable nor deducible. Or let us take a stronger instance. "If one is two, then two are four." Here, I think, we are beyond the limits of legitimate supposition. I suppose the question is whether the interfering conditions necessarily urge themselves so as to hinder us from making the judgment, which the supposition, within its four corners, would justify us in making. *Primâ facie* I cannot at all tell how the system of number might be dislocated if one were to pass for two. One may be taken as added to the value of every number, so that two would become three, or, being also affected by the alteration in the value of one, two might become five. Or again, a fundamental change might turn two into eight, and eight into sixty-four. "But this goes outside the supposition, and we are to keep within the four corners of the supposition." If so, however, we are entitled at least to raise the question whether from so mysterious a change befalling "one" we can affirm any consequence to result in reference to the units which make up two. And if the supposition is to be interpreted by saying, "one in all combinations is to count for two, and no further changes are to be considered," then we are no longer affirming a consequence, but again supposing one, and the affirmation tends to disappear. The following is a similar case, "If sentient beings exist, with perceptions confined within a plane, they see all figures as lines only." The supposition has certainly been brought before the abstract fancy, and consequences of some interest have been drawn from it. Nevertheless, it may reasonably be said, " You cannot really form any judgment about the supposed state of things ; if there are sentient beings in no thickness, they are without material organs of sense, and you cannot apply your conception of sentience in the absence of material organs." And if we are to be strict, this objection seems unanswerable. If you cut away out of a supposed reality a central attribute of the actual reality, such as having the properties of matter, you may lose your right to the consequence which the actual reality would afford you, and be unable to replace it by any other. Whether in any special case you do lose this right is another question. Of course, in the above instance, the conception is made imaginable by approximation.

Thus, though I do not take back what I conceded above, that supposal as such is not affirmation of the reality which is supposed ; yet I must insist that the arbitrariness of supposal is more limited by reality than we are apt to recognize. From the moment that you have, so to speak, fixed your eye on the spot in the real world at which your supposal is to be made, you fall under the dominion of fact. In formulating the hypothesis you are beginning to draw consequences ; in carrying your suggested idea into detail and adjusting its parts with a view to affirming its consequence, you judge at every step. It is not merely in the consequence that flows from the hypothesis, but within the hypothesis itself, that the compulsion of reality is felt. "If a railway were laid from Suakin to Berber"; such a hypothesis as this sets us at work constructing by means of judgments, merely in order to realize our own hypothesis. Termini so many miles apart, such and such gradients, such and such a water supply, so much risk of interruption, and the like. In supposing, as well as in affirming on the basis of a supposal, we are always under the compulsion of reality. And whether the supposal embodies an aspect of reality or merely illustrates one is a question of degree. It is not true that everything which can be couched in the hypothetical form is pure illustrative supposal. The essence of supposal is abstraction, and if sometimes employed to express the abstraction of unreality, it is also capable of being adapted, though with degrees of constraint, to cases where the abstraction is no more than belongs to all definite apprehension of reality.

Thus I contend (i.) that supposal is rather the intrusion of a non-logical feature into cognition than a logical attitude which excludes affirmation of existence, and (ii.) that supposition is always in some degree controlled by fact, and is not always merely illustrative of a latent quality. For these reasons I think it allowable to scrutinize the material content of even universal judgments, whether in categorical or in hypothetical form, before pronouncing the categorical or the hypothetical element predominant in them.

Before passing to such an examination of content, I wish to say a word on a point of the merest verbal usage, but one which, on account of the prejudices it invokes, is not unimportant. I think that English custom has always recognized "*fact*" as to some extent a middle term between Thing or reality, and the knowledge which is in our heads. Fact is always conceived as relative to knowledge, whereas thing and reality rather imply independence of knowledge. True, any reality may be called a fact, but not, I think, simply *qua* reality. Fact is opposed to thing, as perceived event to indifferent permanence ; and when, by what we feel to be a license, a thing is called a fact, it is understood to be designated as a definite manifestation of reality, *of which we must take account.* An "*existing* fact" is almost a contradiction in terms. We introduce statements of fact by such phrases as " The fact is that—" " I know for a fact that—" " What I am about to tell you is absolute fact." Thus we regard fact as belonging, no doubt, to reality, but as existing for us by construction and especially by abstraction, as the embodiment of it in judgments conclusively shows. I have little doubt that most men would unhesitatingly affirm the existence of *things* apart from percipient intelligence, but if asked the same question about *facts* they would be puzzled and would probably decide in the negative. Unknown facts, although a simple process of reflection forces the notion of them on the mind, are felt to be a troublesome conception. Thus I think that common-sense recognizes the true nature of that (viz., fact) on which it chiefly relies, far more correctly than we admit if we confuse fact with thing and reality, or on the other hand with the unformed datum of sense.

8. I shall conclude this chapter by suggesting a point of view in accordance with which it might be desirable to modify Mr. Bradley's distinction between categorical and hypothetical judgments. Reality or real, Mr. Bradley maintains,[1] cannot be a predicate, because Reality is the subject in all judgment, and thus the ideal content of the judgment is *ipso facto* by judging pronounced real. This view forms a remarkable contrast with Lotze's saying,[2] " In fact, however, *real* is an adjectival or predicative conception," and has, I should imagine, been formulated partly by way of criticism on the latter.

We must remember that Mr. Bradley's reality is not simply presentation, but is the systematic whole with which we come in contact through presentation. It appears to follow from this that Reality owes something to the judgment which analyzes it, besides lending something to that judgment. It gives a good name, but

[1] " Principles of Logic," p. 81.
[2] Lotze, " Metaphysik," sect. 31.

receives solid cash.   Reality is for us such as our judgments have made it and maintain it.[1]   Our consciousness may be regarded as a permanent judgment, which
is constantly, with more or less wakefulness, predicating
the detailed content which is our ideally constructed
world, as an interpretation and extension of the present
perception and general self-feeling in which we from time
to time find our contact with reality.

Thus though the subject may be reality, we must in
every case consult the predication to see what the reality
is.   The real world as it exists for us includes many
modes of being,[2] and confusion between these modes is
the only form which a false assertion of existence can
take.   This being so, it may be held that a judgment is
categorical *in as far as it is definitory.*   The form of
supposal need not arrest us ; we should investigate not
the form merely, but the content of judgments.   We
should thus be enabled to account for the grades of
constraint which unquestionably attend the embodiment
of universal affirmative judgments in hypothetical form.
The shape of a proposition "beginning with ' If ' and
going on with ' Then ' " can indeed be forced upon all
abstract judgments, but is obviously not in the same
degree appropriate to all.   This " plain " fact should
make us pause before alleging the analysis of this class

---

[1] *Cf.* " Principles of Logic," p. 86.   " The real which in a variety of
judgments we have already qualified by a certain content."
[2] Ibid., p. 41.

of judgments as an analysis valid alike for all. You
may translate "All trespassers will be prosecuted" into
"If there should be any trespassers they will be
prosecuted," and the rendering is adequate. But take
such a judgment as "Planets are cool bodies revolving
round central incandescent ones." The natural translation of this is not into "If there are planets they
are," etc., but into "If you observe any planet you
find," etc. The hypothesis does not touch the existence
of the planets, but only our contact with it. The supposal
relieves this feature of the case—our contact with the
qualities of planets—from the necessity of being actual
in every arbitrary "now." In doing this it pointedly
embodies one feature of the universal judgment, which
does not refer, as we have repeatedly seen, to the time
*of* predication, but only to the time *in* predication. The
hypothetical judgment insists on this aspect ; the alleged
content need not, for all it says, be *always* actual. But
it is a fallacy to infer from this that the universal affirmative does not assert its subject to be *ever* actual at
all. The definitory content shows that the judgment
embodies an analysis of the planet as an aspect of
reality, as *the* reality in question, independently of time.
Supposal, we saw, is simply intentional selection which
leads to abstraction. But there is always abstraction
in defining any aspect of reality and predicating its
analysis about it. And the difference between arbitrary
selection together with isolation of a content, and the

unintentional abstraction or isolation which results from
the defining action of thought, is a matter of degree and
not of kind.

Indeed, Mr. Bradley's "individual judgments" fully
bear out the principle I have suggested. Where the
subject goes beyond the "here" or "now," where, for
instance, it is a man or nation, or, again, something
that is not in time, the reference, which indicates the
subject, is effected by ideas, is definite and explicit, and
therefore is formally abstract. Without a demonstrative
pronoun, or some such limitation, ideas, as Mr. Bradley
shows us, must be abstract and general in their reference.
In order to ascertain what sort of position in reality is
held by the subject to which they refer, we must examine
the actual matter and substance of what is predicated
quite apart from its outward form. Or, why should not
" God is eternal " = " If God is, He is eternal "?   I only
propose to extend this analysis to every judgment, in
whatever shape it may meet the eye, and to treat every
affirmation which analyzes a substantial aspect of reality
in a way that maintains and announces its substantive
character, as an explicit embodiment of actual fact.

There is a fallacy to be avoided at this point. It is not
enough to have a predicate which involves, say, sensuous
reality. As Mr. Bradley has insisted, " All trespassers
will be prosecuted " may remain true, though there are
no trespassers. And yet, in order to be prosecuted
a man must actually exist. The difficulty is that the

E

predication cannot get itself applied apart from the abstract subject, and the abstract subject is not bound to appear within any specific limits in the series of space or time. It must be remembered that the application of the too familiar notice is by its surroundings limited in regard to space, and by its tense exclusive in regard to time. If the judgments were made in a truly universal sense, *e.g.* in a treatise on the rights of owners or occupiers of land, and it was set forth that "Trespassers are always prosecuted," I do not think that this judgment could be true, supposing trespassers not to exist *in rerum naturâ*. But the matter of the predication, being an event in time, is such as somewhat to resist the attempt to elevate it it into a definitory judgment. Supposing, however, that in advocating the prohibition of man-traps [1] and spring guns, some one were to say that " Trespassers, after all, are human beings," I think there can be no doubt that the general Reality which is ultimate subject is defined by this predication as actual reality. In these cases the predication breaks through the limits of abstraction, which formally confine the grammatical subject, declares the abstraction to be no more than a

---

[1] Scott's country squire, it will be remembered, had man-traps such that "if a man gets in, they will break a horse's leg." This hypothetical judgment is so purely illustrative that it not only sets out to illustrate the quality of the trap by its effect on any man who should get in, but it substitutes for the true consequent a different one more forcibly illustrative of the strength of the trap. This is a case of supposal entering into the affirmation of a consequent. Here, however, it does not limit the affirmation, but extends it. See above, page 42.

means to determinate enunciation, and denies that it is meant to isolate the subject as an adjectival content.

I must observe that the difference of "extension" between subject and predicate does not touch the present question. I do not say that you have trespassers wherever you have human beings, although even this distinction tends to disappear as we approach the definitory judgment. But I say that if trespassers are defined — as *inter alia*, human beings, then reality is *ipso facto* pronounced to be actual reality.

Two difficulties occur to me.

(1.) A definition, it is sometimes said, may be nominal. It may state the meaning of a name as used, *e.g.* in a certain science, and may not allege the existence of any corresponding reality. The *vraisemblance* of such a view depends wholly on the comprehensiveness of Reality, which allows predication to be absolute in any sphere so long as there is no confusion of spheres. But, where no sphere of reality is presupposed, a complete definition must furnish a statement of one, and any definitory judgment that confuses the spheres of Reality is *false*. It must always be borne in mind that the consideration of isolated propositions, which is necessary in logic, is as far as possible removed from the interpretation of judgments which takes place in living thought.

I do not hesitate to say that a proposition which neither has a literary context, nor refers to the fixed standards of science, nor is uttered in answer to any question expressed or implied (" implied " as when we exchange news about a subject that is in our thoughts), is a proposition that can hardly convey a distinct judgment at all.   How seldom and with what difficulty do we introduce a subject completely new to the hearer, and not already possessing a place in his intelligence ! The way has to be paved, and the whole province in which we are about to move mapped out to him, before he can really follow what we have to say.

In narrating Greek legends one may truly say, "A Centaur was a creature combined of man and horse." But of course the proposition becomes false if transferred to zoology.   As stated, it is simply elliptical, and does not represent the complete judgment, which, in its true context, it evokes in our intelligence.   It should run : " A Centaur is a fabulous being, whom the ancient Greeks imagined as," etc.   " A chiliagon is a plane figure with a thousand equal sides."   This, or whatever the correct definition may be, is a geometrical judgment, true in geometry, in the science of certain properties of space.   If we take it to mean that there is, or ever has been, or will be, a chiliagon drawn on paper in black and white, we commit a confusion of spheres, and make the definition false, and moreover assign the judgment a meaning which, in fact, it would never bear.   If we mean that a diagram of a chiliagon has this or that peculiarity, we should say so, and our judgment would then be false if no such diagram had existed *in rerum naturâ.* But, neglecting the diagram and going back to the figure, we may be asked, "Then *how* does it exist? As a statue in the block of marble before it is carved? This is no actual existence; it is nothing." I do not think this question at all easy to answer precisely; and I will point out the extent of its reference before proceeding to answer it.

It applies equally to triangles, parallel lines, the multiplication table and the properties of logarithms, to all the aspects of space and number. It is not made easier in the case of triangles or of logarithms by their existence in books or probably at every moment in the head of one or another student. We should only delude ourselves by looking in these existences for that which the judgments affirm, which deal with geometrical truth. I suppose that what is affirmed is that certain principles are rooted in the nature of space, and in that of our power to count, and that these definite principles result in distinct properties which govern all manifestations of space and of number. "Then this *is* pure hypothesis; you mean, *if* there is a chiliagon, the nature of space will endow it with such and such properties." But I mean more than this. I mean that these properties *are, though not in relation to any time in particular*, and exist *for us* as deducible attributes of space, which in our constructed Reality, we have qualified by these attributes. It cannot be demanded of me here that I should say how Space itself exists; but in whatever way it is *for the intelligence*, in the same way these its properties, which cannot exist for sense-perception, are too, not as ideas in the head, but as matters judged true of reality. They are permanent because and in as far as space is permanent, not because fact must be permanent. It follows that if we were speaking, say, of the æsthetic impression produced by a chiliagon in black and white filling a certain area, we could not define the subject truly without affirming its existence for sense-perception. We might still predicate universally, but the universality would be that of a fact whose manifestations though not essentially related to one part of time, are intermittent. The statue yet in the marble is a stronger case of the latter kind ; its properties cannot be exhausted beforehand in a principle ; and its existence is not for the intellectual vision but for the sensuous perception of beauty. It therefore, to exist as we mean existence in its case, must be given to sensuous perception ; and it is false that the statue exists in the block of marble. A definition, then, is never nominal unless it says so. Of course we may define the use of a word, but we must explain that we are doing so. Otherwise, all definitions analyze the reality of their subjects, and all judgments must be tested by their context for the degree of their approach to definitory completeness. The attempt to assign a place in reality contradicts the isolation of the subject which is essential to a hypothesis or supposition.

(2.) But may not the place in reality be itself

assigned on a supposition or subject to a condition ? "A man who has run a mile in three minutes and a half is an actual existing human being." Here, if anywhere, the predication has for its content actual existence and reality. Yet existence is not asserted of the subject ; the judgment is not false if there is, as there is in fact, no such man as the man described. We must not be misled into treating the proposition as a singular judgment, which of course in one sense it might be. Then it would be equivalent to "An actual person has run a mile," etc. But we are pledged to keep to the abstract, and to avoid the singular judgment. And keeping to the abstract we must, I think, pronounce the form of the judgment awkward. We should like to replace "is" by "would be" or "must be." We do not see the reason for insisting on an essential attribute like humanity. The relative clause, which is all but hypo-thetical in expression, indicates that we are not dealing with an individual of knowledge, but with a fiction put together at random. All these awkwardnesses might be justified by a peculiar context as, for instance, if the judgment was an answer to such a remark as, "He looks like a ghost." Disregarding the above indications of constraint, as, if pressed, we should be forced to disregard them, we should have to allow that the judgment is hypothetical, and in spite of the impossi-bility that its subject should exist, is not false.

But this only shows what is obvious in any such

inquiry, that you may have judgments made with one intention which ape the form of those made with another. The perplexity was caused by the fact that though merely based on a supposal, the above judgment mimicked the shape and content of a definitive affirmation. Taken as aiming at completeness or at an analysis of reality, the judgment would be false. As a matter of fact, I think that the shape of such a proposition would seem ambiguous to us, and in the absence of a special content we should call upon it to make its election between hypothesis and definition, and should treat it as true or false accordingly. A definition which puts a fiction on a par with a fact is false. "The wrath of the Homeric gods is fearful," is false until you add "in Homer"; only in conversation or light literature we readily understand "in Homer" to be implied in "Homeric." In fact, we know by a thousand indications about what sphere of Reality we are talking, but all these indications belong to the judgment, and must not be forgotten when we analyze its truth.

I have pointed out before how exceedingly inappropriate the hypothetical form becomes when applied to a genuine definition, and how it throws its doubt not on what the abstractness of the judgment is intended to leave open, viz. the time of particular manifestation within the sensible series, but on the entire existence of the content which the definition brings into the light of reality. You can say, "If space is, it is three-

dimensional"; " If Europeans are, they are civilized";
" If gold is, it is heavy"; " If the soul is, it is a subject";
" If God is, He is eternal." The hypothetical shape
seems to me equally possible and equally constrained in
all of these.

I should therefore, not without hesitation, suggest
that there may be no impassable frontier between the
hypothetical and the categorical judgments. I would
attempt to approach the relation between them in this
way.

Affirmation about the unanalyzed present perception
may be considered as one extreme ; supposal, having
its subject indicated by a mere idea, definite but
fictitious, as the opposite extreme. The forms of proposition from which the kinds of judgment have respectively drawn their names, are most precisely adapted
for the expression of these two contrasted activities.
For the true region of human knowledge, which for the
most part lies between the two, neither form of sentence,
neither class of proposition, or even of judgment, is, if
pressed home, absolutely and unrestrictedly appropriate.
Definiteness grows into abstraction ; abstraction passes
into detachment and isolation ; and concurrently with
this transition the element of supposal, of taking or
choosing a content with a view to noting its consequence,
appears *within* the categorical judgment, in which it is
active *long before the judgment has become abstract*, and
therefore long before any one would propose to call it

hypothetical. From the very beginning of judgment we know, however obscurely, that we take the subject *as* we take it, for the sake of a connection which, when so taken, it has with the content of predication. And, in a corresponding way, when the judgment has become abstract in the sense of having a not obviously and concretely individual subject, the categorical nature persists *beside the hypothetical* in the abstract universal judgment, which can at this point be exhibited as hypothetical only by a good deal of constraint. It is only as analysis of reality gives way to arbitrary illustration of the real, that the element of free selection or pure experiment conquers, and the judgment diverges from its true development into the type based on *pure* supposal. But a definitory judgment, *qua* definitory, is never hypothetical, consisting as it always does in the analysis of reality ; of that solid construction neither wholly sensuous nor purely intellectual, which, however incomplete, is all that we can save out of the fleeting sensible series.

# CHAPTER II.

## THE JUDGMENT OF NUMBER AND MEASUREMENT.

1. I FIND an emphasis—nothing more—which calls for notice pages 172–173 of Mr. Bradley's work. The observation that intension and extension are relative to our knowledge "is fatal to" the "Kantian distinction" between synthetic and analytic judgments. I do not feel sure how far this criticism is warranted as against Kant's precise view. But it seems to me hardly imaginable that Kant did not know how knowledge grows. However this may be, I desired merely to draw attention to what I should call the *psychological* tone of Mr. Bradley's comment. It is *not* necessary, in order to give value to the distinction between synthetic and analytic judgments, that "the meaning of a word" should be "confined to that attribute or group of attributes from which it sets out." It is only necessary that in each epoch of knowledge there should be a fairly fixed value given to what used to be called essence and accident. The distinction may be hard to justify on metaphysical ground. But it is one without which science cannot

move a step, and not even common sense can easily think a distinct thought. It is a purely logical distinction ; I mean a distinction wholly relative to knowledge as knowledge, and wholly independent of the question whether I, the individual, happen to be familiar with this or that attribute of a thing. Surely the question for logic is never what a name means for you or me, but always, what it ought to mean. And surely, if Pilate's question is to have any answer, we cannot set down what a name ought to mean as wholly unknowable. And this, which has always a considerable relative fixity, is the gauge for distinguishing analytic and synthetic judgment.

A more important comment, because it has a logical bearing, is involved in Mr. Bradley's remark that "a synthetic judgment, so soon as it is made, is at once analytic." Taking analytic in the scientific sense above referred to, I do not admit this to be true. *Not* everything "which is added to-day is implied to-morrow"; this does not take place unless what is added is also established, and established as true independent of time, and as of permanent value in relation to the content before us. I think, too, that even common practice draws a distinction between what we put in the meaning of a word, and what we remember about the thing meant by the word. This is the rudimentary recognition of a *right* or scientific meaning of words.

But Mr. Bradley's observation contains the truth that

every judgment on scrutiny is found to be at once an analysis and a synthesis. Which of the two characters is predominant in a given judgment *for me* is a matter of chance, of my knowledge; which is predominant for the purpose of classifying the judgment in the light of the theory of knowledge, is a matter of the state of science at any epoch in the world's history; and the same judgment would not shift so lightly from the one title to the other if it were not simply a question which of two inseparable features of all judgment is to be given the greater prominence. One may say with Mr. Bradley that Kant really meant to ask about the kinds of synthesis, and the principle of unity in each. I do not object, but I think it unfair to slur the special reference to the different degrees in which predicates "belong" to their subject, as if it were a mere matter of individual ignorance. " In pure cases, or with conditions properly assigned," it may be said, "all predicates that belong at all belong equally." First; I do not think this is true; perfect knowledge would not, we must suppose, annihilate the structure of things, and, if not, some predicates would still belong closely to the function of a thing, while others could only be connected with it artificially, so to speak, and for the sake of curiosity. And secondly; if it were so, still the conditions of im- perfect knowledge are the conditions of human know- ledge, and in a sense therefore of knowledge as such ; and such conditions are a proper subject for logical

formulation ; while the mere accidental state of ignorance of an individual is not so, except in as far as it
may illustrate general conditions of knowledge.

2. Number belongs to meaning in various degrees.
Simple counting relates to Extension ; Measurement,
which is latent in counting, to Intension.

I shall speak in this section of (i.) Number and
Extension ; (ii.) the extensional meaning of Proper
Names.

(i.) Mr. Bradley writes as follows :[1] "It is an elementary mistake to suppose that number confers particularity and destroys intension.  And the error reveals
a deep foundation of bad metaphysics.  Number is
surely nothing but an attribute.  And how can the
addition of an universal quality force us to take a judgment merely in extension?  You may say, perhaps, that
nothing is numbered save actual phenomena, but such
an assertion would be incompatible with fact " (comp.
p. 171).  "If the intension signifies the meaning of a
word, and the extension is the number of actual objects
of which the meaning can be truly predicated, then both
extension and intension are relative to our knowledge,
and naturally fluctuate with altering experience."

I do not hold the view which I understand that
Mr. Bradley is arguing against.  But I seem to myself
to trace in his argument the influence of the conception
which he is combating ; the conception of extension as

---

[1] "Principles of Logic," p. 170.

a peculiar and independent kind of meaning. Number, he says, is an attribute. Certainly. Therefore it does not destroy intension. Certainly it does not. Therefore it does not force us to take a judgment merely in extension. Not "merely." But it does force us to take a judgment in extension, and it does *enable* us to dispense with all but a minimum of intension.

If extension refers to "actual" objects (meaning, I presume, objects existing at the present time only [1]) then every predication of a connection of content must go beyond extension, must refer to many objects not included in the extension, and thus cannot submit to the limitation which would on this view be characteristic of judging in extension. In this case "to take a judgment merely in extension" has a meaning, and one opposed to taking the judgment in intension, and it is intelligible how the addition of a universal quality could *not* confine the judgment to extension. But on any other view of extension,[2] I cannot understand how to take a judgment *merely* in extension has a meaning ; nor how, on the other hand, *so far as a special prominence of extensional meaning is possible*, the addition of the universal quality of number should *not* produce such a prominence.

And thus as I can see no justification for the limitation of extension to actual objects in the sense of objects

---

[1] See above, p. 22.
[2] *Cf.* " Principles of Logic," p. 155 note, and p. 168.

existing in present time ; as extension seems to me to be simply an element in intension, the element which when made precise takes the shape of number, I hold the phrase " mere " extension in the sense of excluding all intension to be a contradiction in terms ; and I see in the hypothetical character of a universal connection of content no bar to an equally hypothetical reference to what I am prepared to call the attribute of extension, *i.e.* of existence in the shape of units distinguishable from one another.

The reason why the introduction of number as qualifying the whole content of a subject (not merely as qualifying one of its predicates ; " six men " must be the form ; not "a man with six fingers ")—why this must force us to think mainly in extension, mainly of the particular, and enable us to forget much of the intension, is not that it is a number, but that we do not know it to be the right number. It interferes with the rest of the intension, not because it is not an attribute, but because it is one. An extension confined to actual objects *must* be discrepant with a universal connection of content, and therefore cannot, in my judgment, be taken as its meaning ; cannot, that is, affect its meaning by reason of discrepancy. The general attribute conveyed by an assignment of number *may* (or may not) be discrepant with a connection of content, and therefore can affect its meaning. Every intension, every connection of content, has one number, and one only (or, it might be urged, none in cases of recurrence which we have no reason to limit) which would express its attribute of extension rightly, and we hardly ever know what that number is. So, although in judging universally we may think of the externality of the units to one another, we cannot, as a rule, give the thought precise expression. If we knew the number demanded by the intension, it would harmonize with the intension, and our thought would be complete in both aspects. Such a number is "three" in "the three angles of a triangle are equal to two right angles." But in an ordinary numerical judgment "six men came by the last train," the number not being perceptibly essential to the subject as determined in the judgment, kills the relation of ground and consequent which we anticipate in a judgment, so far as the intension of the general name man is concerned, and attracts attention to itself, an attribute indeed, but as regards that general name contingent and unaccountable. And this attribute *is* extension. Not that the men are, or are presumed to be, "actual," but simply because we are instructed to consider them especially as distinct individuals entering into a certain kind of whole, not the whole of mankind, but another, framed *ad hoc*, and in its most noticeable feature, the externality to each other of its units, a whole of extension.

I conceive that Mr. Bradley has pointed out in this work the true nature and limits of subsumption; and this I hold to be an epoch-making achievement,

F

at least in English logic.  Where we employ the unity of an individual subject to establish a relation between attributes, not being able to allege a ground of connection between the attributes *per se*, there, and there only, as I read Mr. Bradley, we have subsumption.  Now when mere external unity, the unity of units in their distinction from other units, *i.e.* in their purely numerable aspect, is the most prominent ground for our use of a general name, we are said to use it in extension.  Thus it is plain that subsumption and extension are closely connected ; for in subsumption we argue from that kind of unity in a subject, which is the aspect under which units constitute the extension of a name.

And this same attribute is the root of the system of number.  When we say, " Six times six men are thirty-six men," and " six times six pounds are thirty-six pounds," we *seem* to employ in these arguments no attribute drawn from the intension of man or pound respectively.  The denomination of the result appears in each case self-evident, and it is only in more complicated cases that we see how some intensions will resist some processes.  I suspect (if I may venture for a moment quite *ultra crepidam*) that among mathematicians the sound thinker is he who always clearly envisages the capacities of his units, and that the unsound mathematician (for I seem to have heard that there are such) is he who does not sufficiently consider what units being subjected to what processes will issue in what denominations. In errors arising by such neglect (we have all heard of the question whether you can divide money by money),[1] the neglected remainder of the intension would be avenging itself.

The element of intension which is indispensable to the kind of argument called calculation is the characteristic of being a unit, i.e. *ad hoc* an individual, though in artificial measurement not necessarily a concrete, separable thing.

Therefore it appears to me that what we accentuate in number and rely on in calculation is essentially the attribute which is extension. It is true, however, that to separate this as *mere* "extension" from the intension of a name would be to cut away our employment of the name from all reference to its meaning, and to argue as if results in concrete numbers were obtainable by calculations in abstract number. And the reason why numerical precision interferes with the intension of a concept or name, is not that we are using the concept in question in its mere extension, but that we have created what professes to be a new concept differing from that indicated by the general name solely in having a different extension ; which necessarily conflicts with the full intension of the general name, and for purposes of calculation must prevail over it.

If we had in the form of a number the true extension

---

[1] *Cf.* De Morgan, "Budget of Paradoxes," p. 417.

of the concept as such, we should be able to show ground for connecting it with the full intension. Such a number approaches to a characteristic or essential number; "the three angles of a triangle," "the twelve cities of the Ionic league;" and can even by implication of context become a general name: "the All England Eleven;" "the Three;" "the Ten;" οἱ ἕνδεκα.

I cannot but think, then, that number does draw attention to particularity, if this means or results from the externality of units to one another; that it is rooted in the same characteristic as extension and extensional argument, and as subsumption ; and tends to oust the true or full intension of concepts, which in extensional argument tends to become, and in calculation does become, the mere denomination of numbers.

I may add, that *I* do not say that we "get to Existence" by number.  But I find a preconception, which appears to me erroneous, indicated by Mr. Bradley's thinking it worth while to deny that we do.  Whether we get to existence or not does not seem to me to depend on whether we employ number or not, but on our employing it, or any other determination we may use, in a complete and consistent construction.

The view taken above will be further illustrated when we discuss the relation between counting and Induction.

(ii.) The doctrine, "that proper names have no connotation," Mr. Bradley holds to arise from not observing that Extension and Intension are relative to our knowledge and fluctuate together. In this dispute I am on the whole with Mr. Bradley, as is obvious from my taking Extension as an element in and consequence of Intension. Nevertheless, it appears to me that he treats the question a great deal too cavalierly.

First, of course, I must protest against taking extension to fluctuate simply with our knowledge of the actual objects which bear a certain name. I should have thought that in putting a meaning to actual objects *for knowledge* we could not stop short of all the possible objects which are indicated by the intension when thought as realized in individual instances. The extension of "mammals" does not vary, for me, with the number of actual mammals I have seen or now see. Supposing I say that it varies with the number which I know by inference to be now existing, I really am not sure if Mr. Bradley would call these "actual" or "possible" mammals. And moreover, I could not draw the line there. I could not exclude an extinct species from the extension of the concept, or deny that it is for me, as referred to its proper gradation of space and time, an actual fact. Otherwise I must restrict actuality to the atomic present; and that I cannot do, if I hold facts to be ideal constructions including many elements drawn from the past.

It might be said that these elements only affect our vision, that no doubt it was in the past that we learnt to see them, but that nevertheless we must actually see them now if we are to be justified in pronouncing them existent.   But this, though true in part, has a very limited truth.   Many—*most* of the attributes with which we undoubtingly invest present objects, are not evident in this moment, and are only ascribed as real to the present on the faith of a past in which we judged them real.   Thus the solid reality, as it faces us in the present, involves a judgment which assigned reality in the past, and a present judgment pronouncing (not explicitly and in the abstract, but by its inevitable universality[1]) that the present reality, perceived under one aspect, is continuous with that past reality which was judged real under another aspect.   Whether this present judgment cancels the past reality and substitutes for it that of the present, thus destroying the ladder by which that present rose to its place as reality, is a further question.   For us, at all events, the complete reality of the present rests on the reality of the past, and if that is a now non-existent reality, as no doubt in one sense it is, still it cannot be dispensed with in the interpretation of judgments.   The judgment must take us wherever its content belongs ; nothing can restrict its application in time, except a time relation implied *in the content.*

Then I must suppose extension to fluctuate, not with my special experience of actual objects that embody the intension, but with the range of objects

<hr>

[1] *Cf.* " Principles of Logic," pp. 61, 271.

which my knowledge warrants me in accepting, as, at whatever time and place, actual embodiments of the intension.

Then, secondly, does the extension of a proper name fluctuate with the intension, with the meaning? and so, first of all, has a proper name a meaning?

After what I have said, I need not go into this. Of course, a proper name has a meaning, in the sense that it stands for something, enables us to recognize something, is a current counter both in written and spoken language. And of course this meaning is, *qua* meaning, an intension. And although in proper names the same combination of letters is applicable to different individuals, not in virtue of the same intension, but in virtue of different intensions, this is the case also with the names of Homonymous things (things whose name is the same but their definition different, the sameness of name being, therefore, apart from history, a mere coincidence), and is, therefore, no absolute distinction between proper and general names.

It must be this feature, I think, which Mr. Bradley indicates by the words " here [in proper names] as everywhere intension and extension fluctuate together ; " that is, speaking generally, the meaning of a name regulates its application, and this is true of proper names as of others. So far I am with Mr. Bradley.

But if the parallel intended is between all the individuals designated by a proper name and—not homonymous individuals but—the extension of a single general name belonging to its one meaning or intension, then I can no longer follow.   The extension of Brown or Jones, Henry or Charles, London or Boston, fluctuates not in the same way as that of man, vegetable, or tiger, but in the same way as that of "cricket" as including the game and the insect, or "plant" as including a vegetable and the apparatus of a factory.   Excepting in this latter sense, the extension of a proper name does not fluctuate with our knowledge; and this is just the characteristic difference between a proper and a general name.   In so far as general names are made subservient to pure recognition and then have a fixed extension independent of their intension, they are degraded towards the rank of proper names.   Such are the Linnæan terms of classification for plants.   In some modern works they stand as an index, for the mere purpose of "hunting down" specimens, while the natural system is adopted in the body of the work as exhibiting the true affinities and nature of the plants.   Here we have the most graphic illustration of the incipient proper name.   In all the mass of intension it is possible for plants grouped under the same Linnæan name to be wholly and utterly different ; but, no doubt, we always find the slight unity of an abstract mark binding together all objects to which the name applies.   In the true proper name this has disappeared.

" The meaning," Mr. Bradley says, speaking of proper

names, "is not fixed, and this leads to the idea that no meaning exists." Now I do not say that no meaning exists, but I say that the meaning is a means, and not an end. I am content to put my view thus : A *proper name* is strictly a contradiction in terms. The adjective "proper" indicates a purpose which a name as a significant word can only fulfil by means that contradict the adjective. Therefore Mr. Bradley's remarks are, up to a certain point, incontrovertible. Every name has a meaning, and its meaning governs its application. But a proper name exists for the sake of the application, a general name for the sake of the meaning. It is not true that the two functions are the same, though it is true that either vanishes if the other is destroyed. The ideal function of a proper name is recognition ; the ideal function of a general name, definition. "Name" contradicts "proper," because name implies meaning, and under a meaning there can always be subsumption ; but "proper" has for its purpose to avoid subsumption. For a proper name we want a mark that shall distinguish, and no more ; but we find that the vehicle of distinction *will* take a value of its own and tend to admit of subsumption. It is originally general, and is always tending to become general again. I suspect that the conception of proper names, as we understand them, is not a very easy or early one. We now actually attach to names, written and used in a certain way, a mental reservation that we are to look for no meaning in them. As regards the names of men and women this is quite a modern state of things. The surname still in some cases retains an intension of family and character, and is always of course more significant than the Christian name. But the law now admits no purpose in names but that of distinction ; and permits any one to have any name which he makes it clear that he is to be known by, and to change it at pleasure subject to the same condition. The history of Roman,[1] and I suppose still more of savage, names proves that far more predicative significance attached to the actual name-word in early times than now. And the origin of English surnames illustrates the same truth.

I may remark that the most frivolous of all disputes is that which connects with this question the etymological meaning of certain name-words. The etymology of a word almost always indicates something that it does *not* mean now. The true cases of proper names which, acquiring intension, are ceasing to be "proper," are such as—"a Daniel come to judgment," "the Rupert of debate," " a Crœsus," "a Solon," etc.

In short, then, when we use a proper name we want

---

[1] *Vide.* Mommsen "Röm. Forschungen." All elements of a Roman name were more predicative than distinctive. The prænomina (fore-names) in use among patricians towards the end of the republic were very few, and far more characteristic of descent than distinctive of the individual. Women had at that time as a rule no prænomina (as if, now, they should have nothing but a surname). The name of the head of a household added in the possessive case was very likely in its origin not a distinction of family but a predication of ownership (Marcus Marci filius. *Cf.* Δημοσθενὴς Δημοσθένους. The filius is suspected of being later in origin).

to produce recognition of an individual ; and though this must be done somehow with reference to the individual's identity, yet we do not think nor care how it is done. When we use a general name we want to convey a connection of content, and we let the content take care of itself as regards the individual it may apply to. A proper name, then, must have "intension" (hardly "*an* intension"), but is most proper when it has least.

Is not, it may be said, "to produce recognition of an individual" the same thing as "to convey a connection of content"? I have admitted that the matter is one of degree. It is difficult to distinguish such an announcement as "Mr. Fawcett is dead," in respect of its significance, from such a sentence as "The Postmaster-General is dead." But it must be remembered that ordinary proper names have not the significance that is possessed by those of eminent men. The question is one of tendency, and I think that it is fair to say, that by help of a proper name as such you do not convey a connection of content, but rather point to an indefinite content, and omit to select or to connect.

If I have made my view clear, I do not much care to fight about words. And yet one does not like to surrender important phrases to a usage one cannot approve. So I add that I do not at all admit the propriety of applying the words meaning and intension, which I understand to designate kinds of knowledge, to mere recognition which has no definite ground or motive.

I am disposed to stand by the old colours and to maintain that "no one has knowledge but he who can give an account" of the matter known. I do not mean a theoretical account; I mean an explicit statement of his conception. Mr. Bradley and Stuart Mill—"strange fellowship!"—admit unconscious functions into knowledge to an extent of which I cannot approve, and of which in discussing Mr. Bradley's account of inference I shall have something to say.

3. The analysis of the act of counting is of interest, for it illustrates the effect of extreme abbreviation on an act of thought; and also of importance, for counting is the process of making number, and lies at the root of mathematics.

I said above that it appeared to me to be true that number favours argument in extension, and tends to reduce the intension proper of a general name to the place of a mere denomination of the objects which we number. I have now to propound the suggestion that this characteristic of number has unduly affected an argument of Mr. Bradley's relating to the amount of inference contained in the common process of counting.

I understand Mr. Bradley to deny [1] that there is such a form of inference as Induction by simple Enumeration, if that means simply summing up particulars. From particulars as such, he maintains, there is no inference. To get an inference, you must have, in

---

[1] "Principles of Logic," pp. 326–330.

however rudimentary a form, a connection of content, a
general result left by the contemplation of the separate
cases or objects. So far I am thoroughly with Mr.
Bradley.

The point on which I wish to offer a suggestion is
his treatment of simple enumeration, considered as the
mere summing of particulars, and as thus obviously
equivalent to counting; which latter process, it is
assumed, gives a *mere* collection, without a warrant that
the collection is complete, and without—what is essential, as I agree, to inference—" a selective perception of
one connection of attributes throughout our whole
subject-matter:" "The counting by itself *is* not the
induction," etc.

I doubt whether, in theory, the operation of counting
could be made intelligible on this basis. One might
even appeal to page 426 of " Principles of Logic," where,
as I read it, Mr. Bradley rightly maintains that you
cannot have discrete units without a relation to a
common centre. Is not this to say that you cannot
count mere particulars, and that therefore " the discriminative analysis which goes with the counting " is essential
to the counting? I do not wish to rely solely on this
abstract argument; I may have misread page 426. But
let us look at the act of counting. Of course you may
say to me, " Count ten," and I may run over the natural
numbers from one to ten inclusive; and if I am then
asked, " *What* have you been counting?" I might find

it hard to answer. I suppose in such a case I have been counting the names of the numbers counted—in fact, the vehicles of the process of counting. Or it may be implied that I have counted the intervals of time necessary to pronounce the names of the numbers, at a rate fixed by habit. In either of these cases it is only just possible to trace a continuity or common feature in the series, which would, if each act of counting were a full judgment, be embodied in a predicate for the sake of which we are counting, in connection with a unit by which we are to count. Obviously the limit up to which we are to count is supplied by the predicate for the sake of which we count, and the rule for the differences which we are to enumerate by the unit of which we are interested in asserting the predicate. I do not think that any act of enumeration, however rapid or however abbreviated in thought, is without these elements of meaning. We "count," indeed, by saying "one," "two," "three," and so on ; but what we mean is made clear if we have to instruct others to count for us. Every one knows how hard these instructions are to give and to observe, and how dangerous in consequence is the use of statistics, which are the records of other people's counting. I take it that this is because, in counting for ourselves, we are not in the habit of instructing ourselves explicitly ; we do not find precision necessary in order to apply correctly a rule which springs from our immediate interest, probably bearing on matter which is familiar to us.

But when we count, there is always a limit up to which we mean to count and no further. If I have a telescope, and am asked, "How many men are there in that boat?" I count aloud, "One, two, three, four, five, *six!* There are six men in her." Can it be maintained that my answer goes beyond the essential function of counting?

First, the privative judgment,[1] "No man in the boat is uncounted," is progressively approached by each enumerative judgment. I cannot move a step in counting without a judgment closely allied to this, or why should I not keep counting over and over again? Enumeration has no meaning unless it involves distinguishing what you have counted from what you have not counted. Unless we do this, one number of objects cannot be distinguished from another. The enumerative judgments form a series which exists for the sake of characterizing a certain totality; they cannot fulfil this purpose unless we may convert the last from "Six men are in that boat," to "The men in that boat are six." It may be said that our interest need not be in the number of men in the boat. It may be simply to know if she is carrying more than some given number; and in that case we should not count all, but should stop short. The answer is that then the instruction for counting runs, "Count the men *up to* (the number required, say) *four.*" Four is then taken into

---

[1] "Principles of Logic," p. 330.

the limiting or interesting predicate, owing to some external circumstance; perhaps the boat is only fit to carry four. I can also imagine that it may be said, " It is one thing to say, ' These six men I have counted in the boat,' and another to say, ' Beyond these six I can see no more.' " (The possibility of mistake in declaring an enumeration complete does not bear on the argument; I am only speaking of what we wish to do and believe ourselves to do in counting.) But the line, if there is one, is very subtle. If there was a seventh visible you could not but be able to distinguish the six already counted from him; or, as pointed out above, you would be liable to count them over again, and the process would be futile. And if there is no seventh visible, to distinguish the six you have counted from that, *i.e.* nothing, which is left you, under your instructions, to count, seems to me to be only a form of the same perception as to distinguish them from a seventh. The totality of a certain matter is what you set out to measure; your units exist as units only in reference to it; I think that the process becomes idle if held incapable of furnishing its own warrant of completeness.

Secondly, " the discriminative analysis which goes with the counting " is to my mind the actual essence of the enumerative judgment. It consists in the connection between subject and predicate, which is furnished by the question asked, or instructions given or implied, and therefore is the basis and essence of enumeration as such.  Before I can count you must tell me not only up to what limits I am to count, but by what units.  I cannot set out to count things in general; not only is there no interest in the task, but I do not know what is to be reckoned as *a thing;* I have no principle on which to perform my analysis of the world around me into units, nor do I know how long I am to go on counting.

Sigwart has said that in judgments of number, the number is really a predicate.  Undoubtedly this view has its truth ; especially after the warrant of completeness has been given by pronouncing an enumeration exhaustive.  According to the ordinary reading of the judgment, the number then becomes a predicate true of the subject.  Formally, considered as an attribute, number may be alleged either *in* the subject as a determination, or *of* the subject as predicated.  But perhaps the fact is that the common distinction of subject and predicate cannot do justice to the complication of the enumerative judgment.  It may be said that all attributes are alleged of the subject, only under some condition.  But number tells us so little about its condition (which I have hitherto called the predicate, or matter of interest) that we cannot dispense with the explicit declaration of that condition.  And then our interest attaches to the number for the sake of the condition or determinant which thus retains an essential feature of a predicate.  Thus I cannot help thinking that number is more "formal" and less "material" than other attributes.  Its conditions do not pre-suppose and explain themselves as do those under which other attributes are ascribed. It bears the character of a relation, and is not intelligible without an indication of the whole within which it is a relation. There is a number for every subject under every condition. It primarily records the recurrence of a mental act, of a judgment of perception; while the content or application of the perception is entirely for us to guide or determine. Thus I do not like making number a predicate, except where by implication in a content, *e.g.* in a characteristic measurement, it carries a definite significance. "The temperature of the patient is 102° Fahrenheit," only means what it does, because I know the normal temperature and the danger of excess. And all number is in any case, if a predicate, an element in a complex predicate; it cannot stand alone any more than "in," "to," or "for." In "The number of the names together was about an hundred and twenty," 120 is not more independent than "from" or "of" in, "They went out from us because they were not of us," where also the predicative emphasis is obviously on the signs of relation.

Of course I am not denying that number is "objective," any more than I deny that relations are objective; I only say that, to tell us anything material to be known, it needs more strict and explicit statement of conditions than other attributes—at least, than all other attributes except complex relations. Therefore, apart from characteristic number, which is the *result* of careful inference, I should prefer to describe number as such as the abstraction of the act of counting and as primarily indicating the number of times we have judged a certain predicate of identical but distinguishable subjects. Number is, then, rightly ascribed to things and units of all kinds ; but, like the meaning of signs of relation, it is only intelligible when the component parts of the whole to which it belongs are definitely assigned.

Therefore, while I agree with Mr. Bradley about induction, I suggest a doubt whether his view of enumeration is adequate. I take all enumeration, if fully analyzed, to consist of judgments like this, " *This* book is one of the books on that shelf ;" " *This other* book is one," etc. You may, of course, count two or more at each judgment, but this is simply complex counting or multiplication ; each two or more is known by its quality (*e.g.* the pips on a card by their arrangement), and counted as a unit, the result being got by reference to a known series.

The "selective perception of one connection of attributes " is, then, to my mind, of the essence of enumeration, and enumeration being essentially relative to a totality, has a right to the final judgment, " All the sheep in that fold have been dosed,"[1] for enumeration implies a distinction between *counted units within a certain limit* and *uncounted units within that limit* ; and

---

[1] *Cf.* "Principles of Logic," pp. 330–1.

if the uncounted are zero, enumeration must surely be allowed to warrant that fact. In meaning, indeed, every enumerative judgment may be taken to imply something more, viz. a double counting resulting in a *ratio*, for the judgment distinguishes between two factors in the content, here, "sheep in the fold," and "sheep in the fold dosed ;" and this, a ratio, is the most complete form which the numerical relation between the factors can take. Obviously such a ratio is only a more precise form of the distinction between counted and uncounted. Instead of saying, "Fifty have been dosed, and that is not all in the fold," we could then say, "Fifty have been dosed, and there are one hundred in the fold." But when you come to "One hundred have been dosed, and there are no more in the fold," the two modes of enumeration acquire the same precision in that one case, as the direct perception that there are no more takes the place of the second counting and consequent ratio. I may remark that if we state the answer as a ratio, then, though we still need the content as a denomination for the numbers, we have swerved from the path of connecting the attributes as such.

The true distinction between Induction by simple Enumeration and genuine Inference is not, as it seems to me, quite where Mr. Bradley puts it. It is really parallel to the distinction between connections of content by way of subsumption and the rational perception of grounded connections of content. It is not that the cases supposed to be argued from are mere particulars, for *it is impossible even to enumerate* mere particulars. It is that they are unanalyzed individuals connected by an indefinite identity, which is, as a rule, suggested to our minds by some general name which applies to all, and which, as the appellation of concrete individuals, we subsume under another predicate. We presume a connection between the predicate under which we subsume the individuals in enumerating them, and something or other in the intension of the concepts by help of which we indicate their concrete nature as individuals. Our ready-made knowledge thus supplies us with a sort of rough hypothesis.

I observe, in several cases, that *this* plant and others, having leaves which are always under water, also have them finely divided. Here, I assume that we can as yet *see* no rational connection between the complex concept, "plants with leaves under water," and the predicate, "with finely cut leaves," under which we subsume it. But the two characters being noticeable, if they are fairly constant, we are apt to presume a connection between them; and it is this presumption which forms the essence of the argument, though hidden under the form of subsumption, *i.e.* of the allegation that the attributes are together merely as a matter of fact in the same individuals. If simple enumeration means something simpler than this, I do not believe that there is such a process. But it is fairly named, as I have held above that a " proper " name is fairly named, from being completely antagonistic in tendency and purpose to inferences, as a proper name is to appellations, which rest on precisely assigned content ; although the significance of content cannot, in any intelligible assertion, be wholly done away with.　The contrast may be illustrated in the above instance by suggesting the idea, " Finely divided leaves, like the gills of a fish, sift the water more effectively to get at its oxygen."　Here at once we pass out of the region of presumption, subsumption, and enumeration, into that of suggested causation.

Finally, I do not think it makes any difference of principle that in the simplest cases of simple enumeration the number does nothing, and can be dispensed with.　To make the number, as such, significant, it must be compared with other numbers, which enter into a ratio as explained above.　But even in the simplest cases the process which makes number is involved, and to state the number explicitly is always a safeguard, because it means that each unit has been considered separately and the uncounted at each moment carefully distinguished from the counted.　We can, however, and do establish the empirical "all" by a mere *coup d'œil*, as in the perception that " all those birds flew across the water."　There is a peculiarly negative aspect in this judgment.　What we rely on is obviously that we saw no bird that did not fly across the water.　It corresponds to the judgment " (some, or) none are uncounted," which we saw to be implied in counting; while the positive part of the judgment corresponds to a single perception of the number of units, only that in this case we are not able to reduce the quality to quantity.

4. In simple counting we characterize units by their number. In measurement we characterize a whole by the number of units which it contains. Measurement is implied in all counting. We do not speak, indeed, of "measuring" a crowd when we count the people in it. The unit, a human being, does not present itself to us pre-eminently with reference to quantity. But undoubtedly in ascertaining the number of units of a certain description, within a certain space, we are ascertaining a quantity. In common usage the term measurement is restricted to the process of counting units of space, and is distinct from weighing; but in science it includes the reference of any quality or its physical cause to a standard unit; in this way we measure time, heat, velocity, quantity of electrical action of various kinds. Thus the idea of quantitative comparison seems bound up with the idea of measurement, and the idea of measurement, as reference to a unit, includes the idea of counting.

What Mr. Bradley says on pages 370–1 may very likely be true as a matter of fact. I wish to point out that it again is to my mind somewhat too brusquely put. The mistake is, Mr. Bradley holds, to assume " that the perception of differences in quantity implies the power of counting units." The real fact he takes to be that long before number could come into the world, the perception of more and less, of the whole and the parts, already existed. They existed in an un-analyzed qualitative form. The reader should compare with this what is said on page 370 of the two senses in which degree may be used.

I am not sure that I can imagine what this qualitative form is like. It is a tremendous paradox, at least in words, to speak of perceiving more and less in a quali-tative form, as "the mere vague sense of a more and a less, of a rise and a fall, of a swelling and a shrinking."[1] I do not wish to intrude a captious analysis on plain facts. But I cannot help thinking it worth while to try and distinguish a sense which is but vaguely a sense of more and less, and is also, though dimly, a sense of measurement, from a strictly qualitative sense, such as should not have in it any traceable element of com-parison by means of a unit, and should yet be a sense of more and less. The latter is what Mr. Bradley's paradox seems to require; the former is all that I can well imagine. The beginning of counting, as of measure-ment and quantity, I take to be the establishment of the unit; and I suppose in the first perception of more and less the less is itself the unit, against which the greater is "that and more." When you have not the setting off of one against the other I cannot imagine to

---

[1] "Principles of Logic," p. 370.

myself how you should have the vaguest sense of more and less.  And where you have such setting off, there you have the essential element of counting and measurement.

But below this there is a different kind of qualitative sense that might conceivably come in question, and I do not feel sure whether Mr. Bradley has sufficiently attended to this distinction.   I think there can be no doubt that in cases where we ultimately go on to form a judgment of more and less, we begin, or we may begin, with a judgment of mere *qualitative difference.*   I mean a sense of difference which does not, however vaguely, pass into the direct sense of more and less.   Differences of shape, of musical tone, of colour, and of pleasure or pain strike us, I think, at first as mere differences ; as immediate qualitative impressions which are not the same, but are like or akin, *i.e.* according to Mr. Bradley's phrase, have points of identity mingled with points of difference.  What has shape to do with the matter ? I may be asked.   Shape is not size, and cannot be analyzed into size.   I think that shape is a very good instance of the perception in dispute, just because it is primarily a qualitative perception, but is in various degrees referable to quantity.   First come perceptions of difference in shape like those between a highly dissected pattern and a square, into which no idea or implication of size is likely to enter, the comparison of areas being so very intricate an operation, supposing for the sake of illustration that the area over which the pattern spreads

is in fact somewhat larger than the square with which
the pattern is compared. The perception of difference
between these shapes is purely qualitative. But now
turn to slightly more comparable objects. Compare
a square and a narrow rectangle no longer than the side
of the square. The one is massive, solid; the other
slight, slender. If no one has asked us about the
relative areas, we need not think of them at all. Or
compare the column from the Erectheion in the Elgin
Marbles room at the British Museum, with the enormous
drums in the neighbouring room from the pillars of the
Artemision at Ephesus. The one is slender, almost
frail, the other (even if we imagine the whole column)
immensely solid, heavy, and strong. Here, I think, is
the point where our issue must be decided. "Why, you
are saying," Mr. Bradley may reply, "you are actually
saying that you have in these cases a quantitative perception in qualitative form." But I think not. We
have here a qualitative perception which subsequently
can be shown to rest on quantity (or rather on proportion; but we must go through quantity to get at proportion); yet I do not think that in as far as it is qualitative
it is also quantitative. The feelings which arise on
looking at the two objects are different, and their kind of
beauty distinct. This is all that is essential to perception
of their difference, and though analysis may introduce
the perception of quantity, I do not think this is natural
or indispensable. And in all measurements of intensity

there is great difficulty in ascertaining what is a change in kind, and what in degree. Quantities primarily range themselves as simple differences, and what are quantities of the same is a late and different investigation. We are told that pink is a light purple; but in our qualitative perception of the two we were surely not aware of this "more and less."

Now, I do not think that instances such as the above justify the paradox of alleging that we can perceive more and less *(in) a qualitative form.* Between a qualitative perception and a vague perception of quantity there is a gulf which I cannot get over. In quantity there must be sameness, and degrees, however rudimentary, of the attribute which is the same in both objects of comparison. In quality there may be a generic sameness, such as that common to all coloured surfaces; but this sameness is not the attribute in respect of which the two qualities are distinguished.

I do not know the authority for Mr. Bradley's allegation about nice perception of quantitative differences on the part of savages who cannot count. And supposing that the instance he gives is one of true, direct perception (all suggestions of what has been *done* being excluded), I admit that so strong an instance surprises me. "Take one from a flock of forty sheep, and in a moment they (the savages) perceive the difference." Nor do I know, assuming the general correctness of the fact, how Mr. Bradley would more precisely interpret it. I feel that there is something wearisome in detailed analysis, which must be purely hypothetical, of an isolated fact; but I cannot help thinking that such analysis, conducted, if possible, in presence of the fact, and so as to interrogate it, is much wanted in Anthropology. I will therefore illustrate the difficulty in which the above statement places me, by suggesting two interpretations.

Of course we are not to suppose that the savages count one, two, three, up to thirty-nine; to allege that would be to accept Mr. Bradley's *reductio ad absurdum.*

But how am I even to be sure that in the recorded case there was not simply a perception that the pattern made by the beasts as they were scattered about was altered?  It is no feat to say, "There was a sheep by that tree, and he is gone;" or, "There were three sheep in a row on the left, now there are two."  But that is not saying that the sheep is nowhere in the field, and the savage can do that.  Well; can he?  But if he can, it may still be of the nature of what I should call a "pattern" perception, *i.e.* a perception of symmetry and its opposite, or of a definite change.  Of course, any one would see in five seconds if a book was taken out so as to leave a gap in an orderly bookshelf; one could review hundreds of volumes in a few seconds for such a purpose, or to find a book in a known binding. Or, again, any one would see at once if an angle was cut off a good-sized tessarakontagon by a straight line joining the extremities of its containing sides, those two sides being themselves erased; or if a spoke were missing in a bicycle wheel. And in all these cases we should have a pure perception of position or quality *carrying probably consequences known by experience to relate to quantity;* but not in itself of the nature of quantitative comparison at all. These are no more quantitative perceptions in respect of the contents directly perceived than it is a quantitative perception to say of one book that it cost 10*s.* 6*d.*, and of another that it cost a guinea; or to say, as an expert in tone-discrimination can of the knives of a steam planing-machine, " The pitch of the note they make shows them to be revolving so many times in a second."

But a wholly different interpretation is possible of the savage's alleged judgment; and I suspect this is more nearly what Mr. Bradley would adopt. Let the sheep be massed in a fold, so that no striking pattern is possible, and let forty so massed be seen first, and then thirty-nine of those forty; if the difference is then perceived, without inference from an act of removal observed or suspected, we must suppose that there is a direct perception of the difference of the two quantities, one of them being taken as unit and set off against the other. In this case, again, the detection of the differ-ence, and still more its being estimated [1] at one sheep, is no doubt remarkable.

---

[1] I assume that it is so estimated. What form does the complaint take—" You have touched my sheep," or, specifically, " You have taken one of my sheep"?

I compare with these interpretations a hypothetical case in which each applies to a different part of the same process. It is, or was, said that the man who counted the sheets of the *Times*, in the *Times* office, proceeded by tens, as we often do by twos or fours. Now, in interpreting these processes, there are many subtleties; but I do not think that counting and judging from quality ever merge into one another, though they may go on together. I think that in counting by twos or fours we often do *see the number* in the lots we count by, *i.e.* do make the enumerative judgment of perception about every individual unit, though we only take the time to put it into words at certain short intervals. Within every four, *e.g.* there would then be a short reckoning, conducted in silence, but still a set of four enumerative judgments which then is added on by a separate operation to the former sum. But in counting by tens, I should very much doubt if the single papers are perceived at all. I should think that they are merely *judged* to be there from certain feelings of the operator (assisted, perhaps, by some symmetrical disposition of their edges), and that the unit whose recurrence is really counted is the mass of ten. In such a case the operator employs an empirical inference from a qualitative judgment (for this purpose a pattern judgment ranks as a qualitative judgment), with reference to the single sheets, but actually enumerates, as the units by which he measures, the masses of ten sheets each. In the former element of the process, if this account were right (and if it is not right of this process, it certainly is of some), no unit is applied or employed, there is no tendency to counting, and no idea of it. Ten sheets must, indeed, have been often counted to acquire the power in question, but *ex hypothesi* they are not being counted now. In the latter element we have true counting, a recurrent judgment of perception about an identical, though distinguishable, unit.

Now, if the savage really perceives a difference of *quantity* between the thirty-nine and the forty, then the thirty-nine are to him as one of the masses of ten are to the operator in the above instance; *a* mass, an unit. It is not counting by single sheep as units; it is the point of first establishment of a unit by direct perception and comparison; and the unit is the mass of thirty-nine sheep.

How does this essentially differ from the qualitative perception of which I spoke as not directly involving measurement, or more or less? In this way: the difference in quantity which we infer from the directly qualitative perception is attached to it *ab extra*, and refers to units which lie outside the characters directly attended to in perception. And thus the judgment of qualitative difference—of a defect in symmetry, or of a discord in tone—does not in itself tell us which of the elements compared has the more, and which has the less. Whereas, when a unit is established, and a comparison, however rough, made in respect of it, we cannot but come to a judgment directly and properly involving more or less. And here, in so far as we have a unit, we have not only the essentials of measurement, but also of counting.

I may note that one would like to know whether the flock of sheep in this instance is the man's own flock, and whether, consequently, he knows the particular sheep severally [1] by headmark; if so, the process, though still marvellous in its way, becomes again quite different from either of those which I have suggested, and analogous to looking round a room full of people for a person that one knows; an act not absolutely instantaneous, if the numbers are large, but incomparably quicker than counting, and wholly unconnected with measurement.

No doubt the perception of a relation between the whole and its parts, when that relation is of a particular kind, does take the form of a judgment of qualitative comparison. And I have no objection to Mr. Bradley's moral that, "in considering number, we have no right to strike out the qualitative side." The unit and the limit which are, as we have seen, involved in counting, are, no doubt, a survival of the qualitative relation of part and whole. But in taking the quantitative form, the relation of part and whole *has not so much developed as diverged*

---

[1] Mr. Sully, "Psychology," p. 357, states the matter thus without hesitation.

*from* the type in which it gave rise primarily to a perception of qualitative difference. For this latter form persists by the side of the other—that in which the parts are homogeneous ; and the perception of quantity is due, not to the relation of whole and parts as such, but to the perception of homogeneousness of the parts, which is *pro tanto* a *deviation from* the ideal of the whole and its parts ; although, indeed, to make it possible to count the parts in a whole, so much heterogeneousness must remain as to distinguish the one part from the other. But the relation of whole and part in perception of symmetry or function is not one of quantity at all, and does not tend to become such. No one but an American humourist thinks of a man as diminished in quantity by the loss of a leg or an arm. The parts are here not apprehended as units. It is the apprehension of a part as a unit that indicates the initial point of this divergence into the judgment of quantitative comparison ; and where or in so far as this is absent, there can be no perception of more and less. The unit may be but roughly defined, yet there must be an interest in the process, feeling, or perception *as* homogeneous, and for the sake of that in it which is homogeneous, and for the sake of *its modifications* qua *homogeneous;* and this, however unanalyzed, I cannot call a perception "in a qualitative form."

5. We have seen that measurement rests on homogeneousness or identity. I shall now consider some

observations of Mr. Bradley's on the relation between Identity, Likeness, and Equality. Identity is always abstract.[1] The identity of individuals or of indiscernibles implies different contexts or different qualities in or by which the identicals are made distinguishable.

Therefore, for any exact purpose, it is necessary to specify the degree of abstraction with which an identity that we predicate or presuppose is to be understood. As it is not usual to do this in set terms, but at best to indicate the precise nature of an asserted identity by the emphasis laid on qualifying phrases, a demand makes itself felt for distinctive expressions which indicate the nature of an identity without further explanation. Such a term is "equal," which is said to mean "identical in quantity." I shall have to consider below what is involved in this conception of equality. But I wish to suggest in the first place that a somewhat similar justification may be alleged for the English use of the word "like" and "likeness," or even "exact likeness," as equivalent to one kind of identity.

I quote from "Principles of Logic," pages 261-2, the passages which are the occasion of these remarks. "Likeness and sameness should never be confused, for the former refers properly to a general impression. Similarity is a perceived relation between two terms which implies and rests upon a partial identity. If we say that A and B are alike, we must be taken to assert that

---

[1] "Principles of Logic," p. 263.

they have something the same.  But we do not specify this point of sameness, and the moment we do that we have gone beyond mere similarity." . . . " In mere general similarity the identity will be indefinite, where the likeness is more special it must be at least partly defined, and where the similarity is called ' exact,' I understand that there is a definite point or points, in respect of which the sameness is complete."

I may anticipate the point which really suggested the following comments, by saying that " like " and " similar " in the above passage correspond to the German " ähnlich," of which Mr. Bradley's remarks hold good beyond question.  But it is the practice, and in my judgment quite unavoidably so, to employ the English " like "[1] in correspondence with the German " gleich," which in some cases it is quite impossible to represent either by " same " or by " equal."  There is room in modern use for " identisch," " ähnlich," and " gleich," which have distinct and well-marked meanings in German.  English has only " same " and " like "[2] to represent these terms.  Like, to the best of my belief, covers two distinct meanings, as we shall see below.

Identity is, for us, a result of abstraction.  But it

[1] If " similar " could be kept out of this use and reserved for " ähnlich " it would be well.  I think that as a latinized and, so to speak, more artificial form, it has a tendency towards expressing the perception and not the simple fact.

[2] I count " identical " as equivalent to " same," and " similar," subject to my last note, as equivalent to " like."  " Gleich," in the sense of " equal," does not come in question here.

is sometimes predicated with a reserve which recognizes the abstractness of the identity, and sometimes not. When predicated without such reserve it is individual identity. It is then, I suppose, based on a partial identity which claims to be of an essential and dominant nature ; such an identity as that in virtue of which notes of the same pitch but of different quality are called the same note, or in virtue of which the man is the same individual as the child. (The precise nature of continued concrete identity is interesting, but cannot be gone into here.) Individual identity seems, then, as a rule, to be reached by inference ; it is predicated of a whole which includes much more than the partial identities on which the inference is based, and is compatible with varying degrees of inferential nexus to the extent of which it gives no clue. Thus it may cause us momentary surprise to be confronted with things that are identical without being like. Lotze[1] points out that the same thing in different states need not be " like " itself (" gleich "), but only " identical " with itself (" identisch ").

It would be inconvenient if in such a passage we had no English term at command except "same" and "identical." We should then require a cumbrous periphrasis in order to avoid an actual contradiction, and by such a periphrasis we could as easily dispense with the term " equal." If we are not expected to do this I do

---

[1] Lotze, "Metaphysik," sect. 19.

not know why we should give up "like," as signifying, not a perceived relation based on partial identity, but a special and limited kind of partial identity, viz. such identity of quality as excludes difference ; or identity, in some abstract respect, both of quality and of degree. In other words, if the proper meaning of likeness is a perceived relation based on a partial identity, it seems to be applicable, by abstraction out of this meaning, to mean a perceived or external identity, as distinguished from an inferred, individual, or essential identity.

When Mill, for instance, is condemned for arguing from likeness, it is fair to remember this justification. It is true that an unspecified likeness is no ground of argument, and it is true that when you specify points of likeness you really come to partial identity. On the other hand, it is also impossible to argue from an un-specified identity. "This is the same flower as that" does not justify the conclusion that the two flowers are the same in colour or in certain other details ("same" meaning here according to usage " of the same *species*)." You can indeed argue from this sameness on the ground of a system to which it refers, while in " this flower is like that" you cannot do so. But I doubt whether this is a *logical* distinction. I think that by any one but a botanist more legitimate conclusions could be drawn from "this flower is like," than from "this flower is the same." From the former we could infer "The second flower is beautiful, is fit for decorative design, is purple, is double or single." From the latter we could only infer certain essential matters of the structure of the flower, which are compatible with all sorts of variations of colour, size, and perfection of development.

And in the case of Mill in particular, we always find, or find at least in the crucial places of his doctrine of inference, that the points of likeness are to be specified. I therefore complain of a certain harshness in Mr. Bradley's insistence, against the English school, on the futility of arguing from likeness, when in interpreting Maas he construes likeness, as a matter of course, to mean partial identity. I may add that, to my mind, Mr. Bradley is more apt to fail in specifying his identity than Mr. Mill in specifying his likeness, and an unspecified identity is no better ground of inference—perhaps worse—than an unspecified likeness.

Even in defence of the term "exact likeness" I have something to suggest. Exact *and incomplete* likeness might, of course, include individual identity ; but from this fact none of the absurdities would follow, which Mr. Bradley deduces from the notion of exact likeness being equivalent to identity. Exact likeness would naturally be understood in the sense of likeness *measurably* exact, and excluding difference *in the respects to which the likeness extends.* This is the true meaning of "*gleichheit.*" Even the use of "*gleich*" in mathematics, though exactly corresponding to our use of equal, carries with it, I strongly suspect, a true shade of meaning which in our "equal" is forgotten. The simplest case of "*gleichheit*" is, perhaps, that of a colour-match. Here it has its full and, as I suspect, really universal meaning, viz. "identical in quality and in degree." In defining "gleich,"[1] Lotze calls the two terms so related *a* and *a*. We naturally speak of two "equal" terms as *a* and *b*. Of course the common as distinct from the mathematical rendering of "gleich" is supposed to be "*like*."[2] It is the usual word by which a comparison or simile is introduced.

I think that these usages are instructive. Colours pronounced "gleich," *i.e.* colours which match,[3] are in the full and proper sense "equal," and I regret that we are debarred by usage from calling them so. They admit of more or less, but are not more or less, and so must be considered as having the same number of the same units, which I take to be the definition of "equal." In other words, they are measurably identical in quality. The phrase "colour-equation" has recently come into use, but perhaps refers rather to the composition of the stimuli than to the quality of the colour, although the act of equation is effected by a comparison of quality.

---

[1] *Vide* Lotze, "Metaphysik," sect. 268. *Cf.* note on p. 47 of the English translation.

[2] "Gleichung" means "equation," but "Vergleichung," "comparison" in general.

[3] You may say the colours are "gleich," or, I suppose, that the objects are "gleich" in colour. You must not say simply that the objects are "gleich" because of one aspect of them. This would take you into the loose meaning which Mr. Bradley ascribes to "like," including points of difference in the basis of the relation of likeness.

(The question is, *e.g.* what mixture of red and green light is seen as a match to a given yellow.) Our word "equal," however, is far too degraded to give any such meaning its full prominence ; we think it enough to say with Mr. Bradley,[1] that "equality is sameness in quantity." But I do not see how there can possibly be sameness in quantity without an identical unit, and therefore without sameness in quality.[2] And so I cannot follow Mr. Bradley when he says,[3] "To use the sign = for qualitative sameness is surely barbarous ;" unless he means a generic or specific qualitative sameness which has not been established by comparison amounting to measurement, and which is therefore what I have called individual sameness, and does not amount to exact likeness. I should be inclined to say that, but for our abstraction, vicious in theory if convenient in practice, in the use of "equal," the sign = was the right sign for absolute qualitative sameness. But as we cannot use "equal" in the extended sense of "gleich" which brings out the aspects both of equality and of likeness, whether it is used for "equal" or for "like," I

[1] " Principles of Logic," p. 24.

[2] *Vide* sect. 3 of this chapter. The places quoted there show that Mr. Bradley is well aware of the relation which units must bear to their whole or centre. I may point out for the benefit of others, that in saying a gallon of water and a gallon of wine are the same in quantity, we ascribe to both the identical quality of filling space ; when we speak of equal weights of sugar and flour we ascribe to both the identical quality of gravity ; when we speak of two objects as equal in value, we ascribe to both the identical quality of being exchangeable, and, probably, exchange-able for money.     [3] " Principles of Logic," p. 24.

think that much confusion may be avoided by the use of "like" and "exactly like."

I will give one or two illustrations. "These two notes are the same," means that certain sounds, which from their main feature go by a name indicating their place in a scale, have the same place in that scale. The affirmation only concerns the pitch, leaving quality and loudness out of the question. If we wish to predicate about *them*, we must say, "these two notes are exactly alike." We then retain the word note merely as the *name* of the sound in question; but we say of the sounds as a whole[1] that they produce the same immediate impression on us, and thus assert much more than in the former case. By help of the latter assertion we could infer from the pleasantness or the unpleasantness of the one to that of the other; the former would not enable us to do this. No doubt we might attain the same result by saying, "These two musical sounds are identical in pitch, quality, and loudness." And it is a counsel of perfection always to speak accurately. I only say that equality is reserved as a short term for one kind of identity; I do not see why likeness should not be reserved for another.

So with the same thing in its different states. If we mean that it is perceptibly alike in any two states, we must say so; for such likeness is not implied in its

---

[1] If "these" creates a difficulty, we might substitute for it a mention of the different instruments on which the note has different qualities.

being the same. The determinants which in common speech indicate the nature of an identity are very subtle, and would repay inquiry. If we say, " I have found the same flower that you found," we mean a flower of the same species. I suppose this depends on the purpose which governs the degree of distinction we desire to make. As a rule, it seems to me, " a flower," " the flower," " that flower," means a species,[1] and not an individual ; and so does "that Rotifer," "that Polyzoon." This seems not to be so with the higher animals or with human beings. The same man never means anything but the same individual. The same butterfly or beetle seems to mean the same species. This is, of course, always apart from special contexts which may confer a special interest on any object. I do not feel sure if it would be intelligible (supposing it to be true) to say, " The Scotch ptarmigan is the same bird as the Norwegian ptarmigan." I think we should say, " the same species as." We should say, "This is the same gentian that grows in the Engadine." We should not say, " This is the same horse that runs wild in the prairies." If we say, " These silks are of the same colour," I think this does mean that the colours are exactly alike ; it might easily mean that the colours are of the same class, *e.g.* both blue, and not exclude their being of different shades. In " shades of the same colour " we have this meaning.

---

[1] I think it is quite good, or at least quite usual, English to say, " These are the same flower, but they are not very like."

Therefore it seems that we are to judge from custom and context, *i.e.* especially from the purpose of a judgment before us, what kind and degree of identity is alleged in any affirmation of sameness. I think it natural that we should try and help ourselves out by giving one kind of identity a special name.

It follows further, from the meaning I have given to likeness, that it refers to the kind of identity, viz. the identity of indiscernibles in direct comparison, on which, I should think, all other identities must rest as inferences. And therefore one might say that it is as true that all identity rests on likeness as that, according to Mr. Bradley's view, all likeness rests on identity.

To repeat the main fact to which I wished to draw attention. The most accurate German writing requires "gleich" besides "identisch" and "ähnlich," and in a sense which is not precisely represented either by "equal" or by "like," but combines, in a way justified and demanded by theory, the meanings of both. The definition[1] of "gleich" in contrast with that of "ähnlich" leaves no doubt that it means qualitative identity, the identity of qualities measured and judged "equal," *i.e.* indiscernible in degree. Inveterate custom prevents us from giving "equal" the full sense of "gleich," though I am sure we should gain in precision by doing so.[2] I

---

[1] Lotze, "Metaphysik," sect. 268.

[2] We should not be so much tempted to manipulate numbers *per se*, and forget that they are only the vehicle of quantity.

therefore suggest that we may not be so far wrong in using "like" or "exactly like," for a kind of identity. This is no doubt immediately perceived identity, external and not inferred (except in the remoter sense in which all judgment involves inference) ; but for all that it is not a feeling in us, or perceived relation *qua perceived.* It is referred out of our heads to the object in an abstract aspect, just as are identity, quantity, causation, or any other relative attributes ; and the metaphysical question, what becomes of likeness if we are not there to compare, is not to interfere with the immediate fact that we refer to it as to any other objective content. We might conveniently retain "similar" in a sense corresponding to "ähnlich," for objects related by having points of identity ("exact likeness," or "gleichheit") mixed up with differences.

6. I add the following remarks before leaving the subject of Number. It is an interesting question in the theory of chance whether the ratio which expresses a chance must express something that actually happens "in the long run." I do not purpose to discuss the question at length, but merely to speak of a minor difficulty which I find in Mr. Bradley's argument.

I agree with Mr. Bradley, who is here in accord with Lotze, that there is no meaning in asking whether every chance must be realized "in the long run," or "if you go on long enough." Every series of experiments "must stop short at some finite number, however large it be."[1]  But in Mr. Bradley's argument I find a puzzle, which does not occur in Lotze, as I read him.  It is arbitrary, I admit, to break off your experiments just when the calculated and actual numbers coincide.  It is obvious that if you went on they might diverge again.  But Mr. Bradley urges, herein differing from Lotze, that not only they *might*, but they *must* diverge.  " If[2] I toss the coin until the numbers are equal, of course they will be equal.  If I toss it once more, then, by the hypothesis, they become unequal.  I might just as well say, ' If I only go on long enough, the events will certainly not answer to the chances.' "

I may begin by pointing out that in the above passage, the " numbers are equal " means that the number of observed throws which come " heads," is equal to the number of those which come " tails," which is what ought to happen *out of any total even number*, if the fraction expressing the chances is one-half for each case.  It may be the merest accident, but bears curiously on my point, that in the parallel place in Lotze to which Mr. Bradley refers, the phrase " the two numbers coincide " alludes to the calculated number coinciding with the observed number.  I do not care whether Mr. Bradley may possibly have misread Lotze or not ; that does not affect the value of his views.  But I very much doubt whether in the case which Mr. Bradley gives, the two numbers of which Lotze speaks, *i.e.* the

<hr>

[1] Lotze, " Logik," sect. 286.　　　　[2] " Principles of Logic," p. 214.

calculated and the observed number, do cease to coincide. Mr. Bradley's argument goes to saying that no ratio can ever be realized in a fraction of a cycle. But (I am no mathematician) this *seems* to be a paradox, and to involve classing together cases which are wholly distinct. The distinction cannot, indeed, appear with the ratio one-half, but in another instance is visible at once. Say I have thrown a single die thirty times, and each of the six sides has come up five times ; I then throw twice more, and two different sides turn up. Surely in this case the numbers, *i.e.* the calculated number and the observed number, do continue to coincide. In one-third of the cycle we have had one-third of the sides. If, on the other hand, we had thrown the same side twice for our thirty-first and thirty-second throw, then we should have had one-third of the cycle and only one-sixth of the sides, and in that case the observed and calculated number would not coincide.

The conception of one-third of a cycle may be objected to as involving an hypothesis, and alluding to the future. You have not thrown the cycle of six (from thirty-one to thirty-six inclusive) ; what right have you, then, to speak of the two throws, thirty-one and thirty-two, as two *out of six?* Or in eleven tosses of a coin, what right have you to call the eleventh, one toss *out of two?* If you allude to the future so far, why not further? And thus any error might be compensated. One can only admit the objection. It is well grounded so far as this, that the hypothesis must not be given out as a fact. We have not two throws *out of six*, nor one toss *out of two;* but simply two throws and one toss, after clearing away all those which enter into equal cycles.

On the other hand, the rule laid down in the fraction one-sixth, is itself hypothetical; and if we will not admit that its condition applies, we must at least not allege that the rule is broken. It says, when applied to a series, of each side of the die, "Once in every six throws;" *i.e. if* there are six throws, any given side ought to be thrown once. But if there are not six throws the rule predicts nothing. If so, there are no calculated numbers for a broken cycle, and you cannot say that the calculated and observed numbers either coincide or do not coincide. Considering the nature of numerical series, I am not satisfied with this result. It is plain that a numerical series reveals its character gradually and by approximation. If you throw once only, and the six turns up, you have formally one in one. But the throw excludes no series in which the six occurs once at least. It does not exclude such series; it is simply undetermined in respect of them. Another throw determines it further, and so on till the limit is reached which we, or the nature of the case, may fix. As it is possible for a series, without being completed, to depart from a rule, it is fair, for the purpose of ascertaining whether this is so, to test it by the rule which we have an interest in judging it by, and which is in this case furnished by the condition of the hypothetical judgment expressed in the fraction one-sixth. In this sense, as a test of compatibility, we *should*, no doubt, be taking account of the future, but only as an hypothesis. The strongest objection to such a treatment is the point which I hinted at above. Even six consecutive throws of the same side of the die are reconcilable with the formula one-sixth, if we look forward to completing thirty-six throws. So, if we are to apply hypotheses, why not apply such as this, and make all series correct? We can only answer that you may apply any hypothesis as long as you state clearly what it is that you apply. But the calculated numbers for any total set of throws, which is not a complete set of cycles, must be either impossible to be made out, and then there can be no question of calculated and observed numbers coinciding, or they must be such numbers as are compatible with correctness at the completion of the next cycle ; and, if so, the calculated and the observed numbers do coincide in some cases of broken cycles, and do not in others ; and therefore it is not necessary that the series should depart from the ratio.

I must end with a warning. We are *not* to take account of the order of cases within the total number of actual throws which we are considering. I only supposed a certain order to give clearness to the illustration.

If in estimating chances we take in conditions which operate differently at different times, that is our affair, and we must put up with the consequent inaccuracy of our fraction during the several portions of the time, for the sake of its accuracy as applied to the total of time. A sportsman's chance of killing his birds may be greater in the morning than in the afternoon; but it may be difficult to formulate this difference, and we may try to state the chance in general terms only applying to the whole day. It is, then, to be expected that the series, even if correct according to the ratio, will only be so over the whole day together, and not in morning or afternoon taken apart. If we want a more accurate determination for the parts of time, we must state the conditions of each separately, and obtain a ratio for each, which we can afterwards, if we like, combine into a result applicable to the whole day.

I have dwelt long enough on a quite simple point; I will conclude with an extreme instance. If there were fifty possible cases of some occurrence, with equal chances in favour of each, the fraction for each being $\frac{1}{50}$; if in the first ninety trials each case had occurred once, and besides this, forty different cases had occurred a second time, surely it would be pedantic to deny that such a series was essentially different in respect of conformity to the ratio, from one in which the first ninety trials gave, say, fifty of one case and forty of another.

# CHAPTER III.

## THE NATURE OF ASSERTION.

1. THE striking view which, in substantial agreement with Sigwart, Mr. Bradley propounds on the relation of modality to assertion, appears to me to admit and demand in two respects a different application from that which he gives it. Let us grant that a modal (*i.e.* possible or necessary) judgment is related to a simple assertion, as a hypothetical to a categorical judgment; that the possible and the necessary are signs of inference, and belong to the content of the judgment, while an assertion is simply bare affirmation as such, which formally claims that reality is qualified by the content of the judgment; we may still, I think, resist both the entire irrationality with which the view before us invests the act of affirmation,[1] and the corollary which denies that apodeictic modality strengthens our assertions.

---

[1] *Cf.* "Principles of Logic," pp. 22 and 14. "This content, we have seen, is the same both in the assertion and out of it. If you ask instead of judging, what is asked is precisely the same as what is judged." It is exceedingly hard to determine such a problem as this by pure introspection; the accompaniments of judgment are so easily confused with

(i.) The relation of assertion to modality depends on the nature of assertion or judgment. Mr. Bradley says, in effect, that judgment consists in alleging a content to be true of reality, and the real or reality is what appears in presentation. I recognize the value of this account of the matter, but have already found stumbling-blocks in the mode and degree of this presentation of the real. It seems that till we have it all we do not have it at all ;[1] and unless we admit degrees of truth, and more and less of fact, I do not see how we can escape the latter alternative, viz. that in no aspect of reality about which, nor in any content which, we predicate, have we any hold on reality at all. But even if we were to admit degrees of fact, Mr. Bradley's account of the act of affirmation would still debar us

its essence. But, so far as I can see, the statement quoted does not represent my experience, nor can I understand it on theoretical grounds. I cannot but connect it with the habit of treating the sentence as the exact counterpart of the judgment (*vide* below, chap. iv.). I believe that it would be worth considering whether every idea that comes before the mind is not really in some modality, a modality varying with the attachments which its content furnishes to the world of our knowledge. I also entertain a doubt whether a question is a form of knowledge, an act of thought, at all, and not rather a form of language in which the desire for a certain act on the part of another moral agent is embodied. A question has, I incline to think, no more meaning *for knowledge* than an imperative sentence. Neither, I suspect, can be addressed to oneself, or have any meaning apart from the presence of a moral agent external to oneself. I hope to treat of this subject at greater length elsewhere.

[1] *Contrast* "Principles of Logic," p.,51. " Nothing . . . . can immediately encounter me save that which is present. If I have it not here and now, I do not have it at all." But of course it turns out that the real cannot be confined within the limits of the present.

from expressing those different degrees in the strength of our assertions. As I understand him, he holds that in judgment we simply claim for an idea in our mind that it is true of reality ;[1] or that reality is "qualified by " this idea, "idea" being taken in the sense of a meaning, which our actual momentary mental image and processes only symbolize—a view allied to Berkeley's. We effect the reference of our meaning to reality by joining it, through some identical quality, with our consciousness of present perception, which is the only actual contact that we have with "the real." The claim based on this reference is not a matter of degree. Belief, our habitual state of mind in relation to a given judgment, is psychological,[2] and has degrees ; judgment is primarily logical, and has no degrees. There is, then, I may observe, just a loophole for escaping from the doctrine of the " Grammar of Assent," which makes assent or affirmation both absolute and irrational, in this agreeing only too well, as it seems to me, with Mr. Bradley's view. He, however, leaves himself belief to fall back on, though the title of a mere psychological state is not very appropriate to conviction proportioned to inference. I am aware that Mr. Bradley is able to account for qualified assertion in another way, which follows from his view of modality.

I do not know if I am right in tracing Mr. Bradley's view of judgment to his practice, which will occupy us

---

[1] " Principles of Logic," pp. 73-5.　　　　[2] Ibid. p. 21.

later on, of taking one "point of identity" to be as good as another for purposes of inference. He habitually, as it appears to me, neglects all considerations arising out of the special nature and limits of different identities; and consequently supposes that where *any* point of qualitative identity enables us to connect an ideal content (a "meaning" in the sense explained above) with reality as given in presentation, we must make this judgment with a degree of assertion which is always the same. This is, I imagine, one element in Mr. Bradley's view. He refuses to entertain the idea of measuring the degree and extent of identity by which the content of an idea is for us attached to reality.

Another element is a metaphysical doctrine. "If S — P is fact, it cannot be more than fact; if it is less than fact, it is nothing at all."[1] I see no *primâ facie* ground for this allegation, except on the assumption that fact is not for us a construction, but is something given as a sensuous phenomenon, immediate, external to thought, and simply mirrored in thought. But if the only fact is ultimate and non-phenomenal,[2] it seems to me that *in an ultimate sense* everything which we assert is less than fact, and that if we wish it to take any character as fact at all we must measure our claim by the degree in which the affirmed content, *as affirmed*, is capable of entering into the ultimate non-phenomenal fact. Such a conception is not wholly alien from Mr.

---

[1] "Principles of Logic," p. 181.     [2] Ibid. p. 180.

Bradley's view, which admits that the real is not summed up in presentation, but only makes itself felt there by us, and which also attaches a certain importance to "finding a place" for an imagined fact in the series of events. The reason of this importance, on his view, I do not quite see, for according to it you may have in your mind an imagined fact, which links itself to present perception by a qualitative identity, so that you know that it stands for something in past experience, and this, as I read Mr. Bradley's theory, would at once justify you in affirming it *qua* fact, in the ordinary meaning of the words which express it. To me such an affirmation appears unjustifiable. To employ the capital instance which Mr. Bradley takes, it would constantly have to be made of the content of a dream, which is recollected with all the quality and character of reality, and is only judged to have been dreamed because we can prove that it was not real, and perhaps that it entered our consciousness in the sleeping hours. I do not mean that this phenomenon is normal, but it is quite common. Normally, I suppose, a dream is distinguished by quality from a waking reality ; but where it is not, we are by no means helpless.

Thus I should like to insist less on the element of arbitrary synthesis and "mere" judgment,[1] of which in my own experience I am wholly unaware ; to negative the idea that affirmation is independent of content, and

<hr>

[1] See chap. i., sect. 4.

therefore, as it appears to me, wholly irrational; and consequently, not indeed to treat modality as formal and a case of assertion, but to treat assertion as a matter of content and as a case of modality. On the question whether affirmation is independent of content, I must refer back to note, p. 114, and add that I believe myself to be wholly unable to judge a suggested content true of reality, without either analyzing and re-thinking it as ground and conclusion, or adding a ground *ab extra*, by which I modify the content as I give it my assent. "The arbitrary synthesis of a suggestion with reality" represents to my mind a contradiction in terms. A synthesis with reality seems to me to be the act of recognizing attachments and systematic relations which we cannot make, but can only find.[1] If space permits, I shall endeavour to point out later how, to my mind, Mr. Bradley altogether underrates the complexity of the act of judgment. For instance, though I have no objection, on the merits of the question, to admitting that there are judgments in which one idea is affirmed, without copula, of present reality, yet I must entirely decline to find cases of such judgments in the cry of "Wolf!" or "Fire!" Another instance which is suggested in the same passage—"Miserable!"—comes nearer to what such a judgment should be. But I cannot recognize the word spoken aloud as any test at all of

---

[1] *Cf.* "Principles of Logic," p. 87, "Perhaps we need not judge, but, if we judge, we lose all our liberty."

what goes on in the mind. The word of command, "March!" is surely not addressed to the environment in general; it is a definite symbol with a precise content and limited reference. "Wolf!" and "Fire!" are, like "March!" each of them merely the emphatic word in a sentence, which being given voice suggests the rest. And then, what is *one* idea? Mr. Bradley knows well how little the phrase tells us, and by using it in the place, as a phrase of controversy, surely turns his back on the faithful reader who has already granted him that no judgment "contains more than one idea."[1]

This, then, is my first gloss on Mr. Bradley's theory. I should have thought that the affirmation of the categorical or assertorical judgment was a matter of content, and homogeneous with the possibility and necessity of the hypothetical, and was therefore capable of infinite degrees, but that the assertorical is worse off than the hypothetical judgment, inasmuch as, though really conditioned, it does not state explicitly the condition on which its truth depends, but leaves us to choose it for ourselves out of a concrete mass.[2] The difference, indeed, is often simply grammatical; but this is not, strictly speaking, a difference between judgments at all. I am perplexed, however, considering Mr. Bradley's treatment of the relation between categorical and hypothetical judgments, to find him here, while identifying the assertorical with the categorical, nevertheless drawing a

---

[1] "Principles of Logic," p. 12.     [2] *Cf.* Ibid. p. 90.

broad line of difference in kind between the assertorical and the hypothetical. The only line which I should care to draw would be that between judgments into the content of which time enters, and those where time is indifferent. The former can pass into the latter, but only with such modifications as would make them practically unrecognizable.

(ii.) The above considerations naturally lead me to differ from Mr. Bradley and from Sigwart as to the relative strength with which we make categorical and apodeictic assertions. But I must begin with a large concession, which may appear to leave nothing worth arguing about. It is true that in "categorical" judging we do not as a rule measure the strength with which we assert, and I should suppose that uneducated or un-civilized men cannot do so. You can only actually measure the strength of one assertion by pitting it against another. If there is no conflict of assertions, and no idea of a conflict, there is, as a rule, no consciousness that the assertion we make has only relative strength. And it may be said, from Mr. Bradley's point of view, that he admits and maintains that any judgment becomes inferential (and therefore necessary, and so modal) when reasserted against a doubt ; but he holds that this modal character is not essential to the nature of judgment as such.

Nevertheless, it appears to me that in the relations of content which force a judgment upon us, we have the standard of measurement of the strength with which the assertion is made.  This *is* the strength, though we may not reflect upon it till denial makes us.  I can imagine that it may be replied, "No.  Not the standard of the strength with which you assert; but the standard of your right to assert, which is a very different thing."  When you judge, the objector would continue you commit yourself wholly; whether you are right to do so is a question for you before you judge, and for you and others after.  But you cannot modify your judgment.

I admit, as I have said, that in the assertions of uneducated or uncivilized persons there is something which seems to bear out such a notion as this.  And yet I believe that it rests upon a confusion; and that if, on being asked how strongly he means to assert, an ordinary person would say, "Fact is fact, and I can do no more than say a thing is fact," this is due to the influence of popular theory, and is not reconcilable with the practice of common sense.  The confusion which I speak of is this.  We are apt not to distinguish what we aim at expressing from what we succeed in expressing.  Now, our absolute certainty always refers to the former, never to the latter.  But the former, as Mr. Bradley has pointed out over and over again, is never got into any act of thought.  What we aim at, what the form of every judgment claims to predicate (I do not say that Mr. Bradley backs me up in quite this notion), is the whole non-phenomenal fact, the whole of Reality. And it is to this, and to this only, that our dead level of certainty in the ordinary judgment applies. All actual judgments are provisional, and provisional in different degrees; and we know this quite well and admit it in practice, or admit it in practice even if we do not know it in theory. Nothing is more striking and obvious than this provisional character even of the most direct judgments of perception. We admit them as true and certain, but for their purpose only. Let the purpose be changed, *e.g.* let legal importance suddenly attach to a statement made in casual conversation, like " I saw A. B. in Victoria Station this morning," and at once every detail becomes doubtful. Not in the least that (in the case I wish to put) we doubt the truth of the statement in an ordinary sense ; rather, the truth which was fearlessly asserted and accepted meant no more than this, that some real incident happened which might be *bonâ fide* so described for ordinary purposes. We do not doubt that *something* happened, but we do not in the least pledge ourselves that that something has been actually or accurately described. And no one resents cross-examination as to precise details or omissions in a statement, when it is clear that a new purpose has emerged since the statement was made. The " something " which is asserted with absolute certainty, and the definition of which our judgments try progressively to give, can never be defined accurately till it is defined completely.  And it would then amount to the entire ultimate Fact.  But in each case we are content when our purpose is served.  This fact, that all judging is relative to a purpose, and that cross-examination is not resented, as a rule, if a statement has to be used for another purpose than that for which it was originally made, shows that we do not really attach uniform strength of assertion even to our ordinary assertorical judgments ; and the absolute assent which is sometimes ascribed to our judgments does not really refer to them, but to the ultimate fact which they do indeed claim to represent, but only *ad hoc.*

But if absolute certainty only attaches to Reality as a whole, why should it attach especially to modal judgments ; and is not Sigwart right in his contention that the strength of assertion with which a necessary judgment introduces its thesis, does not really exceed, but is very apt to be less than, the strength of assertion with which an ordinary categorical judgment is affirmed ?  The "must" which is the sign of apodeictic judgment does, as Sigwart remarks, often in real life indicate a very modest degree of confidence in an assertion ; as when we say, "He must (surely) have arrived by this time."  I alluded above[1] to Sigwart's opinion expressed in the same passage, that there must be ultimate premises of proof which are not themselves proved ; a prejudice of "common sense" by his adoption of which,

[1] See chap. i., sect. 4.

if he really adopted it, Aristotle placed himself on a lower logical standpoint than that of Plato.

Now, I am wholly unable to take Sigwart's point of view in this matter, and the undoubted fact which he alleges as to the colloquial use of "must" appears to me to make against him. You cannot assert anything without a reason, that is to say, whenever you assert, you claim to have a reason, or think you have one; you feel as if you had one, even if on cross-examination it is not producible. Therefore, as it seems to me, every judgment rests on the modal "may" or "must" ("may" if it is a "particular" judgment). The only difference in this respect between a categorical or "absolute" and a hypothetical or apodeictic judgment is that in the categorical judgment you do not say what your reasons are, and they may and often do *fall outside* the content of the judgment as understood by a hearer—this is the case with a judgment collected from the testimony of others—while in the hypothetical judgment you explicitly select and allege the reason or condition, which being granted the thesis or consequent cannot but follow. But now, from the very fact that the two forms of judgment, the categorical and the hypothetical, are not separable by an absolute line (I really do not know in what sense Mr. Bradley uses categorical[1] in this chapter, but as there are in strictness no categoricals, except a class of which he says but little, I take the word to be here used

---

[1] " Principles of Logic," p. 107.

with reference really to grammatical shape or perhaps in the sense that "assertions about particular fact are categorical"), from this very fact it follows that the reason of a categorical judgment need gain nothing by being thrown into hypothetical form. Not the form but the content is what makes the assertion, and a bad reason is no better for being made explicit ; on the contrary, in making it explicit we often detect its badness, and it is this that affects the "must" with an intonation of doubt, and often loads it with an adverb—"Surely he must have," etc. The idle attempt indicated by the adverb to superadd a formal assertiveness to our assertion, frustrates and betrays itself, because strength of assertion depends on content, and no hope or interest of our own can directly affect our vision of the connection of a content with reality.

But the complementary fact to that which Sigwart alleges is still more significant. Where you have an apodeictic judgment with a content at all adequate to its hypothetical form, then no categorical judgment with its confused antecedent will present itself with equal and opposing strength. This is the more remarkable from the fact that every hypothetical judgment challenges comparison with the highest scientific ideal of truth, and so is made with a certain reserve and a sense of its provisional character. And yet if it is opposed to a categorical or absolute judgment which includes in its subject, and so admits, the antecedent of the hypothetical, no one doubts for a moment that it overthrows the categorical. Even between judgments of the class to which Sigwart alludes and apparently assertorical negations of them, it is quite doubtful which we believe. " He must have come " and " He has not come " are in all practical life recognized as judgments of just the same order, and to which of the two we assent depends on the intonation with which they are expressed in language, on the evidence which circumstances show us to underlie one or the other, or on our knowledge of the speakers.

It may be that Mr. Bradley is using categorical, not with reference to grammatical shape, but with reference to one of the meanings which he has provisionally assigned to the term in his earlier chapters.

No doubt judgments such as these, judgments which assert the existence of the things which they mention, and not merely the basis of a hypothetical *connection* of certain elements of content—these judgments have a strength in their very weakness. They assert a momentary conjunction of content and imply its connection, instead of asserting the basis of connection and implying the conjunction. And therefore the universal, *i.e.* hypothetical or necessary judgment, which asserts *imprimis* and explicitly the ground of *connection* of content, cannot get at them to deny them. They rely on no rational connection at all, or else on one which is sheltered behind a prominence of mere actual fact. " The lily which I copied had a triangular stem." Science can do little against such a statement—a stem may get out of shape by being crushed in the corner of a wall; and the universal, "The lily, as such, has a round stem," may destroy in the above individual judgment any element of rationality that it might claim—may show, that is, that "lily" has nothing to do with the matter, and the same thing might have happened with an onion; but it cannot annihilate the actual fact that there was this one particular plant-stem, which was that of a lily, *and* was triangular. It is a grave question whether such a proposition is not a mere summary of two judgments; whether "lily," which is a mere superfluous detail, has a right to be in the subject at all.

Nevertheless, even judgments of this class are theoretically accessible to contradiction; they turn out on analysis, as Mr. Bradley has most excellently shown, to be but lower and imperfect phases of hypothetical [1] or scientific assertion. And as such imperfect phases, they have lower strength of assertion, as they have less rationality. This is no doubt a paradox when we apply it to the simplest assertions, say, about our own feelings, such judgments as Mr. Bradley, following Sigwart, would call analytic judgments of sense, like, "That hurts," "I am hot." Nothing can be greater, it would seem, than the strength of assertion of these judgments. It is one

---

[1] "Principles of Logic," 93 ff. I am unable to reconcile this most valuable inquiry into the import of judgments with Mr. Bradley's views on Modality.

thing to say that they cannot be proved, and another to deny that they are asserted absolutely. But we must bear in mind the vagueness of the purpose which such judgments have to satisfy. It is true that no observer could or dares to deny them, and we ourselves are not likely to criticise their rendering of the something which we feel and wish to express. But we know very well that under a doctor's cross-questioning our descriptions have to be altered. Here, as elsewhere, our absolute assertion refers to the real fact, not to the content of our judgment, which is only relative to a purpose. I admit that the question becomes thorny when we get into this region ; for assertions about pleasure and pain are precisely those which seem to be thrown out at times with the most emphatic insistence. One might ask whether this is not an insistence of feeling rather than of assertion, whether the judgment (though significant speech cannot be a mere interjection) does not in these cases approach the level of the interjection. I. mean that perhaps we do not in these cases think of or attach importance to the precise vehicle of assertion ; we do not especially care what in particular we say, although no doubt the whole state which we have it in mind to express is a certainty of the most present kind. I therefore venture to doubt whether the intense conviction which goes with statements of direct personal feelings is a strength of assertion directed to the content of the judgment. We should, often at least, not meet a cor-

rection with positive denial, but with absolute indifference ; the description, we should say, was nothing
to us, we had the fact in ourselves.   Do I mean to say
that I assert the law of gravity with a greater strength
of assertion than that I am in pain (when I seem to feel
myself to be so) ?   First, if I cannot, it would be because
the second judgment contained absolutely no element
which I could conceive as accessible to denial by a
universal judgment, no connection of content, but simply
a bald assertion that this content is.   All categorical
judgments have this tendency, as we have seen.   But,
secondly, if a judgment were to embody nothing but this
tendency, it could not remain a judgment.   Its *form*, its
*claim*, at least, is to be rational.   Even the judgment that
"I am in pain" carries with it some notion of cause or
of permanence, some implication as to the "I" and the
pain which are thus connected.   Hysterical patients will
complain of acute pain and inability to move, and
though the pain is in a sense unreal, it is not illusory.
The physician does not deny that the patient is suffering,
or that movement causes agony ; but nevertheless he
knows that the content of the judgment is, as a reference
to the real world, false ; that is, the pain and other
symptoms are not of the inevitable and constant character which they appear to the patient to possess.   Not
unfrequently moral treatment will succeed against such
symptoms ; a tone of command or of persuasion will
destroy the state which appeared to be physical and

constant. In a case which turns out thus, the judgment formed by the physician on indications *ab extra*, and therefore hypothetical or scientific, is rightly accepted as obviously the same in kind as the patient's own judgment of his state, but higher in degree of certainty.

I shall be reminded that I was to speak not of right to assert, but of strength of assertion ; and I shall be asked how the patient's certainty of the nature of his own pain, and still more, in simple and common cases, his certainty of the fact of it, is affected by the possibility of there being another judgment which may rightly contradict some element in his.

And my answer is that I did not adduce the case of " nerve-mimicry " of pain to prove that the patient did not assert strongly, but to illustrate the conception that what he wishes to assert strongly is not in fact expressed within his judgment. By the necessities of knowledge, what he succeeds in expressing is imperfect and uncertain ; and his apparent strength of affirmation, where it exists, is due to the confusion pointed out above, between what he wants to say and what he does say. Pain, I may add, disturbs the mind so that the more scientific judgment by which he might test his primary affirmation may not be easily framed. I will take another and very striking instance of analogous confusion. A preacher exclaims passionately, " *I* want no evidence ; I *know* these things to be true "—these things being a variety of historical incidents. He means to assert the great fact of religious experience which has coloured his whole life; but the inability to throw this into rational form drives him to find the precise content needed for explicit judgment in doubtful historical matter, which he asserts with all his force purely by an intellectual confusion. What he really wants to assert is only in the smallest degree present in his judgment at all. "But he *does* assert most strongly, and you said he could not do so without a necessary judgment." I reply that in this case *he makes a necessary judgment*, though a false one, and one resting on a confusion. He says, "If man has religion and a conscience, such and such historical matters must be true." The extreme strength of his assertion has against his will and intention taken him out of the region of the categorical into that of the inferential judgment.

Thus the principle alleged above applies even to Categoricals, in the sense of judgments about individuals which imply the existence of the elements that enter into them. The absolute strength of their assertion does not apply to their precise content, and we are as a rule willing to surrender their precise content at the onslaught of a scientific judgment; the ultimate fact which we wish to affirm returning upon us then in some other form. And thus, as a rule, the more precise we are in categorical judging, the more are we willing to doubt our own assertion. If instead of "I am in pain," I had said, "I have a toothache," I should not for a moment question the judgment of a dentist who should say, " You have not toothache, but pain arising from caries of the jawbone." The more precise the less certain ; well then, I shall be told, necessity and hypothesis, after all, do fall below absolute assertion. Not so ; when once our foot is on the ladder of careful judgment, then the more precision, the more strength of assertion. But before we are capable of measuring strength of assertion at all, there is, of course, an apparent dead level of certainty ; we always mean to speak the truth, and that is all we know about the matter. The apparent weakness of modal assertion is not a descent from absolute assertion, but is the effect of measurement. Absolute assertion is a pure fiction resting on failure to distinguish intention from performance, and discountenanced by common sense. The case of the preacher is the same confusion at a higher grade, after the things confused have long become distinct and divergent. This is not a mere failure to distinguish, but an absolute blunder of identification. He makes his connection of content quite explicit, but " precise enough—precisely wrong." Aiming at a categorical judgment of immediate experience, he uses, in order to get the highest strength of assertion, the apodeictic form of judgment, but gives it a content which has no more rational connection than there is between triangularity and a round stem. The fact is, there is in the sense now under discussion no such thing as a categorical judgment, but there is a gradual approach to one, which reaches its goal at the point where the judgment form disappears and gives place to the interjection. And unanalyzed strength of assertion, as opposed to a consciousness which affirms by virtue of grounds, seems greater as analysis is less, and is just about to reach its climax, as reference and therefore assertion altogether disappear.

These considerations have an important bearing on the nature of historical and legal proof, where we are but seldom able to employ scientific judgment directly. I am convinced that the whole realm of history should be regarded somewhat differently from the way in which we regard it; rather as a means of bringing before us certain well-marked phases and indubitable creations of the human soul, in an orderly setting, than as an absolute record of thoroughly definite fact. If we straightforwardly consider the popular conceptions of prominent men and current accounts of important facts which prevail in our own day, we shall see that, whatever the historian's task may be, its value cannot depend on his account of characters and motives, or even conversations and campaigns, being such that, like a theorem in Euclid, it will stand the hottest critical furnace in every detail.

The conditions of legal proof demand a few words. Here we have *primâ facie* the highest certainty, a certainty on which life and death, honour and well-being, are staked at every turn. Yet the conditions of legal proof exclude, except by an occasional and accidental subsumption, any scientific analysis of data ; and science in court, as I shall show lower down, is really not science, but mere fact. And I do not think that, apart from the narrowly limited purposes of law, the facts on which these issues turn are always or often established in a scientific sense. The evidence which has been adduced for clairvoyance or the Lourdes miracles would have hung a hundred men, but before the tribunal of science it is as nothing. The reason of this is that the purposes of law grant a far greater value to testimony than do those of science ; so far greater, indeed, as to obscure the whole point and function of testimony. Testimony is not, as we come to think it, a sort of prop or buttress added outside a matter supported by it, so that a hundred such props make it firmer than twenty : it is simply a contribution to content ; for all proof is by content. Thus when, in the case of a modern miracle or a psychical phenomenon, we have established what an ordinary eye-witness sees in the matter, no further production of ordinary eye-witnesses assists the proof, except by the fortuitous variety of their evidence which contributes to explanation. Eye-witnesses *as such* cannot resolve a contradiction ; this is the task of scientific analysis, and of nothing else.

But common matters of fact are by convention and *for certain purposes* dissociated from the great world of knowledge in which science has its being. We act upon them in accordance with rules and customs, which

exclude analytic transformation of the content alleged,
and prescribe only a few subsumptions under rough
general rules.  "Not physically impossible according
to received notions;" "Having impressed a veracious
eye-witness as an occurrence of such and such a legal
category;" if we can bring an event within these two
conditions we have about the highest degree of legal
and historical evidence.  An advocate's "theory" of his
case is, I believe, technically a work of supererogation,
except in so far as it indicates physical possibility and
saves the credibility of the witnesses.  He need not
prove his theory, but only make these two or three
features of it probable.  When this is done, we have as
regards the whole occurrence a content of very shadowy
outline, but sufficiently attached to the real world by the
mere elements of content furnished in the above subsumptions.  "Sufficiently attached"—that is, for its
purpose.  We all know that law takes no account of
morality.  I say *no* account; for though it demands
intention for certain crimes, it presumes its presence
from certain modes of acting.  The real principle, *e.g.* of
criminal law in determining facts, seems to me to be, that
if appearances are against you up to a certain point, you
must take the consequences for the sake of protecting
society.  I believe the principle to be a right one.  You
cannot leave practical matters open, to all eternity, as
you can matters of speculative truth.  The practical
needs of decision are met by coming to some decision or

other, and the desire for equity is satisfied by the belief that judge and jury have decided according to the rules of the game.

Two objections occur to me which I will mention shortly. Do I mean that a very improbable content in science is asserted more strongly than an ordinary and probable matter of fact? To answer this we must bear in mind that even matter of fact depends for its assertion on connections of content, and these may conceivably be such as to outweigh an incipient analogy or a rudimentary hypothesis. But here we must avoid a snare. The ordinary fact is not proved *in any and every way we may choose to interpret it* by its ordinary connection with life. And if we insist on this, and only take out what the connection of content really carries, we shall constantly find our ordinary matter of fact a broken reed for any precise purpose. And, *qua* matter of fact, it can rarely conflict with a suggestion of science. The outlines of concrete facts are so shadowy, and their possible interpretation so various, that it is only when transformed into science that they can, as a rule, conflict with or confirm scientific suggestions. But in theory the strength of assertions can be compared in virtue of their connection with reality ; and on this ground the answer to the question is what I have given.

Again ; what are we to say of an unreconciled con-tradiction in science, with very good reason shown on both sides? Such for, example, as the question of

Biogenesis, before the more conclusive experiments had been made. The answer is that two hypotheticals with different antecedents cannot contradict each other, and the grounds alleged for the two conflicting views are different antecedents. You assert both with the full strength of the connections of content which they possess; and the contradiction between them only affects some concrete element which is differently interpreted in the two judgments. "Organic matter which generates life after an exposure to 300° Fahr. does so in virtue of no existing life germs." "Organic matter which never generates life after exposure to 300° Fahr. is only capable of generating life in virtue of existing life germs." It is only when science is degraded into a net result or a mere fact that these contradictions become absolute. That organic matter, apart from supposed characteristics, both can and cannot produce life without existing life germs *is*, no doubt, an absolute contradiction. But it leaves out the contents which form the essence of the scientific allegations in question.

The ideal assertion, which alone could have absolute strength, would be the predication of the whole content of the Real about itself as subject. "Pure cases" and apodeictic judgments have their peculiar strength of assertion because the Real, as we construct it, is a system, and their pure or necessary form is their explicit attachment to the system. The categorical judgment has also its justification and its degree of necessity, which in no way depends on its form, and is *ultimately* of just the same order with, and dependent on just the same considerations as, that of the judgments which are stated as modal. And *it* often or always could be so stated, *as Mr. Bradley has shown.* But the categorical judgment does not tell us in what element within or without the explicit content we are to find this justification. And sometimes, no doubt, for the very reason which is really its weakness, the assertorical judgment (taking assertorical to = categorical in Mr. Bradley's more restricted sense as referred to above, p. 127) arrogates to itself the absolute assertiveness which belongs only to the ideal and unattainable judgment, "The whole ultimate Real S has the whole ultimate real content P."

I may add as a corollary, that strength of assertion, being a matter of content, rests on knowledge, and can only be communicated in the medium of knowledge. Thus in controversy one may see a man of science unable to convey the strength of his assertion to minds which do not possess the required knowledge. Too often he will then have recourse to absolute assertion, the attempt to replace by emphasis of affirmation the true ground of assertion which has proved ineffectual. But emphasis is simply an appeal to feeling; to the hearer's confidence in the speaker's good faith or judgment; and as this has no proper place in science (though it has in matters of fact), it follows that, *qua* man of science, the speaker has put himself in the wrong. Science in law courts, it may be observed, can for the above reason never be science, except where some simple construction, say of a machine, goes home to the intellects of judge and jury.   The testimony of experts, *e.g.* that this stain is human blood, or that the cause of death was an alkaloid poison, is properly treated by the law as evidence or testimony of fact ;  and its value rests almost entirely on the character and reputation of the witness.   This is science brought to a net result, and therefore degraded from the ranks of science altogether. Its judgments are not asserted on the strength of rational grounds, but on the strength of testimony.   Of course the physician's or chemist's mode of forming his opinion is more or less criticised in court, but only enough to establish the general possibility of his forming an opinion, and the fact that he has taken trouble to form it.   This is merely the establishment of authority, and authority has no place in science.

2. The nature of the reference to Reality, which constitutes Judgment, may be well illustrated by comparing Judgment with Imagination.   The general distinction is clear ; in Mr. Bradley's words, "what is merely imagined is not held to be true." [1]

Does this apply fully and absolutely to the peculiar case of artistic fiction, which apes the form of direct judgment, and has sometimes (*e.g.* in Defoe's works)

----

[1] " Principles of Logic," p. 411 ; *cf.* p. 75.

been undistinguishable in style from grave historical narrative? This question has only one or two points of contact with Logic; its interest, as Mr. Bradley points out, is mainly æsthetic, and from that point of view it does not concern us now. I suppose that the essence of æsthetic illusion is not the production of belief, not the intensifying of illusion into hallucination, but the stimulus of emotion by suggestion.

But it must be of significance for logic to ask, " How do we re-think, in what mental attitude do we accept, the direct quasi-historical judgments which make up a story like 'Esmond' or 'Ivanhoe'?" We are able to distinguish, within the content of the book, what we are to take as facts for the purpose of the story, and dreams, and falsehoods; we assign to each class of incidents its appropriate effect. And further, a genuinely historical personage or event will appear on the stage at intervals, in a setting fictitious as regards incident, but with a character sometimes more true than that drawn by grave historians. This, too, we re-think in judgments, with appropriate distinctions.

According to Mr. Bradley's view, which in the main I accept, judgment proper involves two elements, (i.) the symbolic or logical character of the ideas predicated,  and (ii.) the reference of this ideal content to the Reality which appears in presentation.

(i.) Of these two characters the first of course goes with imaginative quasi-judgment; I suppose, indeed, with all the work of consciousness considered as intelligence. I am not absolutely certain, however, how "symbolic" or "logical" "ideas" are related to mere "psychical fact." "A content," Mr. Bradley says on page 76, "may be wholly symbolic, and yet purely imaginary." But he is then speaking of imagination which does not simulate judgment. On the other hand, in speaking of what I suppose is simulated judgment, he seems to contrast it with real judgment as mere psychical fact with affirmation about things. I quote the whole passage from page 411, where he is concerned to show that Imagination can never be inference. " Imagination is certainly not free from logical processes. Its trains no doubt, throughout a great part of their length, may consist of the strictest intellectual sequences. They may contain few images, and but little save the present symbolic ideas. Yet somewhere we find a solution of continuity ; somewhere the identity of the datum is lost ; at some point we pass from the adjectival content attributed to our basis, and slide into an image which is not its predicate. And with this break, wherever it comes, we have left judgment for fancy, and are not concerned with truth but with psychical fact."

There is a transition here which puzzles me ; the transition from a symbolic content which is not predicated of the datum or starting-point, and is therefore imaginary and not embodied in a judgment, to psychical fact as contrasted with truth. Are we to understand that a symbolic idea can be a mere psychical fact? Mr. Bradley cannot mean to identify a symbolic or logical idea with the idea as a psychical state, a particular image whose existence is momentary; he must mean it to be that element in any particular image which we fix and use as a symbol; or more accurately still, the symbolic idea must be the act or habit which thus uses elements of particular psychical images with a determinate reference; and the meaning of the idea is in this reference. The ideas which pass before us in dreams are surely logical and significant in this sense. They have a meaning and reference outside themselves, even if wholly absurd. Whether such true logical ideas can really exist apart from judgment in some modality, is a question which I should like to raise on some other occasion, but Mr. Bradley has over and over again said that they can. Therefore, in a disproved judgment, a negatived ideal content, or an imagination without judgment, when, following popular usage, he says that we have a mere "idea"[1] and not a fact, I take him to mean a logical or symbolic idea, and not a particular image. But if so, the place quoted above from page 411 which actually uses the word image seems to me misleading. Subject to this gloss, I take the passage in question to mean "Imagination cannot be judgment, or lead to judgment in the sense in which a given starting-point of truth leads to a new judgment, and therefore cannot be

---

[1] "Principles of Logic," pp. 10 and 76.

inference." I do take it, however, to assert that in imagination ideas may be employed as symbolic contents, with a view to their meanings. If so, Mr. Bradley agrees with me that a fiction may present the first of the two characters of judgment. A wilful lie must have this character in a marked sense, for though it is not, on the part of the speaker, a genuine judgment, yet he must know what "ideas" he wishes to give out for real to those who believe him.

(ii.) But now we come to the second and more important character of judgment, and we have to ask whether in any possible sense this can apply to fiction. In judging, we predicate of Reality the meaning of an idea. Locksley's archery in "Ivanhoe" is the meaning of certain ideas, or rather consists of certain ideas which *are* meanings in our minds. Their meanings are up to a certain point "objective;" they refer to or are ideal contents, belonging to the common world of meanings by which and in which intelligences communicate with themselves and with each other. But more than this; we seem to think these actions in genuine judgment; they do not simply pass before our minds like the alleged phantasmagoria of imagination; they are presented to us in a form undistinguishable from that of ordinary judgment, and we do not maintain towards them a completely reserved and resolutely unjudging attitude. It is true, however, that we do not predicate them of what I may call *real* Reality; and yet to qualify Reality by ideal contents is Mr. Bradley's expression for "to judge."

There is one simple way—rather too simple—out of the difficulty. We may take account of the various orders of existence, and predicate these actions of real reality, but only in their right place as something which Scott invented, and which we have read.[1] But this does not quite answer my question, though perhaps it suggests the right answer. We think of these incidents thus when we are not reading the book ; but, though I do not think hallucination necessary for æsthetic effect, I cannot abandon the idea that in reading " Ivanhoe " we judge the judgments of which the story consists, and predicate Locksley's acts to be real in another sense than as significant ideas once in Scott's mind, and now aroused in ours. I feel sure that we in some way satisfy the form of predication, of narrative assertion.

Is reading and re-thinking artistic fiction the same logical process as uttering a wilful lie ? I should say not ; you cannot *think* a lie except in some remote moral sense ; you can only *speak* one, *i.e.* attempt to cause in some one else a judgment which you cannot yourself make. For judgment is not arbitrary. But you can and do re-think the judgments in a novel, and you contrast, as I have said, the imaginary lies and fancies of the story with its imaginary realities, and all of them with any grain of historical truth that may

---

[1] *Cf.* " Principles of Logic," p. 41.

L

be inserted.   For which reason the presence of historical truth, standing audaciously on its own merits, and not seeming to need the same justification as truths of fiction, is objectionable in a work of art.   No historical truth should be embodied in art which would not have been put in had it been a fiction.

I think, then, that we judge when reading fiction ; but I do not think that the judgment consists in a reference, at least not in a truly conditioned reference, to real reality.   It appears to me that we then judge in a secondary sense, not of real reality, but of a reality constructed *ad hoc,* related to our genuine reality which is in contact with us through perception, much as the world of a dream that continues coherently night after night for months, is to our waking life.   The process might be termed one of secondary judgment, and might also be illustrated by the discontinuous life of the diseased mind by which Mr. Bradley illustrates the qualitative identity which attaches past to present.   Or if we consider the whole content of a fictitious narrative, in virtue of its coherence, as one idea, then I should concede that this idea as a whole is not referred to reality ; but I should add that within it there is room for the activity of judgment by which it, the imaginative idea itself, is as a secondary reality characterized by the various actions and events that take place within it. In the passage quoted above from page 411, does Mr. Bradley admit that within the imaginative sequence which is at some point discontinuous with reality, there can be judgment? If there can, I do not see how the fact is reconcilable with judgment as a mere reference to the reality presented through perception; and to deny that there can, seems to me a very strong measure.

To illustrate. "The wrath of the Homeric gods is fearful." "In Homer it is so," says Mr. Bradley. Or, again, we may ask, "Does Clive marry Ethel Newcome in 'The Newcomes'?" and affirm in answer, "He does." This is the way in which we judge a fictitious content when we have real reality in our mind, and are assigning the fiction its true place in such reality. Though even in this case there is something noticeable about the present tense, which I think every one's experience will agree with mine in showing that we use. "Does" is correlative to the logical present of science, and we shall hardly be fanciful if we connect its idiomatic function in these judgments with the ideal and universal significance of art. "Did" would indicate a historical fact. It would strike us as nonsense to ask, "*Did* Clive marry Ethel?" But further, *in reading* Homer, or "The Newcomes," we do not explicitly qualify every judgment as we re-think it by the indication of secondary existence, "in Homer," or "in Thackeray:" we judge directly, and within the content of the fiction we do not use the present as in referring to it *ab extra ;* we use tense, and give the events their proper places in the narrative. In judging thus I can only suppose that we refer our ideal content to a secondary world ; in Homer to the world of Achilles or Odysseus, in Thackeray to that of Colonel Esmond or Lady Kew.   Now this is possible if the reference to reality is a matter of content, but not otherwise.   Thus if we wish to disclose the ultimate nature of our secondary judgment, we have only to make explicit the connection of content in which it consists, in order to show the reservation or condition subject to which it is judged.   In short, our secondary judgment in following artistic fiction is made possible by a comprehensive act of abstraction.

It follows from these views that in every judgment, so far as I see, the attachments which constitute its predication are the connections which prescribe its content.   I am therefore quite unable to understand the evident inclination of some for whose opinions I have the highest respect, to treat certain classes of judgments with especial tenderness.   A judgment which is not necessary, *i.e.* not determined to be what it is by its place in a system of judgments, is nothing but a fiction, or a falsehood, *i.e.* a secondary judgment, or no judgment at all.   It is a contradiction to make a formal suggestion about, say, religious mythology, to the effect that, though not true in the sense in which ordinary facts are true, it should neverthess be allowed to pass as essential for certain purposes.   You cannot allow a judgment to pass by wishing to do so ; a judgment is not an arbitrary act.   You can, of course, keep silence, and not criticise others in public ; but this is a mere moral precaution, wholly disconnected with intellectual attitude. If you attempt in a genuine and intellectual sense to let a judgment pass, you have at once and *ipso facto* the half-conscious abstraction of which I have spoken in reference to fiction ; and any importance which comes to attach to judgments so protected must make the abstraction palpable. Here we have the single root of which super-stition and rationalism are co-ordinate stems.

I imagine, however, that there is included in the warnings to which I allude, a material suggestion that, as a matter of content, certain facts can only be expressed in some such way as by what we call mythology.[1] This, as a contribution to definition of content, is at all events a legitimate contention. But I must protest against a system of judgment being called mythological, if that only means that, like all knowledge, it is provisional. It is one thing to be provisional, as are certain conceptions employed by the natural sciences, which metaphysicians have sometimes, not unjustifiably, spoken of as mythological. Such are matter, force, atom, abstractions of knowledge[2] treated as subjects endowed with attributes. It is another thing to be wantonly provisional, and for the actual

---

[1] See " Principles of Logic," p. 318.

[2] I do not mean to say that atoms may not be proved to exist as material particles ; the mere fact of being too small to be seen would not affect the degree of their existence. But I take it that atom as conceived, at least in many scientific doctrines, is not fairly identifiable with a material particle in the ordinary sense of the word.

professors of a science to neglect to criticise themselves; for students of theology, or of the science of religion, to encourage themselves and others in accepting judgments of which the content is not forced upon them by a scientific context. This is not in the least analogous to the wise reserve which metaphysic employs when it abstains from aggression on ideas found indispensable for certain purposes by physical science; it is analogous to a relaxation of vigilance on the part of those sciences themselves, to the neglect of that self-criticism which is the essence and growing point of every science, to the attribution of significance to the merely convenient and mythological form of conception, and to the admission of inaccuracy into the content which is the very centre and fulcrum of the operation by which we know. In short, the warning that there must be mythology in religious ideas, as there is in scientific ideas, is either false and dangerous, or truistic and superfluous. "False," if it means that we may or can assert what no necessary system of judgments compels us to assert or controls us in asserting, and in this case dangerous too; for as every judgment is essentially and inevitably both a conclusion and a premise, the reason will not be baulked of this character; and with every careless phrase, every "metaphor" which we easily allow to pass, we are demanding false premises which may carry it as a conclusion, and forcing on ourselves false conclusions

which it may carry as their premise. We are building
a fabric of superstition of which no one can foretell,
still less control, the extent, and which cannot but lead,
both directly and indirectly, to the worst moral result.
We are at once in scepticism and in superstition; for
our judgments *are not in the full sense capable of being
made*, and knowing this, we have to feign points of
attachment which may enable us to seem to make
them. In short, to interfere directly with the content
of a judgment on grounds of feeling, or with a practical
purpose, *is literally impossible;* but to set the intellect
upon weaving a consistent fabric of superstition, of the
fictitious character of which it is morbidly half-conscious,
and by which a certain content obtains the formal
possibility of being approved, this is only too possible,
and is the most terrible cancer of the mind.

If these somewhat extreme criticisms do not apply,
then the warning, that there must be religious mythology, is superfluous. It can then only mean that here,
as elsewhere, we do not know the last word; that we
make use of conceptions which time will show to be
clumsy in form and inaccurate in matter, and which
already are exposed to differences of opinion. But
this does not say that we do or ought consciously to
adopt a different attitude towards our conceptions from
that adopted by the natural sciences towards them;
rather we are to imitate the working disciples of these
sciences in ever remodelling our ideas towards the

most complete and consistent expression of the matter which they have to convey, in accordance with the demands of the rational system to which they belong.

But, it may be said, the conceptions of natural science are modelled with a purpose, to make certain matters thinkable ; why should not we mould religious ideas with a purpose—to satisfy certain needs of the human heart ?  I reply that this reasoning has no point beyond what it gains from an equivocation ;  the confusion between *a* practical purpose, and *the* theoretical purpose —the expression of truth.  If I model a judgment in the way forced on me by other judgments with which it is connected, I do *ipso facto* subserve *the* theoretical purpose ;  and, as I have always repeated, there is at bottom no choice ; I *must* do this, or labour with but half success to deceive myself.  But if I mould a judgment in a way not necessary to my thought, in order to influence your will, in the first place my judgment is spurious ; I cannot *really* think it, *i.e.* I cannot qualify *real* reality by its content ; and secondly, what do you call my action ?  I have spoken that which I am unable to think, in order to gain a purpose.  This is the general and formal definition of lying, but in fiction, as we have seen, we to a certain extent relieve the directness of the lie, and make it thinkable and even predicable in a secondary sense.  And this is the usual case with superstition ; I do not say that we may not even forget the reservation or abstraction under which we predicated at first, and then we escape from hypocrisy, rationalism, and superstition, from the moral and the half moral lie, at the expense of taking it into our minds and making the lie into our truth. Whenever we begin making arbitrary propositions directed by practical purposes, this is the track on which we have started.

I am not saying that natural science can give us our judgments about religion, or judgments on which we can base religion. This is a question of content, of what the judgments say and of the experience from which they are drawn. The answer to it depends on what we include in natural science ; by what ideas we limit its range. I certainly do not see that we can found religion on the exact measurement of quantities, or on anything but the spiritual experience of man. Still the aggressive denial of jurisdiction even to natural science, much more to science as such, seems to me to betray the same misconception as its aggressive assertion. The relation of one science to the facts dealt with by another presents no theoretical difficulty whatever. We are, I think, sufficiently warned against the view or prejudice that there is no science but that of shapes and quantities. What needs more attention at present is the almost identical prejudice that intellectual apprehension outside the region of shapes and quantities, though it may call itself science, has really no kinship with natural science, no necessity, no systematic rationality. Now, I will not here say that there *is* reliable intellectual apprehension

of the bases of religion or morality.  I will only say that
*if* there is intellectual apprehension, then there are science
and necessity, and contents which are not arbitrary, but
are inevitable.  And if there is not all this, there is no
true judgment on the subject at all ; except[1] in the sense
in which we judge *ab extra*, that *in " The Newcomes "*
Clive finally marries Ethel Newcome.  All I contend
for is that, *if* we go into the matter of religion and make
judgments about it, we must and can be guided by
theoretical necessity and nothing else : and that in so
far as we are guided by anything else, *we are saying that
which we do not think.*

If we were to speak nŏt about ideas of religion, but
about religious ideas, the result is the same.  If they are
mere imaginations, they are on a level with the ideas of
fine art and artistic fiction, and can at most be embodied
in secondary judgments, from which of course they
derive none of their motive power.  If they are to be
judgments proper, they must be referred to reality on
some grounds, attached by some points in their content ;
they must be the conclusions of a *bonâ fide* inference, or
they are not judgments at all.  It is not open to us to
consider the question whether we will for ourselves allow
certain judgments to pass or not ; all we can consider is
whether we are to reserve our views as esoteric dogmas.

---

[1] Of course we may also judge as we judge when under the spell of
artistic fiction.  For the present purpose these two cases are the same, being
both contrasted with reference of a content directly to real reality.

I should be sorry to say anything which could be taken as implying disbelief in the judgment of value in art, morals, and religion. I cannot but think that any doubt of its objectivity which may be abroad is the penalty we pay for encumbering the conception of value with matter which is superfluous for its theoretical purpose.

# CHAPTER IV.

## THE JUDGMENT AND THE SENTENCE—IMMEDIATE INFERENCE.

THE relation between sentence and judgment is a difficult subject. I propose to adduce some considerations tending to show that Mr. Bradley has not in all respects kept the distinction successfully before him.

But first I shall permit myself to comment in general terms on Mr. Bradley's attitude towards "hard facts." There can be no doubt in the mind of any competent student, that when Mr. Bradley applies himself to the analysis of data, his work is distinguished by the most searching subtlety. And hence one is the more baffled and annoyed when such a writer seems to swallow a very hard fact quite whole.

I have already observed on Mr. Bradley's acceptance without, as I thought, sufficient analysis, of an allegation as to the extreme nicety with which savages who cannot count are able to appreciate quantity. I may also call attention to the sheer affirmation that early soul-life is immersed in practice.[1]   Referring, as I presume it does, to human soul-life (*war* being mentioned as a feature of the life in question), the statement is more than I can deny, but very much more than I could venture to assert. I welcome the admission that pure theoretical curiosity probably appeared before man was developed, and regard this passage (page 459) as truer than the allusion in page 32, which tends the reverse way.  I cannot get down to primitive soul-life, and I do not see how any one can.  But in what less advanced soul-life I have observed, in very young children, in uneducated people, and in animals, it has always struck me that there do seem to be perplexities and curiosities, and, having learnt from the author of " Ethical Studies " that the most obvious assumptions about early consciousness (*e.g.* that animals are pure Hedonists) need not always be true, one would be glad to see more clearly whether Mr. Bradley is recording a fact of observation, or propounding a result of inference.

I have mentioned above, also, a metaphor which makes me uneasy, that of the "*point*" of identity, and shall recur later to Mr. Bradley's use of spatial metaphors generally.  His leading conceptions, even of " experiment " and " construction," appear to me to be primarily of this metaphorical character.

In all these respects, I seem to myself to observe what I have drawn attention to in the first of these chapters,

---

[1]  " Principles of Logic," p. 459.

a strange interpenetration of Mr. Bradley's thought with the common notions from which he is fundamentally so far removed, and something capricious in the analysis which melts some of the ground under our feet into thin air, while it leaves untouched the adjacent and seemingly homogeneous soil.

1. I now return to the special subject of this chapter. Over-reliance on the facts of language, and on the sentence as type of the judgment, is the root of the principal errors which Mr. Bradley exposes as arising from the belief in subject, predicate, and copula, or in " two ideas " (*i.e.* that the judgment consists in some sort of procedure with two ideas). And I propose to point out that some consequences of the practice have crept into Mr. Bradley's own views.                                        .

I am not prepared to say that it is possible to judge without the use of language, *i.e.* without the help of signs which have constant reference. *Of course* there is no reason for restricting such signs to spoken or written words.[1] Nevertheless, a false scheme of the judgment is *primâ facie* given by the sentence. In treating the judgment on the basis of the sentence, we tend to dissociate the parts of its single thought, as the words of a written or spoken sentence are dissociated in space or

---

[1] Contrast Lotze, "Logik," sect. 6. The German word "Sprache" tends to confine the meaning of language to speech. I see no logical ground for this, and therefore would draw no inference from the thinking processes of the deaf and dumb, until it is ascertained whether they use any signs, natural or acquired.

in time. We think of its subject primarily by help of a word or phrase, of its copula in the shape of another word, of its predicate by means of a word or phrase.[1] If we are to treat the matter thus, we should at all events do better to take the judgment-sentence as bipartite and not tripartite, holding to the good old doctrine of ὄνομα and ῥῆμα. Then we at least see that the content of the predication is the important thing, and cut away at a blow the trouble connected with " is " and " exists."

But I distrust this way of looking at the matter altogether. I would suggest that we should look at the sentence as merely instrumental to the judgment,[2] rather than as the expression, translation, or copy of the judgment. That the judgment is discursive (Mr. Bradley), that the mind goes backwards and forwards

---

[1] It is a fact not without interest for logic, that the writers who treat, with a view to elementary instruction, of the " Analysis " of English sentences, seem desirous, for their own purposes, to get rid of the copula as distinct from what they call the Enunciation (Predication) in a sentence ; but they do not venture to interfere with the " *logical* " subject copula and predicate, of which they speak with distant respect. It is curious to see grammatical analysis becoming logical by application to an uninflected language and turning out more truly logical than current logic, and thus transcending in grammar whilst admitting for logic a distinction which first came from grammar to logic (or rather arose in a rudimentary science which was neither logic nor grammar as such, and was closely related to the science of rhetoric). The books I have consulted are Mason's " English Grammar ; " Jones's " Analysis of English Sentences ; " and Wrightson's " Functional Elements of the Sentence."

[2] *Cf.* " Principles of Logic," p. 50. " The actual fact which appears in perception is the real subject, *to which these phrases serve to direct our attention.*" The italics are mine. The author is here speaking of sentences beginning with " this," " here," and " now."

between the terms whose relation it judges (Lotze), that predication is to refer an idea (a "meaning," of course, not a psychical image) in my head to the real which is presented in perception (Mr. Bradley), all this has a sort of truth, but is to my mind tainted with spatial metaphor ; I mean, to speak candidly, with the idea of looking backwards and forwards from beginning to end of a printed sentence.

There are many kinds of judgment, and perhaps they are not all to be covered by one illustration. We might, however, gain something by attempting to approach the judgment from another side. We all know that an ambiguous perception, I mean perception in the full sense of the interpretative judgment which goes with all the feelings of an entirely conscious man, is accessible in many cases to argument or suggestion. A given arrangement of light and shadow[1] on a surface may mean a prominence or a depression ; when a better observer than ourselves has pointed out what it really indicates, we are enabled to see it so, and judge accordingly. I do not think that the instrument of conviction need be fresh sensuous detail, which we had overlooked before. It may be merely the reminder that a

---

[1] Plato's repeated references to the illusions of σκιαγραφία (the use of light and shade on a plane surface to represent solidity) taken in connection with the stress which he lays on the analysis of confused concretes of sense into attributes conditioned by relations, seem to me to show how thoroughly he grasped the modern idea of the perceptive judgment, which is the root of modern philosophy.

certain detail in a certain connection can have a significance which we had forgotten. But whatever the instrument of conviction may be, the change in our interpretative judgment is not limited to a vision of sensuous detail.[1] Now our perceptive state of activity, after succeeding in such an interpretation, having been assisted by words, but not consisting in thinking about a sentence, is an illustration, such as I conceive to be useful, of what we actually do in judging. Here we have emphasis, distinction, reference, but no local dissociation. I do not think, again, that it can be denied that to "follow" a piece of music is an activity identical with judgment. As the series of sounds, whether complex or single, is developed before us, we characterize each element in it, each fugitive unit of it, by a relation definite though hardly nameable, to a whole which is itself in process of construction *pari passu.* I am not now speaking of the effect of music on the soul, *qua* fine art; but merely of the intelligent hearing which, like the careful study of a great picture, is a condition precedent of artistic enjoyment. Such instances give us the judgment, perhaps, in its purest form. We here see that the distinction and union which characterize it are intellectual in character, not spatial or temporal; and intellectual not as what we call a mental transition (I spoke of a *change* above merely to introduce the aid furnished by words), but rather as an extension of a

---

[1] *Cf.* " Principles of Logic," p. 490.

thought by thought, or of impression by thought. Nothing, perhaps, in "Principles of Logic" is better calculated to exhibit the radical nature of judgment than the author's account of the early growth of the function, when it or its analogous activity consists in the "extension" of an impression by an idea. Even so, however, we do not quite get at the point which I am anxious to make. In a judgment, each part, though distinguished, is in the other. The notes which we hear intelligently in a symphony, the stroke of bright colour which we see appreciatively in a picture, the commonplace phrase which we find transformed by the handling of a great poet, have their extended significance within them. "Referred to," then, is too weak a term.

The content itself is transformed by our judgment. It is not a datum about which something is said. This is only the external shape of communication. There must indeed be a datum, or to what can the modified content be referred? But the datum's old self is seen in and as contributing to its new self. Change is not of the essence of the judgment. The distinction is intellectual, and can be permanent, for it belongs to the nature of knowledge.

To read the common text-books, and even Lotze (I do not accuse Mr. Bradley of this worst fault), one would think that a judgment is in the form, "This book is that book." Now you cannot say, "This book is that book;" you may say, "This book is the same as that book," but then the two books are the whole concerned in the judgment, and the judgment consists in distinguishing and alleging a certain aspect within this whole.

"*Quorsum haec?*" Mr. Bradley may reasonably ask. "What more can I do than I have done? I have said that in Judgment the true subject is Reality not an idea; that what we predicate may be merely a single idea, without a specified aspect of reality as subject; that subject, predicate, and copula are a superstition; that the grammatical subject is constantly not the logical subject. What more can I do for you?"

What I want in the first place is this, that even these excellent propositions should not be maintained on the basis of an appeal to the written or spoken sentence; not, at any rate, without a special inquiry in each case as to the act which that sentence represents. On this ground I object to two elements in Mr. Bradley's discussion.

Firstly, to his argument that because you can make a judgment with a single word, *therefore* subject, predicate, and copula are superstitions. I should imagine, too, that he argues on the same ground that judgment can exist "without any copula and with *but one idea.*" I object here merely to the expression, as, according to "Principles of Logic," page 12, every judgment has but one idea. And secondly, I object to the assumption that the grammatical subject of a sentence is that about which we naturally raise the question whether it is the logical subject or not.

2. My first objection here may seem trivial. But I believe it to be worth noticing. If "a single word" means, as it naturally does, a truly single word in the language of a civilized people, you cannot make a judgment with a single word. You can only make it with a verb, which is a miniature sentence, or with any word to which context or emphasis lends the force of a verb. Some languages, we are told, have not the distinction between noun and verb. They must, however, have some way of indicating when a word carries a predication, *and this sign, whatever it may be, belongs to language.*[1] It is unjustifiable to confuse a verb, or a word specially indicated to have the force of a verb, with a truly single word of civilized speech. I do not think that this is *mere* tautology ; I am not saying solely that you cannot judge with a single word unless you do judge with it. I am saying that you can utter a single word without judging (though I will not take upon me to say that such a word is significant), and that when you do judge with it you make or presuppose some special sign that you do so, and that this sign belongs to language, and the presumption of its presence to the interpretation of language.

What do I say to "Wolf!" and "Fire!"? I say that they are not renderings of the articulation of

---

[1] See above p. 158.

judgments, but signs for judgments, interpreted by the help of habit, accent, and gesture. We must never confuse these signs, which are more and more used in complex civilization, with the real approach to single-word predication which occurs when we get near the interjection, and probably in rudimentary language, though even in this the "single" word is never truly single. The "Spectator" made a sign of judgment when he saw the fox go away, and silently stretched out his arm ; and this signified a judgment in his mind, though it did not fully convey the judgment even to his friend who knew him. But surely we must not criticise this gesture as exhibiting the elements and articulation of the judgment which it symbolized. I may put a question ten lines long, and be answered, "Yes." Surely that is not a single-word predication.[1] I am not guided by a "linguistic prejudice" that the subject must be understood. I say merely that the particular instances in question are highly defined judgments, which are no more exhibited in their structure by the well-known cry for help or of warning, than the judgment

---

[1] "Principles of Logic," p. 56. "A common understanding or the pointing of a finger is all that serves to limit the reference." Pointing the finger is a sign, and of course makes the word a sentence. As to a common understanding, the question is how much it supplies in definite articulate thought beyond what I say aloud. The relation between explicit language and signals has many degrees. But signals, whose meaning is quite "dependent on a common understanding" which is special, and not *the* common understanding of those who share a language —such signals must be estimated by their meaning, and not it by them.

that it is noon by Greenwich mean time is exhibited in the dropping of a ball on a pole over Dent's shop. " Wolf!" in another context may mean, " This is a wolf-skin and not a bear-skin," and " Fire !" may mean, " I want a light for my pipe." Surely no complete proposition could be so utterly indeterminate within itself. I am of opinion, indeed, that *in these particular* cases we actually think of words which we do not say. The cry is, in fact, pretty nearly an imperative.

This subject is a very wide and hard one. I have already said that Mr. Bradley's other instance seems to me better for his purpose. I quote the whole sentence.[1] " In some moment of outward squalor and inward wretchedness, when we turn to one another with the word ' miserable,' the subject is here the whole given reality." Here the reference is less specified ; the exclamation does not fit into a web of custom ; the content belongs more to immediate feeling, and is more obviously adjectival, and consequently the necessity for a sign of precise reference is reduced to a minimum, and the sign is given by look and emphasis. The sign of predication, which is the true grammatical copula, is always given somehow, if only by the general postulate of language, that if a man speaks, he is saying something. This is obvious if we look at true single-word predication where the words, whether verb or quasi-verb, habitually and by virtue of some *recognized* indication can do duty for the expres-

---

[1] " Principles of Logic," p. 56.

sion of a complete judgment. But where there is no recognized indication, but the word may be described as in " Wolf! " and " Fire ! " as a sham interjection (I agree with Mr. Bradley that these are not real interjections), then because the copula is furnished by accidental and various means, we are able to pretend that it is not there.

What is the *logical* copula,[1] then ? The answer depends on our view of the judgment; for the copula has no content in itself, is nothing but the indication that the act of judgment is performed. It is clearly not the indication of time, which Aristotle took to be the distinctive element of the ῥῆμα, or enunciation. For predication is prior to tense in the history of language, and, although present in the tense-system of the finite verb, again expands into the logical or scientific present, which is independent of time. Aristotle was evidently misled by the connection, which the grammar of European languages would generally tend to affirm, between finite verb and tense. The form of judgment which he himself frequently uses, ὁ ἵππος λευκός, indicating the copula by mere position, might have undeceived him. I do not believe that any word which is employed to indicate a judgment is free from a peculiarity,[2] whether proper to it or superadded *ad hoc*,

---

[1] " Principles of Logic," p. 22. " If the copula is a connection which couples a pair of ideas, it falls outside judgment ; and if on the other hand it is the sign of judgment, it does not couple. Or if it *both* joined *and* judged, then at any rate judgment would not be *mere* joining."

[2] *Cf.* Sigwart, On the element which makes the predication. " Logik," vol. i. p. 93.

which indicates the act of judgment by means that must be set down as linguistic. No doubt we ought to get rid of the idea, to which Lotze affords only too much countenance,[1] that the logical copula is a distinct element of positive content, needing for its appropriate expression a special word or words in a sentence. Aristotle has no such idea, unless it were, as I have said, that he connects predication with the element of tense which he was accustomed to observe in a verb. So far as I know, there is no name for copula in Aristotle.[2] But when we regard the logical copula as the common or formal element of the act which is a judgment, the act of reference, and the grammatical or linguistic copula as the expression or communication of this act, whether by accent, gesture, word, or reliance on the hearer's expectation, excited by previous means,—then it becomes a contradiction to say with Mr. Bradley[3] that judgment can exist without a copula. Copula is a name drawn from analysis—mistaken analysis—of the sentence which represents a judgment, for that characteristic in it, always present, but never most aptly marked off as a

---

[1] *Cf.* " Logik," sect. 37, according to which it is the logical copula that exhibits the particular relation between the object-matters of two ideas concerned in judgment. But this particular or special relation obviously belongs to the content of the judgment, to the object-matter asserted. The same mistake is indicated in sect. 52, where to say that Socrates has or liberates slaves is treated as a case of enunciating the concept " slave " of Socrates, the differences between these judgments and Socrates is a slave falling, as the author must mean, into the copula.

[2] σύνδεσμός is of course conjunction, not copula.

[3] " Principles of Logic," p. 49.

single word, which indicates the act of judgment as such.

"Very well," Mr. Bradley may say, "let there be a linguistic sign of judgment. But this is not a copula in the old sense, not a connection within the content of the judgment, not a sign that one element therein is to be taken as true of or belonging to another. If a sign of connection within the judgment, then not the sign of judgment; if the sign of judgment, then not a sign of relation within the content which is judged." [1]

I cannot agree with this view, which I have represented in my own language, but, to the best of my belief, correctly. It appears to me that the true subject of a judgment, that which is qualified by an ideal content, must be within as well as outside the content which is referred to it ; and that there is no obstacle on this head to the sign of judgment being a connection within the judgment. In the notion that there is a subject, fixed, so to speak, at one point, and an ideal content brought up from elsewhere and joined on to it, I again trace the pernicious influence of the sentence with its dissociated parts, the root of the very errors which Mr. Bradley combats so successfully. "Judgment is not *mere* joining." [2] Certainly not joining as expressed by

---

[1] *Cf.* " Principles of Logic," p. 22, quoted on p. 167, and also p. 14. " In every judgment there is a subject of which the ideal content is asserted. But this subject, of course, cannot belong to the content, or fall within it, for in that case it would be the idea attributed to itself."

[2] " Principles of Logic," p. 22.

the conjunction ; the conjunction is not the copula. But all judgment is at least a kind of joining. When we have said that every judgment is at once an analysis and a synthesis, I do not see how this can be a matter of dispute. It is obvious that there can be connections within a judgment which are not *the* judgment ; a relative sentence, or the condition of a hypothetical judgment, are cases which prove it. But for all that, the judgment is *a* connection, and I think essentially is absolute connection. The connections which are not judgment fail to be judgment because they are not taken as absolute, as capable of summing up the reality that is apprehended in the form of an independent whole. I therefore think that the sign of judgment is rightly called the copula. It is nothing apart from the content which is judged, or rather, which is the judgment on its material side. It is not a link, or a word. If we must have a metaphor, let us rather think of the heat which enables the air to hold vapour in suspension, or of the life of a vegetable cell, which resides, works, and arranges in and by help of certain substances, is not locally separable from them, and yet can pass away and leave them apparently much the same in actual content as before. Why is absolute connection the essence of Judgment ? I answer, because Reality is for us a system, a construction ; and Judgment claims to exhibit, that is to construct or reconstruct, Reality. It is thus not true that Reality is the subject in judgment, if that means that it is not the predicate.

And the notion of a subject which is outside the content that is judged, *and therefore not in it*, seems to me, as I have said, to be wholly unreal in the sphere of thought, and to have a meaning only of a sentence in print, or, as we hear it unfold itself in speaking, from nominative to verb. Reality *is formally* the subject in every judgment ; but materially the real is assigned its actual grade of reality by the content of the predication. The character which is the differentia of judgment is the claim—only the claim—to define a whole complete in itself. The general scheme of judgment, then, comes to this : "The Real, when thus conditioned, expresses its totality thus." The essence of affirmation is not exhausted by the consciousness that an identical quality binds the ideal content predicated to the Real, which exists for us as an ideal structure ; but only in this, together with the farther and rational apprehension that our Real, an ideal structure, as thus conditioned, sums itself up thus and not otherwise.

I will try to explain this in instances. I must, unfortunately, deprecate Mr. Bradley's instance, "The sea-serpent exists." I do not think it an easily intelligible judgment, and therefore I do not know in what sense to take it with a view to analysis. And for this reason. "Exist" is a formal predicate which receives material interpretation from context. When the context is unmistakable, the verb receives signification as against its negative ; but if the context is dubious all signification is gone, for in some sense the predication of existence is always true.   " The men for whom the colonel drew pay did not exist," *i.e.* there were no men to whom he had to pay over the money which he drew in the names of soldiers alleged to be receiving pay.  The purpose and relations of the existence in question are here supplied by the test of receiving pay ; and a counter-allegation, " they did exist," would mean that there were real men entitled to pay on the books of the regiment, though not necessarily that the colonel paid them.  But all meaning is cut away from " exist," if no test of the existence in question is furnished, and if, consequently, it is uncertain what order of reality is covered under the formal verb.  For, allowing to Mr. Bradley that no one cares about my private psychical fact, the idea or image in my head, that its existence is assumed, and is a matter of no interest ; still there are many grades of existence which are habitually predicated, and between which the formal verb does not distinguish.   Mr. Bradley knows this very well,[1] and I cannot understand how, in face of this simple fact, he should give an absolute and unvarying value to the predication of existence.  I do not think that any one would now naturally take the judgment that the sea-serpent exists to mean that it is an animal in the organic world.  This is the highest grade of existence which it could claim, that suggested by the term serpent, a suggestion of which Mill makes

[1] " Principles of Logic," p. 41.

great use in his discussion as to the nominal character of definition. By analyzing " a dragon is a fire-breathing serpent " into " a dragon is a thing that breathes fire," and " a dragon is a serpent," he removes from " serpent " the qualifying adjective which made it obviously imaginary, and causes it to claim existence in the world of flesh-and-blood animals ; and consequently he can exhibit a sharp contradiction when he predicates of it its old adjective fire-breathing, which claims to depress it again to the rank of a creature in fiction. It is a simple fallacy *a dicto secundum quid ad dictum simpliciter*, and does not show that to construe a definition as a matter of fact gives a false conclusion with true premises, but only that to change the sense of a word and replace it in its old context, is likely to generate contradiction.

If I were forced to assign a meaning to the judg-ment, " The sea-serpent exists," I should guess that it must be understood somewhat in this way, " The real appearance named as the sea-serpent has the reality of proceeding from a constant and natural cause ;" *i.e.* " The structure of reality in the respect A, is realized in a constant relation B." Any other connections within the judgment, which only help to explain or to condition our thought of reality, are subsidiary to the whole which is asserted and thus are not judgments. But any such connection becomes a judgment the moment thought is confined to it. The judgment is the special way in which at any moment (I do not say within the moment

and no more), we precisely think our world.  We are
not able, nor do practical life or the conditions of
human knowledge permit us, to be at all times, or ever
perfectly, in possession even of the world which we have
constructed in our intellects.  But whatever may be the
stimulus to attention or the ground of interest which
causes us to judge, and however slightly our intellectual
world may respond to the appeal addressed to it, every
judgment appeals to the whole to pass sentence on the
part ; and it is this rational decision, not an isolated and
particular necessity of fact, that forms the assertion and
warrant of every judgment.[1]  Even in " it hurts," or
" miserable," the speaker sums up all that his intelligence
will do for him under the conditions of the moment ;
we must imagine that when he so judges, a man's whole
being is reduced to the level of quality, has become a
mass of pain or wretchedness.  This may seem wildly
exaggerated for most cases ; I may say " it hurts," as
an indication to an observer who is making precise experiments on my sight or touch for the sake of Fechner's
law ; but then " it hurts " does not represent the real
judgment ; I leave much unsaid which is accurately in
my thoughts, because the observer knows it already.
Complete conception is assertion ; I mean conception
complete as regards the present powers and furniture of
the conceiving intellect.  All fancy is abstract ; wilfully
or indolently abstract.  All judgment is as concrete

[1] *Cf.* below, Conclusion.

as the mind, given a certain stimulus or interest, can make it.

Then why do we not always proceed by definition? How can we judge that a triangle has its three angles equal to two right angles? No one can say that this is the entire or adequate specification of a triangle. Now I believe the intellect, if moving fair and free in a province of knowledge, always makes for a definition. But in the current of thought, some other whole, not the pure scientific whole of which our consciousness has elements in it, is usually prescribed to us by the guiding purpose of the moment. And thus the intellect does its best to sum itself up in an absolute distinction and connection of such an artificial whole, instead of simply reconstructing the natural and constant fabric of reality. I may, for instance, be in doubt about the size of one of the minor angles of a given right-angled triangle, and at the first effort to sum up the total bearing of my intellectual world on this angle I may get no nearer than to see that it is one of three which together = two right angles. The point which makes this mode of conception into a judgment is that it is all I have to say at the moment, that I give it out for the whole reality of the matter. If I see further, *e.g.* that the angle in question is one of two which together = a right angle, the judgment that it is one of three drops into a premise. But is not a premise at once itself a judgment, and a part of a judgment, viz. of the conclusion considered as issuing from the inference as a whole ?   And does not this dispose of any such notion as that propounded above, that the essence of a judgment is to be an entire and independent verdict, the total outcome of a present intellectual world ?   It is clear that a premise is more than a condition.   There is a difference between A, because it is B, is C, and A, if it is B, is C.   "*Because*" it is B seems to be a separate judgment as well as a condition ; while "*if*" it is B is a mere condition.   The former = A is B and therefore it is C ; the latter only = if A is B, then it is C.   In the former case the judgment A is B must be maintained along with and in the judgment A is C, for otherwise the ground for A is C vanishes.   In the latter the judgment A is C is not made ; but only the one judgment A B is C.   In both cases we have the nexus A B is C asserted ; but in the former we have A is B alleged in addition, either as a fact in time or as a necessary nexus.   Is any relation of A and B asserted in the hypothesis "If A is B—" ?   I think that something is asserted, viz. such a connection of their contents as makes the determination of A by B—not really possible, but—intelligible.   In both cases, then, or in the direct argument at least, for I need not press the second for my present purpose, we have a judgment within a judgment.   Is this possible if the judgment is a totality, a conception under all available determinations, a perception of the structure of reality taken as complete *pro tempore* ?

I think so, and I will try to make the distinction plain on which this possibility rests. A premise is of course asserted in the argument which rests on it. But it is not asserted as we write it down, as one of a number of separate sentences. If we begin with it thus separately, we must count that beginning as an incomplete stage of insight, in which we have not yet perceived the nexus of the argument. The argument as a whole, which is essentially identical with the conclusion, carries, when perception has made it a unity, its own assertiveness in its content. The premises are there, but their content is transformed and passes gradually into that of the conclusion. Therefore we do not, as might be imagined from the formal scheme of reasoning in text-books, keep two judgments separate as premises, and transfer their assertive force to a third distinct from them, leaving them still asserted outside it. I do not imagine that any one seriously contemplates the intellect as engaged on three distinct assertions *in* and *as* one and the same act. The point is that the premise merges in the conclusion, is enlarged or developed into it. And then the matter before us is simply the passing of one perception into another, which other takes up into itself the content and therefore the assertory character of the first. If the assertion is that the three angles of a triangle are equal to the two interior angles made by a straight line cutting two parallels, and therefore to two right angles, the proof may take the

N

shape of a perception how two of the angles of a triangle must always differ from the two interior angles spoken of, by an amount equal to the third angle of the triangle, and further how the two interior angles in question are obviously equivalent to the two adjacent angles on the same side of a straight line. Thus the proof does not simply substitute one term for another and transfer the assertion of the old judgment to a new one so formed. It rather modifies the contents so that for certain definite purposes they become identical, and as regards the identity the assertion of the premises is transformed into that of the conclusion. I therefore think that the relation of premise to argument shows that the judgment always *is* the total act of thought ; for as perception or insight into a nexus penetrates deeper and further, we find that judgment necessarily follows it and extends itself to the whole which is perceived to cohere.

The copula, then, is the absolute connection by which thought treats a content, such as from time to time fills our intelligence, as *the* content of that Reality which we meet with in presentation and extend by construction. The "*schema*" of the copula is not the point of contact between two spheres ; not a formal meeting-point of unvarying extent or value ; it is a grasp like that of an electro-magnet, varying in extent of surface, and in the strength which intensity of work affords.

Mr. Bradley, if I may venture to say so, appears to me to have erected into a separable element of affirmation—in assertorical judgments the sole element—what is really but the abstraction of a common feature out of the concrete assertiveness of all judgments. All judgments without exception claim by their form to be true. The truth is the whole ; and they thus claim to exhibit the whole, which they transparently fail to do. This is formal assertiveness, but is incapable by itself of constituting the full assertion of any judgment. It is this that, as an abstract feature, is absolute and identical in all judgments. In addition to this, or rather as the concrete nature out of which this is abstracted, every judgment has its own peculiar degree of grasp or apprehension which embodies in actual content the perception that claims to be the truth ; and this constitutes the material strength of assertion.

I think, then, that the copula is the essence of Judgment, and is essentially a connection, or rather *the* connection ;[1] though I know that there are connections within judgments other than those which are the judgments.

3. The relation of the grammatical to the logical subject [2] is a curious question, and might repay historical

---

[1] *Cf.* Wundt's " Principle of Duality," and his treatment of the Copula, " Logik," pp. 54 and 143.

[2] " Principles of Logic," p. 23, on two ideas in judgment ; p. 50, on " grammatical show ; " p. 271, what subject is the link of connection in certain inferences.

inquiry. I have already indicated that I ascribe the doctrine treated by Mr. Bradley on page 22 and following pages of " Principles of Logic," which makes the judgment consist of two ideas and a copula, to a confusion between sentence and judgment. With his criticism as there stated I have only to agree. But *primâ facie*, I should say that *grammatical subject* is strictly an incorrect expression, though now warranted by usage. In uninflected or but slightly inflected languages like our own it is natural to employ logical [1] expressions in the analysis of sentences ; but if the analysis goes by external shape and stops short of interpretation a good deal of confusion may result. I confess that in grammar, *i.e.* in the analysis of sentences with reference to the relations of their component parts of speech, I had rather talk of nominative case, verb, and object (as we do not happen to want object in logic). Then we might reserve subject and predicate, which cannot be identified by mere inspection of parts of speech, but are aspects of knowledge, for logic, *i.e.* for the analysis of meanings in general, as characteristic of intelligence and independent of linguistic differences. I suppose that the " grammatical subject " usually means the nominative case, whether expressed or supplied, to the principal verb. I know of course that verb ($\dot{\rho}\tilde{\eta}\mu a$) is in Aristotle a logical term ; but we now have a distinction between grammar and logic, and I think it

---

[1] *Vide* p. 159, note on the English works that treat of " Analysis."

should be maintained. The "verb" of grammar is no longer co-extensive with ῥῆμα. It would be interesting to inquire whether the custom of grammar does not on the whole coincide with the counsels of metaphysics; whether the nominative case does not on the whole tend to stand for the true subject, the true identity in differences, and the verb or adjective for some one of its more transitory differences or determinations. I am inclined to think that this is the case.

But in logic we are dealing with neither extreme. We cannot accept the relations of the parts of speech as we find them in a sentence, for a final determination of subject and predicate; nor yet are we justified in denying the relativity of judgment, by which I mean, in this context, the possibility that we may intend to judge, and therefore may actually judge, in an order of knowledge which diverges indefinitely from the order of reality. For *logical* analysis, our meaning is what we mean or intend to affirm. To elicit this from a given sentence is a matter of interpretation. And apart from terms of precision which refer to fixed contexts or to familiar interests, and in the absence of an actual context, interpretation is scarcely possible. But it is clear that there is no presumption at all in favour of identifying the logical subject, *i.e.* that aspect of the real which presses upon our attention as containing matter for synthesis or analysis, with the grammatical subject, *i.e.* in a regular sentence the nominative to the principal verb. In two forms of the skeleton judgment as Aristotle states it, the predicate B is the nominative case with which the subject A is connected through a verb. " B is predicated of the whole of A," " B belongs to the whole of A." The sentence in all ordinary composition, even in scientific treatises, is governed by rhetorical considerations. There is a strong tendency to put the natural or metaphysical subject in the place of grammatical subject or nominative to the principal verb. Any other structure of an enunciation obviously demands an effort of thought which this rhetorical structure avoids, too often in spite of its being necessary. I open Locke's Essay at random, and find in the chapter on " Cause and Effect and other Relations : " " *Relations of Time.* Time and place are also the foundations of very large relations, and all finite beings at least are concerned in them." Here we have three enunciations, " time " and " place " being the grammatical subjects of the first two, and "finite beings" of the third. These are possible judgments, of course ; but they are not the judgments which Locke makes in this passage. He is developing the aspect of reality known as the relation ; we cannot suppose that he hits upon place and time as independent data, and proceeds to analyze them into relations, and then jumps to an independent characteristic of finite beings. The common subject is obviously reality considered in respect of its relatedness, and this is shown to be capable of taking the forms of place and time, and also to be in these forms so comprehensive as to include all finite beings as related points. The immense proportion of enunciations which are introduced in the same chapter with the formal nominative and verb "we call," offer considerable difficulties to such interpretative analysis. But it is clear, I think, that as a rule no special judgment is intended about our mere use of language; though I will not deny that in Locke the usage may be characteristic.

Interpretation of this kind is the necessary complement of written language. For speech it is less necessary, because the emphasis and inflection which form the life of living speech supply it in great measure. And therefore I think that to ask whether the grammatical corresponds to the logical subject is only to ask whether we have said what we meant to say.

Perhaps, however, there is a different and more metaphysical problem involved in Mr. Bradley's suggestion, of which I have been speaking. Perhaps his question is not so much, " What judgment did I make ? " *i.e.* " What did I intend to say in a certain sentence ? " but rather, " What judgment ought I to have made ? " *i.e.* " What ought I to have intended to say ? " in expressing a certain fact. Thus on page 23 of " Principles of Logic " Mr. Bradley says, " Judgment is not inclusion in, or exclusion from the subject. By the subject I mean here not the ultimate subject, to which the whole ideal content is referred, but the subject which lies within that content, in other words the *grammatical* subject. In 'A is simultaneous with B,' 'C is to east of D,' 'E is equal to F,' it is unnatural to consider A, C, and E as sole subjects, and the rest as attributive. It is equally natural to reverse the position, and perhaps more natural still to do neither, but to say instead, 'A and B are synchronous,' 'C and D lie east and west,' 'E and F are equal.' The ideal complex asserted or denied, no doubt in most cases will fall into the arrangement of a subject with adjectival qualities, but in certain instances, and those not a few, the content takes the form of two or more subjects with adjectival relations existing between them."

Let us take the instance, " A is simultaneous with B." The interpretation of this sentence depends on the question which it answers, *i.e.* on the rudimentary disjunction which it brings to a conclusion ; in other words, on the actual relation of datum and synthesis which it is meant to render. There is not the least presumption from the mere form of the sentence that A is the logical subject of the judgment. In considering the enunciation before us *as an instance*, we may indeed take the nominative as the guide to the subject, simply because we have no context to suggest anything else. But otherwise, any of the readings which Mr. Bradley suggests on this page, "A and B are synchronous," " Simultancity exists in the case of A and B," are no less natural meanings of the sentence as given, than that which makes A the sole subject. To model the sentence so as to exhibit the intended judgment is a matter of tact and scholarship only. The rhetorical investiture, by which speech appeals to feeling or recognizes common usage, has to be stripped away, and the logical skeleton duly articulated. The answer may rhetorically keep the shape of the question, " Who did it ? I did." This correspondence makes apprehension easier, and perhaps indicates authorship and responsibility. But logically " I " must be predicate here. Take, again, "It was a grievous fault, and grievously hath Cæsar answered it." I can hardly doubt that the logical subject all through is fault or ambition ; the *saltus* from fault to Cæsar is unnatural. The judgment is that if there was a fault, it was no doubt grievous, but also was expiated. Cæsar becomes subject *in grammar* because he is a person, but he is logically a factor in the predicate. So in Mr. Bradley's instance, "A is simultaneous with B " may clench any one of half a dozen disjunctions according to context : " A or C," "with B or with C," "simultaneous or in succession," "is or is not." And in each of these cases I should say that the logical judgment or intellectual synthesis actually performed, had for its subject or datum the element of reality assumed in the previous disjunction, and for the matter of its synthesis the disjoined member which it affirms as against another possibility.

It is quite a different problem to say what the

judgment ought to be ; what datum and what synthesis represent the scientific order of thought. This is a matter of the theory of knowledge, and here is the problem which Mr. Bradley is mainly discussing, not the grammatical subject and the logical subject, but the given or taken, and the true or ideal, logical subject.

So on pages 49, 50. I quote the passage. "In the simplest judgment an idea is referred to what is given in perception, and it is identified therewith as one of its adjectives. There is no need for an idea to appear as the subject, and, even when it so appears, we must distinguish the fact from grammatical show. It is present reality which is the actual subject, and the genuine substantive of the ideal content. We shall see hereafter that when "this," "here," and "now" seem to stand as subjects, the actual fact which appears in perception is the real subject, to which these phrases serve to direct our attention."

I thoroughly agree with this passage, but I can see no reason for the distinction between fact and grammatical show. There is no grammatical show *of a judgment*, if we treat the sentence as merely instrumental to the judgment, and the judgment as essentially concerned with reality. A name, and the grammatical subject may be treated as a name, does not suggest an idea *qua* idea, but a reality. If we consider the judgment as that which we intend to assert, we shall have no difficulty on this score. On a different level we may, indeed, find a difficulty between reality as it is *for us*, and our ideas as the means by which we get at it. But at least in judgment, what we mean is always some feature of Reality.

As I have already said, I do not understand how even the true or ultimate subject can fall outside the content of a judgment. In saying this, I may be proving that I have not really apprehended Mr. Bradley's conception. "The real subject to which these phrases serve to direct our attention." This is to my mind the character of the subject in all judgments. I have said that on Mr. Bradley's own principles I cannot follow the distinction between categorical and hypothetical judgment. At least, I can only understand it as equivalent to the distinction between the affirmation of facts in time, and affirmation into which time does not enter. No more can I grasp the idea of a subject which falls outside a judgment, *except in the sense of the one ultimate subject, reality or the non-phenomenal fact*, which all judgment is an attempt to define, and this falls within the judgment in as far as the latter is true. It appears to me that in stripping away the accidents of the sentence Mr. Bradley has torn off some essentials of the judgment, and has done so because he has not kept the intellectual act sufficiently distinct from its linguistic instrument. In getting rid of subject and predicate as two ideas we ought not to tear away the datum of analysis and synthesis from which the judgment starts.

4. The above considerations have an obvious bearing on questions of immediate inference. We can only get at the judgment in a formal way by means of the sentence ; and now it seems that within certain limits the same judgment may be conveyed by different sentences. It may be said that this is ridiculous, for the judgment is the meaning of the sentence, and if the difference in the sentence means anything, it must alter the judgment. We shall be speaking to some extent of cases in which perhaps the difference in the sentence does mean nothing ; but I may point out that the modification of a sentence might affect the content of the idea, though not the main relation of datum and synthesis. The grammatical subject is apt to be thought as a person or at least as an agent, or a thing. In speaking of immediate inference we are met on the threshold by the question, "Do such and such changes in the sentence imply transition to a fresh judgment ?" [1] There may be transition to, or at least adoption of, a fresh judgment without inference, but there cannot be inference from one judgment without transition to another.

I have spoken above of the effect aimed at by

---

[1] *Cf.* "Principles of Logic," p. 387. "If they (the immediate inferences) are mere tautologies, rearrangements of words without alteration of ideas, they cannot be inferences."

rhetorical modifications of the sentence which do not alter the structure of knowledge, though they may affect the colouring of the ideas. I must add, that in course of ages the growth of interpretative skill and the perpetual wear and tear of language have an effect, which we cannot disregard, in neutralizing differences of grammatical structure. The process results in a sort of subsumption, by which certain forms of sentence are taken as equivalent because we have been told—or have frequently inferred—that they are equivalent. Standing where we now stand, I do not think we can refuse to treat sentences as meaning what they are employed to mean, even if, as is not impossible, we should find different forms of words more sharply distinguished in earlier stages of speech. I mean that if to us now there is no appreciable difference between " No fine art is manufacture," and " No manufacture is fine art," then the question what difference there may have been before the disguise had worn so thin, would only have historical and not logical interest.

It appears to me that in comparison with the analysis which drags to light the inner nature of so-called categorical judgments, the treatment of immediate inference and of negation in " Principles of Logic " is guided by too great a respect for given grammatical forms. I will illustrate what I mean from the account of conversion that involves the negative judgment, and from some further questions about negation.

I shall also try to point out that Mr. Bradley is not, in my opinion, sufficiently careful in handling the sentence when it is really to stand for the judgment in inference. His premises, or rather *data*, are stated with a negligence of form which I take to be intentional, and to have the purpose of removing them as far as possible from the suspicion of implying a major premise. But the data of a conundrum are not the premises of an inference. They are at best the material out of which such premises can be formed.

(i.) I begin by quoting [1] Mr. Bradley's summary of his view of conversion where the negative is not employed. " The truth is, that if you keep to categorical affirmatives, your conversion or opposition is not rational, but simply grammatical. The one conversion which is real inference is modal conversion, and that presupposes a hypothetical character in the original judgment."

So far I thoroughly agree with Mr. Bradley, subject to a protest on one point. That point is the *consensus* with which logicians, following herein the example of Aristotle, disregard the convertible affirmative judgment, and thus reduce all assertion to the type in which a concrete subject has ascribed to it some casual or generic attribute, without implication of ground and consequence. If I say " A. B. has come to town," "One of C. D.'s pictures is by Turner," no doubt I am content

---

[1]  " Principles of Logic," p. 390.

to leave the predicate as an attribute which is not
peculiar or characteristic. But in most serious argument, in making the observations which are to enter
into a science, or in endeavouring to read the riddles of
social and political causation, we indicate either by
context or by some trait of language, that we hope and
intend that our judgments shall have characteristic
predicates. I am persuaded that the fallacies of "un-
distributed middle" and "illicit process" are hardly
ever committed in actual thinking ; and that apparent
cases of them arise from the captious ignorance of
critics who find it easier to point out that an argument runs formally from predicate to subject, than
to weigh the assertion that the predicate is characteristic and therefore, presumably at least, convertible.
Of course such an assertion is hazardous in proportion as its content is deep ; but for the doctrine of
conversion the question is not whether it is true but
whether it is made. We do not habitually invert our
judgments so as to put the characteristic predicate in
the place of subject, and thus bring argument from it
under the common rules. Partly, I suspect, we prefer
not to have an attribute as subject (this is due to the
metaphysical instinct of common language, of which I
spoke above), partly the caution of science prefers to
retain the form of common judgment while implying
a characteristic predication. It is thus that we light
upon arguments which are formally fallacious, but

materially as good as our classification at any moment can make them. If a logician condemns such arguments on purely formal grounds, he only condemns his own ignorance. *Per contra*, of course such arguments are hit by objections which are formally irrelevant. It is almost always, not indeed a flat denial, but a grave objection to a judgment which claims any high degree of significance, to allege cases where the predicate is present without the subject. Such objections show how far the judgment is from embodying a "pure case," which is the ideal of every judgment. If it is affirmed that "The Scotch crofters are always distressed in a bad season," it is not at all beside the mark to reply that many people are distressed in a bad season who are not Scotch crofters. So far from being irrelevant, this reply picks out for denial the very core and nerve of the affirmation, viz. that being a crofter is *a* or ideally *the* specially determining condition of misery in bad years. If, indeed, the affirmation can then defend itself by explaining that the more general conditions of misery in bad years, which the objection shows to exist, are in some special form involved in and condensed into the position of being crofters, it can of course rehabilitate its case.

Even Lotze gives an uncertain sound on this point. 'Mere logic," he says,[1] "does not justify simple conversion of a universal affirmative;" reciprocal

---

[1] " Logik," sect. 80.

judgments, he continues, are found, but they must be established materially. This gives an air of mystery to the matter which is quite needless. " Mere logic " here represents nothing in the world but the custom of low-grade thought. There is no reason in the nature of things why the reciprocal judgment should not be recognized in logic, and if recognized, it would be recognized as simply convertible.

I do not doubt that the quantification of the predicate and the equational logic have been greatly favoured by the circumstance that they alone seemed to recognize the true intention of carefully made judgments, viz. to be characteristic. But their kind of reciprocity is not what we want ; it is got by levelling down, not by filling up. What we want is more like definition ; and logic, indeed, always treats of definitions, and says that they are simply convertible, but never, so far as I know, points out how closely the purpose of all judgment is connected with the definitory form.

Do I want to introduce a fresh class of universal affirmations, and to alter the rules of conversion and syllogism where this class is concerned ? No ; but only because it is not worth while to tamper with the rules of formal logic which have now little more than a historical interest. It is, however, important to bear in mind that logical technicalities have been formed by reflection on the most trivial and everyday uses of thought. We must, therefore, always be ready to re-test them when

O

we apply them to functions which they did not originally contemplate.

I have now to speak of some forms of Conversion in which the Negative is concerned ; and then, pursuing the subject of Negation, to say something on its alleged "subjective" character, on Double Negation, Excluded Middle, and Disjunction.

My purpose in speaking of Negation will be to insist upon its strictly logical significance; that is to say, its function as an element in a system of knowledge and the character which that function imposes on it. I shall attempt to point out that Mr. Bradley's account of conversion where negation is concerned, and of double negation, is needlessly artificial, and too much trammelled by regard for the grammatical sentence ; and that his treatment of negation as such, of Excluded Middle, and of Disjunction, betrays a tendency to look at Negation psychologically and in its origin rather than logically and in its function. In all this I seem to myself to trace that desire for plain and immediate foundations of knowledge on which I have already commented. I do not believe that such foundations are to be had.

In entering on questions occasioned by " Immediate Inference," I must first guard myself by a reference to page 25, where I have indicated my view of what may be called true immediate inferences, such as Distinction, Recognition, and Abstraction. I have no doubt of the existence of these inferences, and should wish, as I have there explained, to classify all judgment as belonging to one or other of such types of Inference. But the more I recognize an inferential process as subsidiary to the making of an ordinary judgment, the less I am inclined to find a fresh act of this complex nature in every variation of linguistic embodiment.

Thus I cannot agree with Mr. Bradley that there is a real passage made by inference from " A is not B " to " B is not A." " A is not B " means that A has a quality which excludes B. This is Mr. Bradley's analysis of significant negation, *i.e.* negation which is (and all negation in actual thought is) more than bare denial. And I have no doubt that this analysis is substantially right. But, if so, how can we construct the judgment without a definite perception of the incompatibility of A and B? The quality $x$ of A cannot exclude B except by reason of some quality $y$ in B.[1] The act of judgment must consist in perceiving

---

[1] An interesting point arises here. How is it easier to see that $x$ is not $y$, or not B, than to see that A is not B? Is there not a risk of falling into an infinite series? Does not $x$ is not $y$, or not B, come under the same analysis as the original judgment A is not B (which might be taken as = A is A and therefore not B)? And then, why should the latent predication of a positive quality be ascribed to every negative judgment? The fact is, that if the negation " — is not B " remains a bare denial, it cannot be based on a positive quality; in order to be capable of connection with a positive ground, the negation itself must be assigned a determinate meaning, and it is this meaning, not the bare denial as such, which is capable of being positively asserted on a specific ground. We shall find, however, that important consequences follow from the fact of all negation being, in

these qualities in their antagonistic relations; whether antagonistic in the nature of things like a triangle and a square, or antagonistic on the authority of some rule which is taken as valid, such as that the attribute of having a "superior." corolla excludes the attribute of being a Ranunculus ; (because a Ranunculus has an " inferior " corolla ; but we need not, from a logical point of view, know this reason, supposing that the rule, " No Ranunculus has a superior corolla " is, in our opinion, sufficiently authenticated). This, I suppose, is what Mr. Bradley means by saying that in negation "we experiment with both our terms." But then, he continues,[1] " We find that, given A, B cannot be there ; but as to what will happen when B is supposed, we have no information."

I venture to think that the phrases, "both our terms," "given," and "experiment," are here fatally misleading, and betray a tendency to take the sentence for the judgment. This we are all apt to do ; we are apt to start from A, and, glancing at only its most obvious features, to overlook a ground of incompatibility with B which may exist in some less striking point of A, and may not reveal itself to our perception till we come to scrutinize B. The error is a common one, and comes from an indolent construction of the precept contained in the sentence which directs our

the abstract, and so far as concerns its outward form, bare denial. The relation of ignorance that something is, and knowledge that it is not, *i.e.* of the privative to the exclusive judgment, is involved in this question, to which I shall return.                    [1] Page 392.

judgment. " Treating is not forbidden by the Bribery Act." In such a judgment we are inclined to represent the subject by sharply defined details freshly brought before the mind, and the elements which are negatived by hazy recollections. But of course there is nothing in the nature of the judgment to excuse such indolence. We are bound to search the Act before we can say what it does and what it does not forbid. For the purpose of the judgment, the "two terms" are not capable of separate consideration. They are not dissociated like the two ends of the sentence. It is true that they cannot be amalgamated in a concrete unity as is the content of an affirmative judgment. Nevertheless, assuming always that we are dealing with rational and significant negation, we unquestionably predicate an intelligible idea ; the phrases, " exclusion," " repulsion," " rejection," are among the forcible metaphors to which Mr. Bradley gives, in my opinion, undue weight. What we predicate is a limited and specified difference ; an otherness which we subsume under the generalized form of negation when we wish to emphasize the distinctness of things and ideas within the world as we know it.

Mr. Bradley would make the passage from " A is not B" to " B is not A," an apagogic inference. " There must be," he says, " a new experiment in which B is taken as real, A suggested, and exclusion found to result. No general principle can give the result, for the principle itself has to be got by the process in question."

Here, to my mind, we come on the weak side of Mr. Bradley's doctrine of Inference, a side about which we shall have much more to say. "An experiment," "finds exclusion." No doubt, especially in inference, what a normal mind finds is what we must acquiesce in. But to say this, is only a psychological account of the matter, not a logical account. I may be wrong, but I seem, even in this trifling matter, to trace the influence of Sigwart and Lotze ; to hear them pronouncing that knowledge is based on an unaccountable necessity, found within the limits of isolated judgments, and that the only reason which can be assigned for ultimate truths is that the mind cannot help accepting them when presented. This seems to me not wholly false, but wholly inverted, and to consist in assigning a universal psychological feature of judgment as the peculiar and rational ground for certain determinate judgments.

Let us look at the experiment.[1] Suppose B, then A is excluded, or is possible. First, let it be possible, and then A may be B ; or again B may be not-B, for B can be A, and A is not B. Thus we prove indirectly that B excludes A, and that the two are incompatible.

It occurs to me, here as elsewhere, that the simple letters are very bad illustrations. They have no content, so that the connection of content on which the whole

---

[1] If compelled to choose between the processes suggested, I should prefer "the explicit perception of a new relation got by abstraction from an implicit whole."

argument turns, simply does not exist in the skeleton instances. On the other hand, I admit that I ought not to take a case in which the reciprocal exclusion springs to the mind the moment the names are pronounced. I am, however, in some difficulty on this head, for I frankly do not believe it possible to go through any such process as is here described before seeing the converse of a Universal Negative. But I grant that this consideration is not decisive, because our seeing the truth might be only apparent, and wrong, and might really demand the steps which Mr. Bradley alleges to be formally necessary, even if we were not in the habit of going through them. I will take an instance which is only too transparent, but has, perhaps, a thin veil of unfamiliarity for readers who, like myself, are not mathematical.

"No parallel of latitude" (taking this phrase not to include the equator) "can be a great circle." Here the first thing that strikes me is that we cannot so much as set about constructing the judgment suggested by the sentence till we begin to test the parallels of latitude by the main criterion of a great circle, viz. being in a plane which passes through the centre of the sphere. Otherwise we should not know in what aspects to suppose or conceive the parallels for the purpose of the judgment in question. But when we perceive the parallels of latitude as in a series of planes which pass outside the centre of the sphere, and are continued in both directions away from that centre, and thus do not cut the sphere-surface in "great" circles—*i.e.* circles having the full diameter of the sphere—then we hold together as a systematic idea the characteristic of parallels of latitude and the discrepant characteristic which we may illustrate by the equator and meridians, and judge of the former that they must always be other than the latter in this essential feature, the relation to the sphere-centre. Now, when we have such an intellectual perception, not as a confused whole, but with its salient points and distinctions selected by the judgment, and clearly defined, I cannot conceive what change can be made by inverting the grammatical order of the terms. In order to convert on Mr. Bradley's plan, I am, *with this judgment in my mind,* for it is the premise on which I go, to suppose B, the great circle, given. (Supposing it "given" is, so far as I can see, only the same as simply supposing it, for this purpose at least ; in order to get the judgment in question I need only suppose the content in question, not any other content such as might connect the great circle with reality.) I am then to consider the question (for of course I must be told what judgment is required to be obtained), can B "great circle" be A "parallel of latitude"? or, putting it in a more correct form, as a question represents no real intellectual state, I must decide on the disjunction "B can or cannot be A." But as I try to bring the disjunction before me it must decide itself ; I cannot really maintain a disjunctive attitude at all ; A is given as excluded. If I am asked, as Mr. Bradley seems to ask me, " Try and suppose A possible, and see what absurdities you get into then ; that is the real proof that A is excluded," I can only answer that I am glad to claim Mr. Bradley's authority for thinking cumulative proof by concordant systematic relations a characteristic of knowledge, and a feature the absence of which must always throw doubt on any supposed necessary intuition, however apparently competent to stand alone. But in the case before us I cannot, subject to the given conditions, suppose that of which the absurdity is required to be shown, though I can see that *supposing I could suppose it*, and yet remain certain of my premise (a combination inconceivable in detail, and only supposable verbally, as we may say " suppose the universe were not "), the apagogic argument would then show that it was impossible.

Would the argument, however, as put by Mr. Bradley, in any case take us round by easier steps than that which it would enable us to escape ? " If A is possible, then A may be B." Here we have a simple conversion, for B is the subject from which we are to start, and so " B may be A " is the only form to which we have an immediate right. " B may be A " is the supposition. What we know is that " A is not (= cannot be) B." I do not see how we are to get from this to the falsehood of " B may be A " without *either* going round by the *very converted negative* (" B is not, cannot be, A ") *which we are endeavouring to obtain*, or else going from " B may be A," to the simple converse " A may be B,' which is then contradicted by " A is not (cannot be) B." Mr. Bradley's other suggestion has not this objection ; it uses a plain syllogism, with the rule or axiom that of premises which correctly give a false conclusion we must treat that one as false which we are not bound to treat as true. Thus we get " A is not B," and (supposing that) " B may be A," then " B may be not-B ; " which being impossible " B may be A " is false, (the other premise being our primary assumption which we are bound to take as true), and therefore " B cannot be (is not) A." This is a fair verbal inference, and does not presuppose its result ; though whether it does not presuppose truths just as hard to come by is another question. The inference, however, *is* verbal ; it omits the element of actual material difference from which the whole judgment derives its import. For, let us put it in terms which have a meaning, " No parallel of latitude can be a great circle," and so " No great circle can be a parallel of latitude," for if it were, then a great circle might not be a great circle. This argument may be understood in two ways. As obtained by Mr. Bradley's process it is a verbal or secondary argument, and puts the cart before the horse. *Why* cannot a great circle be a parallel of latitude ? Because if it was, then owing to what we have just been told, it would not be a great circle. You thus assign the formal contradiction as the ground of the material opposition which causes it, or rather, perhaps, as its own ground. What you want is to assign the material opposition as the ground of the formal contradiction. And the above argument might actually be thus understood, and be appealed to in this sense: "A great circle cannot be a parallel of latitude, for it would then be in a plane that does not pass through the centre of the sphere." Thus, while appealing to the consequence that in becoming a parallel of latitude a great circle would surrender its own differentia, we appeal not to this consequence in its formal aspect, but to the material opposition or contrary relation directly and in the concrete. Thus, and thus only, can we obtain a converse truly dependent on and embodying the content of the original apprehension. And if that apprehension was complete, such a conversion does not alter it, and therefore is grammatical and not logical.

I should like to lay down in opposition to this page of "Principles of Logic," the principle that it is impossible to modify a conclusion without modifying the systematic content of the material reasoning or perception that gives it. Any argument which does not effect this is purely formal and tautologous.

(ii.) The view of contraposition in the passage before us has the same defects. It makes the process purely formal and tautologous, and therefore, I should say, purely grammatical, while alleging it to constitute an inference. It does not consider what the judgment "A is B" is or implies ; and indeed, when framed with symbolic letters the judgment is and implies almost nothing. I do not think that "A is B," as it stands, represents a judgment, I mean an actual judgment with reference to the letters A and B.

The process of contraposition is explained to be indirect, and to rest on disjunction, as the process of conversion did in the last case. Given that A is B, then as not-B is either A or not-A, and it cannot be A because it would then be B, nothing remains but for it to be not-A. "This conclusion removes the alternative Not-B is A, and since but one possibility remains, that is therefore actual, and hence not-B is not A."

I admit that "A is B" being given, the perception "Not-B is not A" follows somewhat less directly than, given that "A is not B," the perception that "B is not A." I do not myself believe that this has much to do with the nature of the judgment from which we start, and at which we arrive. I ascribe it rather to the non-natural grammatical form, of which it is not easy, except for those accustomed to skeleton instances, to make at once a genuine application. We should scarcely admit that we were inferring if we said on the ground of "Every vaccinium has an inferior fruit," that, " If a plant has not an inferior fruit it is not a vaccinium." Again, we are perplexed, especially in the symbolic form, by the feeling for the ideal of judgment from which we *should* be able to infer that Not-A is not-B. Knowing by experience that we are not as a rule formally justified in this inference, we are shaken in our reliance on the judgment-form altogether.

And if we *were* to appeal to the process which is sketched in the passage before us (and I might apply the same remark to the case of the Universal Negative), it could not be as a formal consideration that a plant with a superior fruit could not be a vaccinium, because then its superior fruit would have to be an inferior fruit. We have processes not unlike this where the premise is not distinctly in the mind, or where the quality for which not-B stands is not certainly known to be not-B, because we then have to hold the alleged not-B and B together, and consider whether they really do exclude each other. In such a case the original judgment is not fully made, the sentence not fully interpreted into an intellectual perception, and it is possible that variation of phrase may assist us in apprehending the full and distinct content of the judgment required. But when the judgment symbolized by " A is B " has been thoroughly made, when we have a content A affirmatively determined in respect of a characteristic B, so that the whole may be symbolized by, not exactly A B, for that might mean mere juxtaposition, but by some more complex sign indicating a definite interpenetration of the elements—then we cannot go back on such a judgment, while still affirming it, and suggest that what is not characterized as B may nevertheless be A. We gain nothing by the formal announcement that if not-B were A, it would have to be B. This is only saying that not-B is not A because it is not B. It is, in fact, an argument in Camestres, A is B ; Not-B is not B ; Not-B is not A. The question really comes to this ; is it inference to say, Because A is B,[1] therefore A is not not-B ? I think it is not inference. It is exhibiting by means of a grammatical form an element of the connection of content which every judgment as such affirms. But to complete the transition I need the simple conversion of A is not not-B, into Not-B is not A ; this Mr. Bradley denies me unless by an apagogic inference. I have explained my reasons for differing from him.

I am inclined to think that if we are to come to any conclusion on these points which is not purely arbitrary, depending on the custom of the individual mind, we must direct our attention to distinguishing the logical judgment as such from the efforts which lead up to it. Efforts of inference certainly take place in following a symbolic or skeleton judgment through contraposited or converted forms. It would be hypocrisy in me at least to pretend that I have never faltered at a symbolic conversion and written A for not-A or the like. But we must surely distinguish between formal or interpre-

[1] *Cf.* "Principles of Logic," p. 149, on double negation.

tative inference and material modifications of content. What I contend for is, not that such transitions by inference are psychologically impossible, but that if they are made, that is a proof that we have not yet thoroughly thought the original judgment or premise. We are, in such cases, simply proceeding to organize and articulate the original judgment itself in accordance with precepts furnished by the formal peculiarities of the sentence. We cannot pledge ourselves for the grade of apprehension with which individuals may commit themselves to an enunciative sentence; if we go to extreme cases, where the use of a developed language is being learnt by an undeveloped mind, the question becomes a very hard psychological puzzle. But the logical account of the typical judgment is not to depend upon these historical *data*, though of course their bearing, so far as known, must not be neglected. And I should certainly say that in the intention and usage of careful speakers or writers in European language, all the immediate inferences (in the traditional sense) that can be made from a judgment are present in the definite structure of the judgment itself.

Mr. Bradley's treatment of the contradictory relation of B and not-B as a mere case of disjunction I shall return to later.

(iii.) "Principles of Logic," page 392. "It is by virtue of the same apagogic process that we are able to argue from the absence of the consequent to the absence of the ground." I merely mention this corollary of Mr. Bradley's view in order to point out its bearing upon the question whether a disjunctive judgment can be reduced to two hypothetical judgments. Obviously Mr. Bradley will not admit this; for it is agreed on all hands that to represent the meaning of the disjunctive judgment, "A is either B or C," we must be able to assert four hypothetical judgments.[1] To reduce these to two demands " a process of conversion." The hypotheticals required must have negative elements, and conversion of a negative, according to Mr. Bradley's view, presupposes a Disjunction. I shall comment on this latter idea in speaking of Disjunction.

Before passing from this page 392 I must draw attention to one more point—the relation between the "experiment" and the "general principle." We do not, we are reminded here as elsewhere, get an inference (in this

---

[1] The four hypotheticals are: i., If A is B it is not C; ii., If A is C it is not B; iii., If A is not B it is C; iv., If A is not C it is B. Of these, however, ii. and iv. can be obtained from i. and iii. respectively by processes analogous to simple conversion and contraposition; and I should be disposed to consider each of these pairs (i. and ii., iii. and iv.) as standing for one judgment only. Mr. Bradley makes, I think, a slight oversight on page 121, in selecting the hypothetical judgments i. and ii. as forming the alleged equivalents to the disjunctive judgment : i. and iii. cannot be obtained from each other, and are both required to represent the disjunctive judgment. It is these two, therefore, which would be chosen by those who speak of reducing it to hypotheticals. So Sigwart, "Logik," i., section 37, paragraph 10. But owing to Mr. Bradley's view of the nature of conversion as presupposing disjunction, he would require all four hypotheticals to be given in order to make up the disjunction, though he would not admit that it could be reduced even to these.

case B is not A from A is not B) by any general principle, for that principle must itself first be got by the process in question. Here I confine myself to noting the antithesis, and simply add that I cannot understand how any "experiment" or "process" in the way of inference should have any virtue, except as an operation on our vision, enabling us to see something of a general principle. Thus in the "got by" I suspect an old confusion; that, in fact, of *post hoc* and *propter hoc*. And in the insistence on this relation of experiment to principle I seem to see the same curious attitude, partly assumed, towards the foundations of knowledge, which I observed upon in chapter I. sect. 4. I shall return to the same point in speaking of Subsumption.

(iv.) I am puzzled to know what Mr. Bradley is combating when he contends[1] that "the antecedent in necessity must be universal, but it need not be more universal than the consequent." "There is no more need for the consequent to be more concrete than the antecedent than there is for the effect to be more special than the cause."

According to the ordinary view, the consequent is related to the antecedent as predicate to subject, and effect to cause in the same way. "Deny the consequent and affirm the antecedent." "The same cause always has the same effect, but the same effect has not always the same cause." These popular maxims show that

[1] p. 220.

P

consequent and effect are regarded as more general than antecedent and cause respectively. Mr. Bradley has himself recognized the correspondence of consequent and predicate by his reduction of the categorical judgment to a connection of antecedent and consequent.[1]

I do not say that this is more than a popular idea founded on the conception of the judgment current in ordinary logic.[2] In actual thought and inference I doubt whether this feature is so common as is presumed. Mr. Bradley himself takes the popular view elsewhere. "You cannot reason straight from the attribute to the subject or from the consequent to the ground." Now, from consequent to ground in a pure case, and from attribute to subject in a definitory judgment, you can reason straight; and I think that the judgments which we make in arguing constantly, if not universally, claim these characters.

But this is by the way; the strange thing to me is, that the tendency of popular illusion being, for reasons which would repay inquiry, in the direction of treating consequence and effect as corresponding to the predicate of a common judgment, and therefore as more general than antecedent and cause respectively, Mr. Bradley should select for censure the view that they are less general. I should have thought that antecedent and consequent, as also cause and effect, when adequately

----

[1] p. 43, *cf.* p. 390.　　　　[2] See p. 190.

known, must always be convertible. In a certain sense, indeed, the entire causal process, or nexus of antecedent and consequent, might be looked at as more concrete than any element in it; but this would simply arise from the fact that when we think of the elements apart from the process we are apt not to give them the full determinateness which as elements in the process they possess. But the determinate element, whether cause or effect, implies the whole process in relation to which it is determined, and can be neither more nor less general than that process.

I can only suppose Mr. Bradley to be alluding to some idea of Explanation, but I do not precisely know to what. Mill's account of explanation does not involve any "more general principle," except in the sense just alluded to, that it treats the matter to be explained as a determinate combination of elements, which, *qua* not thus determined by combination, are capable severally of other combinations. But of course, even if such an element were "naturally more knowable," the particular consequent which it gives in combination, and therefore the combination itself which is the antecedent of this consequent, is always a modification of the element considered in the abstract. This is, I suppose, what Bacon calls "Limitatio naturæ notioris," "a modification of something which is in the order of nature[1] more susceptible of being known." And no doubt the isolated

---

[1] Naturæ seems to mean "*to* Nature," a mistranslation of φύσει.

elements to which we refer a process must be known in their relative isolation, or we could not analyze the process into them ; and *in this sense* explanation is always by the more general, which is the same as saying that it analyzes the unknown into the known. And again, the better known an element in an explanation is, or is capable of being, the better we are pleased at bringing something we did not understand into connection with it. The order introduced into knowledge is thereby rendered more complete, and from a number of little worlds of thought we progress towards one great world. This is all that I see in the matter, and it seems to coincide with Mr. Bradley's hint.[1]  "No doubt in the cases where you say 'because' you may find what we call the principle of the sequence, and that, of course, must be more abstract than the actual consequent. But the principle is not the antecedent itself. It is the base of the general connection, not the sufficient reason of the particular consequent." Still, as I observed above, I am perplexed by the following sentence : "There is no more need for the consequent to be more concrete than the antecedent, than there is for the effect to be more special than the cause." There is no need for——. But is it even possible? and has any one maintained it? I should have said it was impossible, and that no one had maintained it, but that popular views do maintain the very opposite, viz. that

---

[1] "Principles of Logic," p. 220.

consequent and cause are more abstract than antecedent
and effect. This view, I think, does require confuting,
in favour of the only possible doctrine, viz. that the
universality of reason and consequent is always exactly
the same.

# CHAPTER V.

## ALLEGED SUBJECTIVITY OF NEGATION.

I NOW turn to ask how far and in what sense logical negation is subjective.  I begin by referring to what I said above as to the stage or level at which we must take the judgment for logical purposes.  Keeping, as I think we ought, to the developed judgment of civilized life, we shall be obliged to assign a high degree of positive value to negation.  The question of stage or level of judgment is fundamental in this matter.  I will take a single test of this from Sigwart's chapter on negation.[1]  "The primary judgment ought not to be called affirmative at all; at the outside it should be called *positive;* for the simple enunciation A is B is only called an affirmation by contrast with the negative judgment and in as far as it rejects the possibility of a negation; but it is not a condition of the judgment A is B that the thought of a possibility of its being denied should have been entertained."

The correctness of this assertion depends absolutely

---

[1] Sigwart, "Logik," sect. 20, par. 1.

on the level at which we take the judgment. The question is one of those which constantly recur in the theory of knowledge, or, indeed, in any account of a continuous growth, and I could wish that a general formula were laid down to clear out of the way once for all the ambiguities which such a question involves. Their interest is not logical, but historical.[1] The issue is merely how far certain features, necessarily implied in a process, or at least necessarily developed in it by a contact which is quite inevitable, become explicit and distinguishable within such a process. The interest of a judgment, no doubt, is not always expressly to correct or even to provide against a mistake ; the judgment may take its rise from the mere positive interest of the content which it affirms, not from an interest in exclusion by means of that content. On the other hand, however, we must bear in mind that communication is not the essential of judgment. Therefore we must not go so far as to say that mere desire to inform another, or to influence his action, can produce a judgment. Strictly, these motives can only cause us to speak our judgment aloud ; the actual making of the affirmation must be accounted for on purely logical grounds ; and though these imply an interest, yet it is a definite interest some-

---

[1] *Cf.* " Principles of Logic," p. 30. " Thus with judgment we are sure that, at a certain stage, it does not exist, and that at a later stage it is found in operation ; and, without asking where the transition takes place, we may content ourselves with pointing out the contrast of these stages."

how bound up with the particular content which is judged, and therefore is itself subject to the observations I am about to make.  In other words, the desire to influence you may make me *speak*, but my ability, and the compulsion I am under in an intellectual sense to affirm *thus and not otherwise*, is guided and confined by a necessity of knowledge, and thus has the side of exclusion which a mere desire to produce a result would hardly display.

The interest which makes us judge and the matter which we affirm in judging, *are* exclusive from the first. This no one denies.  We have, then, only the impossible task remaining to say at what grades of judgment, or how far at any grade, exclusiveness becomes an explicit purpose.  I repeat, exclusion is *in* the purpose from the first ; it is given in the nature of the world, and the only question is how far the intricate systematic relation of object-matters has at any moment an influence on our judging.  Can we really escape from " Omnis determinatio est negatio " ?[1]

If I say " Dinner is at 6.45 to-night," I do not, indeed, imply that you have denied it, or that you will deny it after I have made the judgment ; but I do imply that I think you might have come at the wrong time if I had not told you, *i.e.* that your intellect was in a negative state as regarded the content in question.  If you already

---

[1] I do not say "all negation is determination," because several negations may rest on the same excluding quality.  " Principles of Logic," p. 116.

knew the hour, and knew me to be aware that you knew it, you would resent being told of it again, because it would imply that I thought you likely to forget or to confuse. When our words are less precise, " I am tired," " Oh, how hot it is ! " " I have just seen your brother," it is of course not necessarily the case that we should be consciously affirming against a known or anticipated denial, though we may very well be doing so, *e.g.* in saying, " I *have* just seen," which seems to mean " the judgment ' I have just seen ' is true." We are, however, *in fact* affirming against a possible denial, because, to repeat what I said more generally above, we are abstracting and selecting, and by doing this we commit ourselves both to omissions and to connections of content. No doubt in simply affirming a common fact or feeling we are not careful to guard against omissions which may be challenged, or a connection of content which may be impugned. But every term of precision, every indication of measurement, every qualification by a condition, is a danger-signal of actual or possible denial, and in many cases a record of a denial that has been parried. " Ah ! no," it may be said ; " not a denial, only a mistake." It is one thing to take care to be correct in a judgment, to guard against mistakes, and another to maintain an assertion in face of an actual or possible denial of that particular assertion. It is this latter attitude, I may be told, of which Sigwart is speaking, and which he denies to be a necessary element in judging—judging as he says *positively*, without the special colour of affirmation. Now I do not believe that this attitude of assertion simply against denial of the same content can really exist as a logical factor in an act of judgment. I do not believe that " mere " or ungrounded judgment is possible. And therefore I do not think that we ever meet what we understand as a denial by the unmodified affirmation of the content denied. Either we. see a ground for the denial, or we do not. If we do, we modify our judgment, or while repeating it, yet add explanations, so as to evade the shadow of doubt which the denial seems to us to throw upon it. If we see no ground for the denial, then it appears to us to be either nonsense or a lie. In either of these cases it is *not a judgment*, and does not count to us as a genuine negation. If against nonsense or falsehood we think it worth while to repeat an assertion, we may no doubt do so in identical words, but the assertion is changed in content. It is not changed in respect of its rational ground, for that has not been impugned ; but it has acquired a fresh bearing which would usually be indicated by manner or accent. " What I say is unaffected by your denial ; " " What I say is not wilfully false," are the sort of bearings which a judgment has attached to it by emphatic repetition in face of a negation which appears arbitrary. But this is not the normal attitude of assertion to denial ; the denial in this case is not recognized as a true denial. Whenever we judge affirmatively in face of a denial which we recognize to be *bonâ fide* and to have a meaning, then we never simply unsay the denial, but always modify the content so as to admit what is true in the ground of negation. This "ground" and the modification to meet it, are hard to trace in very simple judgments, but I believe they are always there. And thus the modification which guards against mistakes is after all the normal attitude of genuine assertion against genuine denial. And the presence of this attitude is, as I have remarked, indicated by every note of precision, every measurement or proof of careful selection, which a given judgment exhibits. It is, in short, obviously implied in all selective abstraction, *i.e.* in all judgment ; how far it is consciously operative is a matter of historical psychology. Here again I note the futility of the skeleton judgment. " A is B " and " A is not B " are a scheme of affirmation and negation which corresponds to nothing actual. To assert or deny thus absolutely is to accuse the other speaker of nonsense or falsehood.

I should therefore lay it down that in every judgment which involves measurement or contains conditions, the thought of the possibility of its being denied has deter-mined the shape of the judgment at every salient point. Whether this principle would contradict Sigwart's view I do not know ; but if it does not, his "primary judgment" cannot be actual as belonging to developed thought. Of course we must not suppose that the thought of a possibility is inoperative because we believe ourselves to have guarded against it. The precautions, especially when they are factors in an intellectual act, are embodiment of the thought of the possibility.

I do not think that I differ from Mr. Bradley in my view of the actual character which we must ascribe to the negative judgment as such. His statement is more careful than that of Sigwart, who appears to lay down positively [1] that negation necessarily presupposes actual affirmation. On this point Mr. Bradley is clear, and I think, obviously right. Negation does not presuppose affirmation, though it does presuppose the idea or suggestion of an affirmative relation. I must, therefore, admit the essence of sect. 13 of Book I. ch. 3, the chapter on the Negative Judgment, a chapter, I may say in passing, which appears to me to be a masterpiece of logical analysis and suggestive criticism. I quote the first paragraph of sect. 13. "' Logical negation ' cannot be so directly related to fact as is logical assertion. We might say that, as such and in its own strict character, it is simply ' subjective ; ' it does not hold good outside my thinking. The reality repels the suggested alteration ; but the suggestion is not any movement of the fact, nor in fact does the given subject maintain itself against the actual attack of a disparate quality. The process

---

[1] His account of double negation ("Logik," i. 25, 1) clearly rests on the idea of an actual affirmation prior to the first negation. In 20, 1, he says only "den *Versuch* einer Bejahung," which is right, and agrees with Mr. Bradley's view, but is inconsistent with Sigwart's own account of double negation, as Mr. Bradley in effect points out.

takes place in the unsubstantial region of ideal experiment. And the steps of that experiment are not even asserted to exist in the world outside our heads. The result remains, and is true of the real, but its truth, as we have seen, is something other than its first appearance."

All that I wish to do is to remark upon some points connected with the uses of negation in knowledge, with the view of meeting the question "Why, if 'subjective,' is it natural and indispensable?" Or is it not indispensable? The general doctrine which I wish to uphold is that negation, though belonging in form to a higher level of reflection than affirmation, is yet in actual use not especially subjective or artificial, but tends to become more and more co-ordinate with the affirmative, not by careless usage, but as a necessary element in knowledge.

1. We agreed that negation does not presuppose an existing judgment against which it may be directed. Need it, however, presuppose even a *question* [1] in a sense in which the affirmative need not do so? Mr. Bradley says that it must; [2] and the simple analysis of the negative undoubtedly bears him out. Negation proclaims on the face of it that we do not perceive in the object-matter observed the feature or aspect with reference to which we are testing it. And therefore, *primâ facie*, the predicate which we deny of a subject is related to a criterion

---

[1] "Den Versuch einer Bejahung," Sigwart, l.c. supra. I have expressed above the opinion that a question is not, as such, an intellectual act or state, but must correspond to some form, however rudimentary, of disjunction.

[2] "Principles of Logic," p. 110.

which we bring with us, or which is in some way suggested to us, not by the direct perception of the subject, but by some interest which less directly concerns the subject. If we say, " The men A, B, and C are not up to the standard of height required for the army," the judgment is one which, so to speak, we need not have made. The idea of a particular standard of height is brought to bear *ab extra* on our perception of the men's height. The subject does not challenge us to try it by this especial criterion. We must here, not merely as is possible in affirmation, find the quality or attribute present, be struck by its presence, and pronounce that it qualifies that which we perceive ; we must first bring the external related point up to that which we perceive, and attempt to unite the two in a whole pronounced to be real. In short, in order to deny, "we must have the suggestion of an affirmative relation."[1] In affirming we may, but do not always, begin by a suggestion before we proceed to affirm, though in Mr. Bradley's words, " the primitive basis of affirmation is the coalescence of idea with perception."

2. But for my present purpose, which is to estimate the place of negation in developed thinking, the above admission amounts to very little. In the mature intellect —we might probably say in the intellect of adult human beings—the judgment is guided by acquired interests, to the almost entire neglect of sensuous prominence. I am

---

[1] " Principles of Logic," p. 110.

inclined to think that if the prominence of a sensuous stimulus, *e.g.* a loud noise, attracts attention and causes us to judge, it is rather because some feature of rarity in the fact of its prominence demands explanation, than that we yield attention immediately to the sensuous disturbance. Therefore it appears to me that far the greater part of our actual judgments in developed thinking, whether affirmative or negative, are preceded by the stage of suggestion, in the same sense as is negation. Suggestions come from our interests, and it is hard to say that the judgments which these call forth are artificial or not objective. Let us recur to the instance, " The men A and B are not up to the standard height ; " and let us turn it into an affirmation. " A and B are up to the standard height." Surely it is plain that the stage of reflection and the degree in which suggestion precedes judgment, are exactly the same in both these judgments. Where, as in the above case, the predicate, however important, is not obviously challenged by the constant nature of the subject, affirmation demands antecedent suggestion no less than does negation. Where, on the other hand, the predicate is conditioned by a relation essential to the nature of the subject, then the work of suggestion is done once for all in the permanent nature of our world of knowledge and feeling, and the stage of reflection which denial presupposes is all but absorbed in the direct and natural reference to a standard which we cannot but apply. If, while looking at a college eight, we say of one of the crew, "That man cannot row," we have been provided with the required suggestion by the fact of seeing him in a racing boat.

In fact, at the level of judgment to which I am now referring, denial is always charged with so much positive intention (I do not think the positive *intention* is always one with the positive *ground*) that the question rather is, " Why not express it in positive form ? "   This can generally be done without essential sacrifice of meaning, and the fact that it can be done shows how slight in the fully matured judgment is the difference between affirmation and denial.   It would be interesting to consider how far circumlocutions with "fails to," "is without," etc., can really be treated as positive.   I suppose that it is not fair to do so except where they really allege a significant contrary— a quality of defect so to speak—and are not mere metaphors without positive content, and degraded into simple equivalents for the negative.   "He has not passed his examination," undergoes a real change if we substitute "he has failed in," etc. ; because failed is a definite contrary which may or may not be concealed under the contradictory " not passed."   But to say, "This triangle fails to be equal to that," would be a mere grammatical periphrasis for " is not equal," unless it implied that the two ought, or might be expected, to be equal.

But in spite of the possible substitution of a positive predication, the negative maintains its place in language.

One simple reason, or one simple form of the reason for this, is the extreme convenience of generalizing a set of contraries, *ad hoc*, in a particular point of view, as contradictory to a certain affirmation.  Sometimes negation is the only simple way of effecting this purpose.  In the instance given above, of course we may say, "A and B are below the military standard ;" but this is hardly more than a makeshift for the negative.  In either form of expression the essence is that we erect a number of contraries, the several heights of the men whom we are inspecting, into the absolute alternative or contradictory "not as high as."  A more complete case of the same kind is the generalization of the greater and less as not equal.  And when we come to a criticism like "cannot row," *i.e.* fails to row as any one ought who undertakes to do so, we find that the negative abstraction has reference to a teleological standard, which may be said to be given in the object, although not satisfied by it.  Here, *i.e.* where a thing does not come up to its type, the negative has a value which can hardly be called other than objective. The affirmative relation is directly suggested, and negated in as far as it is suggested, in the object of perception. I am only speaking of the simple teleology of our everyday world, not of any remote final cause.  Thus if we say, "That ship is not fit to go to sea," there is nothing artificial, arbitrary, or in a special sense subjective, in our criticism.  "Fit to go to sea " is suggested affirmatively as an attribute of ship, *ipso facto*, the moment we recognize an object to be a ship; and in the case of unfitness the negation is as really given in the object before us as is the affirmation in the case of fitness.

It appears to me then, that the question of the subjectivity or artificiality of judgments turns actually and materially on the value of the standards by which we judge, and not on the distinction between assertion and denial.  Negation may, no doubt, be trivial and idle. Perhaps it is capable of being so in one degree further than affirmation.  We can deny that a triangle is an elephant, and we cannot affirm it.  But we may affirm that a triangle is a triangle, and that an elephant is an elephant; and these instances exhibit the vanishing point of affirmation when it becomes absolutely free from negation, as does the former the vanishing point reached by negation as it frees itself from all affirmation.  Or, if we go to judgments which have a meaning, it is true that a number of negations may be founded on the same positive quality,[1] and therefore may convey no further information about the subject after the first.  But this is as true of affirmations.  On the number of angles of a triangle we may found all the affirmations that the multiplication table makes about the number three without thereby learning anything about the qualities of a triangle as such; and if it is replied that then we at least develop the content of an attribute which is an

[1] " Principles of Logic," p. 116.

attribute of a triangle, we must bear in mind that to deny on this ground that the angles were four, five, six, or seven, would also be to develop the content of the attribute three.

I have, indeed, attempted to point out [1] that in developed thought, as we know it, affirmation displays a reference to possible negation as distinctly as does negation to the possibility of affirmation. This view, however, and my present contention, refer to the material value of judgments. They in no way detract from the correctness of the analysis which decides, on consideration of their formal character, that in the beginning, negation involves a phase of reflection with which affirmation can dispense. But when a positive judgment has come to bear traces in its structure of the repeated phases of suggestion and negation which have modified it, we can no longer treat it as merely positive.

It might, indeed, be alleged that even in respect to a complex predication, denial is always one remove higher in ideality than affirmation. If an ideal content has been modified a dozen times to make its assertion possible in spite of denials, the thirteenth denial has for its basis the suggested affirmation of the entire content so modified. And so in respect of this entire content, a fresh denial presupposes a suggested affirmative relation, while the affirmation does not pre-

[1] See p. 219.

suppose any special or definite denial, a ground for which can hardly, on the hypothesis before us, be taken as anticipated. I will only remark on this, first, that though no further special and definite ground of denial is implied in the affirmation, yet the fact of having passed through a number of modifications to disarm denial cannot but endow the affirmation with a strong general bent and tendency to be asserted as against a total denial. And secondly, that in proportion to the complexity and precision of such an elaborated content, the actual elements of negative determination which build it up acquire a progressively greater share of its import, as against the mere formal characteristic of being, *qua* affirmation, on a lower level of reflection than a further and fresh negation. I mean, to recur to the rough way of speaking which I employed above, that an affirmation which consciously and intentionally denies twelve negations, has a reflective and ideal character which is but little dwarfed by the fact that the negation which so to speak corresponds to it, which might be directed against it in its fully defined form, would be not on the same level of ideality, but one remove higher. Considered even from this point of view, the subjectivity of negation as compared with affirmation tends to a vanishing point in knowledge. And as we shall see later on, there is a simpler point of view which makes them not merely approximate to, but actually reach the same level. I have argued above without departing from the ground of external shape, on which Mr. Bradley's analysis cannot be absolutely rejected. I have assumed that an affirmation, if it denies, can only deny a negation. But in the concrete structure of knowledge this is not the case. Negation rests, no doubt, as Mr. Bradley maintains, on the common fact of *contrary* opposition, which it generalizes into contradiction. But it does not stop at contradiction. The contradictory negative clothes itself again with the positive contraries out of which it sprang. The true and objective place of negation in knowledge is to exhibit the contrary as the contradictory ; *i.e.* to deny or affirm, for it is all one, *under disjunction.* Here, then, we have the affirmative, not merely as the denial of denial, but as the denial of affirmation. Both negative and positive judgments become double-edged. It is obvious that affirmation which carries the intention of denial as much as of assertion, has, considered as a judgment, the ideal or "subjective" character of negation ; while the negation which carries the intention to affirm has supplemented its "subjectivity" by a positive allegation of ideal content. It can hardly be doubted that all actual thought gives some of this value to negation, and consequently some of the complementary value to assertion. The only negation which has no such import is the idiotic "infinite judgment," such as "Virtue is not square." And some approach to the absence of such import may be ascribed to the forced reserve of mere records of obser-vation.  " On the 25th, no sunshine ; " which, whatever it may *imply*, is taken to *commit* the observer to nothing but bare denial.

I shall return to this aspect of negation when I come to speak of Disjunction and Excluded Middle.

3. But I wish first to say a few words on Double Negation, which Sigwart considers one of the clearest indications of the gulf which is fixed between negation and reality.  He appears, as I observed above,[1] to go further at this point than Mr. Bradley is prepared to follow him.  Mr. Bradley pre-supposes as the indis-pensable basis of negation, *not* an actual affirmative judgment, but only the suggestion of an affirmative relation.  He is therefore precluded from Sigwart's short method of pronouncing that a second negation abolishes the first, and leaves the original affirmative standing.  On Mr. Bradley's view, if the second ne-gation simply does away with the first, nothing need be left but a question or suggestion.  He therefore holds that the reason why a double negation affirms, is that a denial can only be denied on the strength of our knowledge that the corresponding affirmative is true. Thus, as " A is *x* which excludes B " is the true ground on which we assert " A is not B," so " A is B which excludes not-B " is the ground on which we assert that " A is not not-B."

<hr>

[1] See note, p. 220.

I will begin by remarking that in civilized speech the equivalence of double negation and affirmation has so long been recognized, that when we set about interpreting a sentence, either is subsumed under the other as a matter of course.[1]  It is therefore exceedingly hard to construct distinguishable judgments corresponding to the two propositions in question, with the view of considering the logical relation between them.  Practically, therefore—I mean, if we are to analyze language in its rough current usage—I cannot deny that whenever we say "A is not not-B," we already know and are prepared to allege that A is B.  This follows, to my mind, from the simple fact that the two propositions are obviously and transparently equivalent.  I do not believe that either is in the usage of civilized thought prior to the other.  We just as often get at the explicit affirmative by seeing that we cannot do otherwise,[2] as at the explicit double negation by being struck with the affirmative.  I believe these two sides to be involved in every judgment, the distinction between them to be subtle and difficult, and the idea of an inference from one to the other wholly unreal.

[1] It would be worth while to analyze the indications by which we know a double negative from a merely repeated negative, as it occurs in vulgar English, or in classical Greek.  In Greek the true double negation is frequently, I will not say usually, represented by throwing one negative into the form of a positive content, and then denying this, "There was no one who did not."  "No one was so humble that he was not spoken to," etc.

[2] Oddly enough, this is the process to which Mr. Bradley himself, along with other modern logicians, is apt to refer our cognition of simple truths. *Cf.* "Principles of Logic," p. 515.

It may seem captious to add, that to explain our apprehension of the equivalence of double negation and affirmation by an inference from the double negation as consequent to the affirmation as the sole possible ground, *i.e.* by an inference that an inference has been made, seems not only far-fetched, but contrary to the ordinary tradition which Mr. Bradley accepts, that inference from assertion of consequent to assertion of ground is not warrantable.[1]

Leaving these considerations, which appear to me extremely artificial, I will ask the simple question, how we come to use the double negation at all; why it answers, as we must suppose it does, to some logical or psychological requirement?  I see two reasons for the use in question: one ethical, and one logical with a psychological corollary.

Ethically, we feel a need to deny in the form con-secrated to denial.  It is comparatively unusual to apply the double negative in a complete sentence; but in face of a previous negative, say in debate, or in a continuous context, the incisive and rebuking force of the negative seems more appropriate than a mere counter-assertion.  It has all the associations attached to "giving the lie."  In answer to a personal charge,

---

[1] Of course special knowledge may warrant such an inference; but in the case before us, the matter to be inferred being a particular course of inference, I should have thought the special knowledge would have given the presence of the alleged ground as a fact, and dispensed with the inference from consequent to ground.

*e.g.* "You were not in the House when it was counted out last night," it is a mere exculpation to reply, "Indeed I was," but a counter-charge to say, "That is not the case," or, still more, "That is not true." It characterizes the negation as a falsehood, instead of merely falling back on the content which is true.

And logically, we have the case of indirect proof, in which the disproof of the negation is undoubtedly taken as prior to the proof of the affirmation. I wish that Mr. Bradley had dealt explicitly with this point, which no doubt he regards as decided by his remarks[1] to the effect that you cannot disprove "A is not B" on any ground but a knowledge that A is B, unless the number of possibilities with respect to A has been already limited by a disjunctive judgment, "which is not here the case."

And perhaps the question might be raised whether an indirect proof can be erected on a pure contradictory alternative, *i.e.* without a limiting disjunction. Most frequently it is not so erected. I mean that it is assumed that if a certain line does not fall here, it falls somewhere else; it is assumed that if a triangle is not equal to another, it must be either greater or less than it, and the indirect proofs are set up upon these positive assumptions. Even so, I should incline to say that all intelligible negations presuppose some such disjunction as these arguments imply. No one assumes it explicitly; it is held to be conveyed in the nature of

---

[1] "Principles of Logic," p. 150.

rational speech. And then I should admit the argument quoted above, but not the fact. I should say that it is here and everywhere the fact that the content of negation is limited by a disjunctive judgment. But if this were not so, I should still say that double negation shares the fate of indirect proof; and if the absence of an explicit disjunction is not fatal to indirect proof, I do not see why it should be fatal to the priority of double negation. "It did rain yesterday," to take Mr. Bradley's instance, may be got at thus. "If it did not rain yesterday, the ground must be in good order;" "The ground is not in good order," "Therefore it is not true that it did not rain yesterday." Even here, it may be objected, I am, under cover of a consequence, assigning a positive value to "it did not rain," *i.e.* assuming that there was some kind of weather, and that it had some effect on the state of the ground. I can only say that I have fined down the negative as nearly as possible to mere privation; but of course it does assume, not only that no wet fell, but that the world and the ground existed yesterday. It is just possible, then, I think, genuinely to approach the affirmative from the side of its negation, as in indirect proof. The process is, indeed, apt to be fanciful, or wilfully abstract, the relation between the two sides of a judgment being so intimate as it is and so transparent. It is less frequently a true necessity of thought, than a rhetorical phrase which affects the content by an intimation of the speaker's mood.

It may be worth noting, as a corollary from what has been said, that we use double negation not only for insistence and asseveration, as Sigwart has pointed out, but also in speaking with caution and reserve (μείωσις). In the former we characterize the particular, in the latter the universal negative as untrue, thus in each case establishing the contradictory through the ordinary process of logical opposition.[1]

The peculiar insistence with which these judgments are made depends on their affinity with indirect proof and the negative instance. They allege that a content has been scrutinized with reference to its limit; that attention has been bestowed on the specific question, whether a certain content can possibly or does always fail to exhibit a certain attribute, and that the answer has been negative. The denial of a particular negative we may illustrate in the case of, " The three angles of a triangle may be not equal to two right angles," which we deny by pronouncing that " The three angles of a triangle cannot be not equal to two right angles." And the denial of a universal negative by, " In England the sun never shines in winter," which is denied by saying, " It is not the case that, in England, the sun never shines in winter." Of course we have no right to the universal affirmative all A is B (of which No A is Not-B is the converted contrapositive) unless we are satisfied

---

[1] Thus Sigwart's complaint, that double negation has hitherto found no place in logic, appears ill-founded.

that there are no exceptional cases in which A is not-B ;
nor have we any right to the particular affirmative A
may be B, unless we are sure that there is ground for
assuming exceptions to the negative rule A is never B ;
but there is no doubt that looking for the fact or the
possibility of exceptions to a general ·rule, is a peculiar
side of inquiry, and marks an advance in method and
ideal of knowledge.

Then, if I will not have it that the denial of " A is
not B " must rest on the knowledge that A is B, and
yields A is B solely by this implication, and as I have
agreed with Mr. Bradley in rejecting Sigwart's view
that the original positive judgment is simply left standing when the negation is cancelled, how do I ground
the inference from double negation to affirmation ?

*a.* I should prefer not to call it an inference, being so
transparent as it is, and being provided for in ordinary
logical opposition.  But of course it is possible, as the two
judgments (or rather the two propositions) are equivalent,
to point out how their equivalence may be justified, if
justification is demanded.

And then, $\beta$, I should adopt the antiquated view
to which Sigwart alludes in passing, that the meaning
of double negation is a consequence of the law of
excluded middle.  The essence of negation is the
conception of an absolute alternative or contradictory,
and the law of excluded middle simply expresses this
early generalization.  I cannot venture to judge how

thought would get on with mere contrary opposition, in which the only way of ousting one predicate would be to affirm another and leave the two to fight it out in the mind. But it seems to me clear that it must soon be discovered that to fix on or discriminate the content of an idea, in the way indicated by the Laws of Identity and Contradiction, implies a dichotomy between the content of the idea on the one hand and all that is other than it on the other hand. If anything could be found in knowledge which was neither the given content nor other than it, the possibility of having definite ideas and of recognizing them would be gone. I believe, therefore, that dichotomy is involved in true negation, the generalized idea of otherness, and that we cannot have negation cheaper. Hence every denial is under a dichotomous disjunction, the ultimate disjunction between A and not A, in which to deny the one is to assert the other. This appears to me to be the full reason, so far as it falls within the province of logic, for the indispensability of the negative. The capacity of recognition which is involved in the possession of significant or symbolic ideas involves a capacity of rejecting what is alien to the content we are considering. And it may happen as I pointed out above,[1] that the common character of being alien to some particular content is a character which it is necessary to predicate with distinctness.

Then I think that Sigwart's notion of the especial

[1] See p. 223.

subjectivity of double negation is grounded on a gravely imperfect view of knowledge. It omits to consider the element of limit or distinctness, which in science takes the shape of the negative instance, and which forms a problem and aspect of knowledge complementary in practice, although essential in principle, to distinct and discriminative apprehension. We should see this more clearly if we might write as the equivalent of A is B, not only Not-B is not A, but Not-A is not B, which for reasons mentioned above, common logic does not allow. In science these complementary negations express the work of the negative instance; in that at the point where, and in as far as, you leave A, you also surrender B, and at the point where, and in as far as, you surrender B you *ipso facto* lose A. To affirm by double negation may be regarded as an imperfect attempt to render this aspect of fact.

4. We have seen so far that Negation is necessary to the structure of reality *for us*, and that double Negation is a simple consequence of Negation. I now turn to look more closely at the positive meaning of negative judgments.

"If we confine negation to mere denial,' it is the exclusion of an idea by an unspecified quality; and if we confine the denial to its negative side, it is the mere exclusion of an unsuggested idea." "A bare denial can never be found; for when A excludes some relation to B which is offered in idea, there must always be a ground for that rejection.    The base of the denial must be a positive quality, unspecified but necessary."[1]

With these views I thoroughly agree.    But I would subjoin two remarks.

First, it appears to me that the bare denial, which is never found, is the only kind of denial which is secondary or subjective.    The moment you begin to allege a positive content you depart from the purely subjective denial, the denial which is secondary because it only exists in order to reject an affirmative.    Such a denial, as the author here says, is not found ; or, as I said above,[2] an ungrounded denial is not a judgment.    The best case of bare denial is the "infinite judgment"[3] when it does not imply a rational ground.    If it does imply a rational ground, then I presume it is not a true case of the infinite judgment.    I mean that "the soul is not a triangle" might be a rhetorical way of saying that the soul is not in space, and this would be grounded in the positive quality of the soul as mind, and would not be an "infinite judgment."

This brings me to my second remark.    I wish that Mr. Bradley was as clear everywhere as he is here, that an ungrounded judgment (he only says it of a negative judgment) is no judgment.    We should then get rid of mere judgment and of "arbitrary synthesis of suggestion with reality," and have a different light thrown on

[1] "Principles of Logic," pp. 255, 256.     [2] See p. 218.
[3] See p. 226.

the position of those Inferences whose centre is not explicit.[1]

I pass on to speak of the positive value of negative judgments. Mr. Bradley places this in the positive ground, on which, whether specified or not, they base the rejection which they pronounce. I doubt, however, whether the positive ground need exhaust the positive purport. I incline to think that in the analysis of every judgment, whether affirmative or negative, three elements are traceable : the ground, the content actually employed in judging, and the consequence, *i.e.* application or bearing. Can we not, then, it will be asked, simply say what we mean, without employing a content that is in excess of the application that we require ? No doubt we often can do so, especially if the judgment appeals to feeling. If we say " The sunset is beautiful," " The Australians have won the match," we seem to acquiesce in the content affirmed without drawing any further and precise conclusion out of it. But when we come upon an enunciation, however carefully expressed, in its place in an argument or exposition, we cannot avoid interpreting it by the context. I mean that, besides what it says, there is something which it more especially *does ;* some link of argument which it takes up, or some salient point of exposition on which it insists. Without being properly ambiguous, the same proposition is susceptible of very different significations.

<hr>

[1] See ch. I. sect. 4.

In addition to the question what certain words mean, we always have in our minds the question what the author means by them, or why he employs them here and now " Psychology is a theoretic as distinguished from a practical science." When Mr. Sully uses these words he is speaking of the relation between Psychology and other sciences. The content of "theoretic" is of secondary interest, though essential as an instrument of the distinction required. The author's intention at the moment is not so much to indicate of what nature Psychology is, as to bring out the degree in which it is necessary to certain other sciences. The distinction might, on the other hand, have been drawn in the same words as subsidiary to an account of the nature and belongings of a theoretic science as such. When the " bearing " of a statement is very precise, it ought perhaps to be regarded as a suppressed conclusion, after the fashion of the " enthymeme." " This is the shortest way (so we had better take it)." " The proposed Railway under Hyde Park will not pass under any trees, (so would not risk spoiling any)." "This letter is over one ounce (so it requires another halfpenny stamp)." This is not merely a feature of sentences; it attaches clearly to the judgments themselves ; we use a content, symbolic idea, or meaning, which comes to hand, but the precise bearing and point even of this meaning, *i.e.* the meaning within the meaning, is given by context. It is possible that in Logic, as we deal perforce with isolated judgments, we may have to neglect this feature of all living thought ; but I am sure we ought not to forget it.

To return to the negative, suppose we are told, " The ordnance map of Manchester is not recent." The ground of this statement will be the actual date of publication of the latest map we can find ; the actual content employed in judging is this date considered as excluding recent publication ; but the bearing or application of the judgment is almost certain to be that the map is not to be relied on for recent details. Of course the ground of negation may include or coincide with this consequence ; I only say that I do not think it need. Supposing that it does not, the complete analysis of the judgment then is " The map A bears an old date $x$, which excludes the quality of being recent B ; and if it is not recent, it is so far unreliable $b$." We have here two hypothetical judgments involved. " If $x$ is, B is not," and " If B is not, $b$ is." About neither pair of terms, it may be observed, do we pronounce the equivalent of a complete disjunction. We do not say that " If $x$ is not, B is," nor that " If B is, $b$ is not." But if the ground and consequence coincide, we then have given to us the elements of a complete disjunction. " The signal-light A is green $x$, and therefore is not red, the danger-signal B, but is green, the safety-signal $x$." Here our two judgments would run, " If $x$ is, B is not, " and " If B is not, $x$ is." In other words, we here suppose ourselves to know that green and red have their significance from being the only two alternatives, and thus green is not merely the ground which excludes red, but is also the consequent which we desire to assert through the exclusion of red. Why, then, should we deny red instead of asserting green? More than one reason is possible; I select the chief. It may be because we wish to confirm green as positive ground by green as consequent. The perception may be more or less doubtful. It may be "a colour which I take to be green, but which is certainly not red;" in this case the consequence of "not red" at once ties the colour down to be green. Thus ground and consequent must be different, to account for the employment of negation; slightly different at least, or in need of mutual corroboration. But we often like to have corroboration where there is no practical doubt. And this leads to the other possible reasons for employing denial. We *say more* by denying, in such a case, than by affirming. For in the positive we can rest, in the negative we cannot. The negative must have its ground; the positive is compatible with an indolence of thought which may never go on to accentuate its negative and systematic import. "That is a green light, and means safety," does not force us to realize, though we may know, that there is only one other light, which is red and means danger. It does not force us to reflect that the alternative which we perceive to be fact is one of only two.

Now, all actual negation owes its significance to

hypothetical and disjunctive judgments, like those considered above. And in every case, I think, there is a positive bearing as well as a positive ground, though the two may coincide, and I presume that Mr. Bradley means them to do so. The *material* difference between affirmation and negation (for the reasons assigned above for preferring negative expression become merely rhetorical *in face of exact and realized knowledge*), the *material* difference tends to vanish, not merely because negation has become positive, but because the judgment which was originally positive has been invested with definite powers of exclusion.

5. But the formal difference between affirmation and negation remains, and has consequences as to which I cannot wholly follow Mr. Bradley. The mere formal Negation, which represents nothing but my personal failure to find a certain attribute in a certain object, tempts us sometimes to say, " This is not visibly impossible, and therefore it is really possible," and sometimes to say, " This is not visibly possible, and therefore it is really impossible." Mr. Bradley treats these two temptations in the same way.[1] I agree with his treatment of the former, but differ from him as regards the latter.

From the " privative judgment," " So far as I know, the nature of things does not make $x$ impossible," we ought not to conclude directly that " In the nature of things $x$ is possible." Before passing to such a con-

---

[1] " Principles of Logic," pp. 198 and 515.

clusion, we ought to show that in the nature of things, as I think of it for this purpose, there is a basis for the real conditions, which, if realized, would bring $x$ with them.

In short, to pronounce a thing possible requires a positive affirmation ; an affirmation that of the conditions which would bring that thing to pass, some, or some element, or some yet remoter antecedent, conditions are real. On the ground of sheer and mere ignorance whether the thing in question has or has not any basis of hope in reality, we cannot properly make the material statement that reality to some extent at least favours it. It is not enough that reality as we know it should be impartial. Impartiality in such a case is nothing, and so the negation carries it, not because privation amounts to exclusion, but because nothing can come of nothing, and so there is nothing to exclude. We may say in such a case, " I cannot show it to be impossible ; " but we must not say, " It is therefore possible." I believe that these remarks reproduce the essence of Mr. Bradley's contention, which appears to me to be right, and to dispose of a very dangerous fallacy. You cannot get something out of nothing, or knowledge out of ignorance.

But the other case does not seem to me quite parallel. We have just been comparing Privation with Affirmation. We are now to compare Privation with Exclusion. Here we find in common at least the external form of ignorance and failure. However demonstrable an exclusion may be, yet the ultimate " not " can never be directly deduced from its positive ground.　I imagine that this must have been the meaning of the old saying, that you cannot prove a negative ; for, a negative premise once granted, nothing is easier than to prove a negative conclusion.

Thus, when Mr. Bradley lays it down[1] that " A privative judgment can by no handling become an exclusion," I am obliged to rejoin that, though out of a pure negation ("privation ") you cannot get a positive, yet except by the instrumentality of a pure negation you cannot ultimately get an exclusion.　In favour of the most positive rejection that can be pronounced, you can have *in form* no warrant but the privative judgment, which *per se*, as we saw, amounts to nothing.

The material difference between privation and exclusion, between " I do not know that A is," and " I know that A is not," is easier to recognize than to explain ; and I somewhat grudge Mr. Bradley the wealth of spatial metaphors he expends on it.　In a bare privative judgment, such as has no meaning and cannot affirm a possibility nor ground an exclusion, " the subject is confined to something without the sphere of the predicate." To say of ultimate reality "it is without the rejection of x " is to say of it something which has no meaning, unless, so to speak, the place left empty by this mere privation is occupied by a positive attribute.　" In the content of the subject there may be an empty space where the quality should be," or, again, there may be no such space.　I do

[1] " Principles of Logic," p. 515.

not know what this space in a content means. And though I wish not to be captious, I must advert to Mr. Bradley's instance (page 112). "In a privative judgment the predicate red would be denied of the subject simply on the ground that red was not there. The subject might be entirely colourless and dark." But if red were excluded by green, that would be opposition. Surely this is a slip. If the subject can be dark (colourless in that sense), it has surface capable of colour, and the exclusion of red is exclusion by opposition.

I suppose Mr. Bradley's meaning comes to this, that Exclusion rests on opposition. In that case, the space which the excluded attribute would fill, *i.e.* its special relation to the content, is filled by a different and positive attribute. Or the space may be empty, *i.e.* we may know that the content must have some attribute in the genus of the doubtful attribute, but we do not know what. Or there may be no space, *i.e.* we may know of no conditions operative on the subject which would generate any such attributes as that supposed to be in question.

But the metaphor of a space and what fills it makes the matter far too easy. The question is really about just the point which is here slurred. What attributes *are* opposed? What are the limits and shape of the "space," and how do we know that it would not hold both the attributes, or which of them it would hold best? " The dimensions of space are not four" excludes four, we may say, on the ground that they are only three ; but this will hardly do, for in order to prove that they are only three we must prove that they are not four.  And the only way of getting at this is to say that I *do not see how* to construct the dimensions compatibly with their being four.  A number is needed, and I can make it no number but three.  "Not four" expresses my impotence to make it four.

What I wish to point out is, in the first place, this formal analogy between the privative and the exclusive judgment.  And the moral I wish to draw is, that here invincible ignorance ought to go for something, that where the more we try the less we find a positive result we should cease to pronounce the matter inquired into possible or even not impossible, and should at length be permitted to shift the negative from the position which it holds in, "I do not say it is so," to that which it holds in, "I say it is not so."  We use in this sense, "I do not think," "I do not believe," etc.  Mr. Bradley will say, "If you have a positive ground of exclusion, show it, and make your privative judgment into one of exclusion ; if not it cannot exclude."  But this seems to me to be very hard, because, as the author points out,[1] we may have a possibility alleged in a region where our knowledge supplies us, and where the allegation furnishes, no condition or attribute of any sort bearing on the suggested possibility.  And in such a case

---

[1] "Principles of Logic," p. 199.

it will be, *ex hypothesi, impossible to discover a positive ground against the suggested fact or possibility.* An allegation can only be disproved out of itself; if it alleges nothing positive, you can find no positive ground against it. You cannot disprove that of which no proof can be offered. Then we should only have to be wild and fantastic enough, and we could at once demand a suspension of judgment. This is no visionary danger. It is the essential vice of popular superstitions. "This is my view, and if you are really impartial, you will at least suspend judgment." I reply, "No. Suspension of judgment is for a conflict of proofs, not for their absence on both sides. Nothing can come of nothing, and in the absence of proof the attitude of judgment is not suspension but rejection." Of course there is a general ethical obligation to be open to all proof when alleged ; and a presumption that proof can or will be had is itself a degree of proof. My object is merely to effect a slight *rapprochement*, an admission of at least generic identity, for the privative and the exclusive judgment, to insist on the fact that the ultimate transition from positive to negative form is always privative ; and therefore to claim more exclusive force for the mere privative, and to concede less finality to the exclusive judgment, than popular usage permits in either case. The true logical denial, common to both, is, " I see no reason to think," which is as strong a negation as knowledge can furnish. " I see every reason to think—not" has only a rhetorical

advantage over the former.   Both involve a reference to
all the knowledge we can command ; neither is able to
indicate what that may amount to.   Thus we should not
regard " I cannot see how two straight lines can enclose
a space " as absolutely different in kind from " I can find
no case in which an unknown language in an unknown
alphabet has been successfully interpreted."

It may be said that the two set of cases which I
have treated as opposite are really on all-fours with
each other.   Mr. Bradley has regarded them as being
so.   Considering Exclusion as depending on a positive
quality, he treats the inference from Privation to Exclusion, which I wish in some degree to justify, as identical
in principle with the inference from Privation to real
possibility or affirmation, in favour of which I have, as
explained above, nothing to say.   Of course, indeed, by
treating impossibility as a positive quality, and the
failure to find it as a Privation, and by regarding real
possibility as the exclusion of exclusion, *i.e.* as something
negative, we might *verbally* reverse the above reasoning,
and treat the assertion of impossibility as affirmation
(this Mr. Bradley does [1]), and that of real possibility as
exclusion.   I have tried to point out that there is a gulf
between the two which cannot be crossed in this way.
If you formulate real possibility as the exclusion of
exclusion, you reduce it from positive knowledge to the

---

[1] By saying that "We do not know that S—P is impossible," is or
rests on a privative judgment.   "Principles of Logic," p. 188.

necessity of ignorance. If you state it as a positive condition or attribute, you leap the gulf from ignorance to knowledge, and make a statement to which the form of exclusion could never have committed you. In inferring from true privation to true exclusion you keep within the form of ignorance, however much you may weight it with the matter of knowledge.

We do not seem yet to have grasped the material difference which undoubtedly exists between " Privation " and " Exclusion." Can our apprehension of a definite contradiction by which the quality $x$ " repels " or " rejects " the quality $y$ be brought under the head of ignorance? If we judge by ordinary usage, it would be idle to attempt this. The impotence of inevitable necessity does not seem to us to be the same as the impotence of mere seeking without finding. And yet the inevitable necessity of a contradiction manifests itself to us as seeking a way of conciliation, and finding none. Many such contradictions have not been final; I do not say that none are, though I incline to think that in their present form none are. The matter comes to this: in the judgment of exclusion the negative embodies a definite distinction warranted and supported by a classification which must be modified, or perhaps annihilated, if the distinction is denied. In the judgment of privation we are in a chaotic unsystematized region ; the negation is such that it may be reversed without further modifications of our system of reality. Both fall under the common expression, "Conceiving the matter completely, I cannot conceive it so ;" but the absolute completeness of conception is different in each, though in both it is all that we can make it. Does straight exclude curved? It is of no avail to say that straight occupies the place which curved would occupy, and therefore repels it. This is only a metaphor expressing a matter of fact. That which decides is geometrical classification, and according to the answer it gives we either can or cannot see how a straight line can be a curve.

6. I explained above[1] the view which I take of the principle of Excluded Middle. I have no strong objection to the expression in which Mr. Bradley follows both Lotze and Sigwart, when he says that Excluded Middle is one case of Disjunction. I quote the whole passage from page 412, partly because of its merits of expression. "Excluded Middle is one case of Disjunction ; it cannot be considered as co-extensive with it. Its real and contradictory alternative rests on the existence of contrary opposites. The existence of exclusion without reference to their number is the ground of disjunction ; and the special case of assertion and denial is developed from that basis in the way in which contradiction is developed from exclusion. Common disparate[2] disjunc-

---

[1] P. 236.

[2] Mr. Bradley uses "disparate" as equivalent to "incompatible," or "contrary," and without reference to the meaning "incomparable."

tion is the base, and the dual alternative of *b* and not-*b* rests entirely upon this." [1]

I have remarked above, and shall return to, the small store which the author seems to set by a general principle. In one sense a general principle rests, no doubt, on the facts from which we happen to abstract it. But in laying down a general principle, we do not consider that we are simply dealing with one among the facts, though it may and will take the same shape as cases on which it throws light. This occurs, for instance, with statements of proportion compared with their application in particular cases, and perhaps with the general explanation of proportion as such compared with statements of proportion. And in the same way Excluded Middle appears to me to be *the* case, not *a* case, of Disjunction. It is not merely that we have two alternatives in the one case and several in the other. It is that the skeleton disjunction A is either B or not B lays down the condition to which predications must conform in order to be truly alternative. I will not lay stress on the alleged "reduction" of disjunction to hypothetical judgments, which Mr. Bradley does not admit. But I think he would agree that the hypotheticals, though not in his view sufficing to constitute disjunction, yet represent elements without which there can be no disjunction. Now, these elements are a knowledge of the positive

---

[1] *Cf.* "Principles of Logic," p. 129. "Disjunction" does not rest on "Excluded Middle."

ground and consequence of the rejection of a certain predicate. That "common disparate disjunction is the base" is true in the sense that the whole matter rests on the existence of qualities from the presence and absence of which conclusions can be drawn about the absence and presence of others. If you have qualities which you know to be thus related, you have a Disjunction, and the thing is done. But it is not true in the sense that to find a number of predicates, each of which claims to be the predicate, or rather *a* predicate, in a certain judgment, is enough to make a disjunction. You must arrive at a certain stage of precise knowledge; you must be able to affirm, on grounds which seem to you valid, that not only the assertion but also the rejection of any one predicate has consequences as regard the other or others. The number of alternatives does not affect this requirement. Out of three alternatives, A, B, C, to reject C will not establish either of the other two ; but it will affect each of them by making it one out of two and not one out of three. Whereas if you do not know that the exclusion of C reduces the field to A and B, you have not got a disjunction at all. It may be said, as Sigwart has said,[1] that when we know that "If B is not, A is," we already know that "either B is or A is." This is not true ; no provision is hereby made for the cases "If B is— " and "if A is— ;" it is therefore possible that the two, A and B, may be

<hr>

[1] "Logik," vol. i. p. 257.

compatible. But waiving this point as trivial, I say that the fact, if true, makes no difference, for I am not insisting that the hypothetical is prior to the disjunctive (though it is prior to the disjunction of A and B simply), but laying stress on the element of knowledge which is brought to light as essential to the disjunction ; the knowledge, in Sigwart's words, " of a Negation as ground of an affirmation." This is the material fact in the structure of our world which makes Disjunction possible, and which is *formally* expressed in bare negation and nowhere else. For " disparate " disjunction conceals this feature of its positive predicates, which do not contain it in our rudimentary knowledge of them or exhibit it in their form, but are endowed with it by our defining thought in virtue of precise systematic relations. The skeleton form " either B or not-B " exhibits in its abstract nakedness this relation of mere exclusion, and thus forces us to recognize an essential aspect of knowledge. The Law of Excluded Middle drags to light and holds up to us in the abstract a principle which, though in various degrees unrecognized, is at the root of all discrimination, and therefore of all intelligent apprehension.

7. In Mr. Bradley's discussions of the disjunctive judgment there is much which surprises me. It is only too probable that I have not succeeded in grasping his meaning. I think it worth while in the interests of clearness to put forward my principal difficulties at the risk of exhibiting a want of comprehension.

I have alluded above[1] to Mr. Bradley's analysis of the categorical element contained in Disjunction. I only recur to the point in order to express a doubt as to the exact feature which he takes to be superadded by the Hypotheticals. I quote from page 124, " Being sure of our basis, the quality $x$, upon this universal we erect hypothesis. We know that $b$ and $c$ are disparate. We know that A is particularized within $b$ and $c$, and therefore as one of $b$ and $c$. It cannot be both, and it must be some one. So much is the fact. To complete the disjunction we add the supposal, " If it is not one, it must be the other ; if A is not $b$, it must be $c$ ; and it must be $b$, if it is not $c$." This supposal completes the " Either—or."

I cannot understand what the supposal adds to what is taken as fact. I even doubted at first whether the selection of the supposal with negative antecedent was or was not a mere slip. That its converse is repeated as a separate supposal is explained by Mr. Bradley's view of this conversion as a genuine inference.[2] However this may be, the case " If A is $b$ it is not $c$ " is not given as a supposal, and as it, *à fortiori*, cannot be derived from the case which is given, I conclude, though doubtfully, that *it* is held to be included in the basis of fact. But what a narrow line between fact and supposal ! It is fact that A being $b$ excludes $c$, but supposal that A being not $b$ accepts $c$.

---

[1] P. 27.          [2] " Principles of Logic," p. 392.

I do not rely on the above argument.  Mr. Bradley may have meant in this place, for the sake of brevity, to let each hypothetical stand for its converse also, and may have written down a convertend and converse instead of two complementary supposals by a slip which is only too easy with symbolic letters.

But I should have thought that the fact obviously included the assertion of both, or, in Mr. Bradley's way of speaking, of all four supposals.  We are taken to know categorically that " A cannot be both B and C," *i.e.* that its being either excludes its being the other, and "that it must be some one," *i.e.* that its not being the one ensures its being the other.  What can be gained by repeating these determinations in a hypothetical form ; and more especially, if we hold to the obvious interpretation of the passage, what distinction can be drawn between them according to which " A cannot be both " (*i.e.* if it is B it is not C) is fact, and A must be one (*i.e.* if it is not B it is C) rests on supposal ?  One might say that the " ifs " put more clearly the experiment which must be made in inference ; and perhaps it is more (though not much more) than a grammatical variation of phrase.  But they only state something of which we must have been satisfied before we had a right to judge " Not both but one."

I go on to speak of the Inference involved in Disjunctive Judgment.  As I understand Mr. Bradley, there are three ways in which we may regard Disjunctive Inference.

S

*a.* We may think of it [1] as syllogistic, reducing " A is *b* or *c* " to " A not-*c* is *b* " (which, however, does not tell us anything of A which *is c*), and arguing " A is A not-*c*, therefore A is B." But this process, as Mr. Bradley says, and I agree, tells us nothing of the point of main interest, which is how we get the explicit statement of alternatives. The inference as here described is a subsumption under a major premise, which is treated as given, and is not accounted for.

*β.* " Before " the syllogistic argument " in time, and before it in idea, comes the actual process, and we must see what this is." This, the actual process, starts, as I gather from a remark on page 385, with " an explicit exhaustion of the possibilities of A," though I do not find this laid down in the account of it. We also know, to begin with, that A is nothing which excludes *a*, *b*, and *c*. We then learn successively that A is not *b*, and that it is not *c*, and conclude successively that it falls within *c d*, and that it is *d*. This conclusion is not proved from the major, " What is not *b* or *c* must be *d*." On the contrary, the process which establishes the conclusion also establishes the major.

I suppose that the process so described is hardly a definite inference till we come to the last step. You have three judgments expressing possibilities for A ; you deny one, and the other two are left standing, still as possibilities. We seem to have done nothing at all

[1] " Principles of Logic," p. 384.

to them, and yet I admit that, as pointed out above, there has been a modification of their relation to knowledge, and therefore an inference. The chance of each possibility is now half, whereas before it was one-third. The inference consists in giving out these two cases for the whole content of the judgment, instead of the former three, and the process is like that of perception or rational analysis by which we remove the irrelevant matter in a scientific observation, and set down what remains as the truth.

The last step, however, deserves the special attention which the author bespeaks for it. By abolition of the last possibility but one, the survivor changes from possibility into fact. Mr. Bradley sees in this an illustration of a principle to which he recurs more than once, " the principle that a sole possibility is actual fact." But even this principle is not the premise, but is known as the result of the argument.

What I wish to point out in this representation of the disjunctive process, and also in the conception (page 385) of inference from the mere survival of an idea, without asking whether all possible ideas have been suggested, is the stress laid on the *fact* of survival without reference to its grounds. An idea is not accepted as fact because it survives ; it survives because it is accepted as fact. And why ? Why, for some material ground which favours it and disfavours other ideas. So with the " sole possibility." If there is ground to pronounce it fact now, after the rejection of the opposing possibilities, there was ground before, but for the opposing possibilities. Before, the opposing possibilities were able to use the evidence which they shared with it, and thus of course neutralized part of the evidence for it. But now they are abolished, it, as sharing in the characteristic which made the whole disjunction certain, is now certain on the ground of that characteristic, which could not help it against the others while they existed.

Thus I confess that I cannot see my way to the principle that a sole possibility[1] is fact ; except in the sense that a truly sole possibility must have had such a fight for its place, that it is pretty certain to have made good its claim to be judged a fact. If Mr. Bradley meant that out of *any given* set of suggestions the survivor must be taken as fact, I should be in despair. But as long as the sole possibility is something which it is not certain that we shall ever light upon, I do not so much mind. And I seem to trace the view which I prefer in the distinction between two interpretations

---

[1] *Cf.* "Principles of Logic," p. 451. I am almost driven to suppose that I have failed to understand the nature of this principle. I do not seem to myself to be aware of its operation. It seems to me quite possible to doubt all suggestions on a given matter, and I see no reason for accepting any that is not positively established. *If such non-acceptance is treated as a judgment,* and thus as the sole possibility in question, the principle is reduced to the formal necessity that consciousness, in relation to any matter which draws attention, should pronounce a verdict guided by its entire apprehension of the then real world. But this is no special principle of inference.

of: " I must because I can not otherwise "—viz. " I must not otherwise because I do thus, and I know that I do thus because I cannot do otherwise," and, " I must do this because I do not perceive that I do aught else." As we saw above, it comes to this ; you cannot exclude on the ground of mere privation ; you must not say, there is no other alternative, simply because you have not found one.  You may exclude on the ground of a motived privation ; that is, when you can say, " I have before me a positive quality involved in a positive systematic construction, which is essential to the subject A ; it admits of such and such alternatives, but, *so far as I can see* (for here comes in the inevitable element of privation), any other would upset and contradict it."

It seems to me that Mr. Bradley's genuine disjunction and his principle of the " sole possibility " are so con-structed as to favour mere privation.  He describes the principle as dealing solely with the form ; he makes the surviving idea fact because it survives.  I would almost venture to suggest that this is as bad as, indeed is a case of, the superstition which refers every conclusion to a major premise.  Mr. Bradley himself, following, I presume, in the track of Hegel,[1] has drawn attention to the error involved in extracting the form of an inference, and placing it as content of a major premise, under which is subsumed the whole content of the inference ; the employment of the form as content of a premise

---

[1] Hegel, "Wiss. der Logik," ii. p. 151.

being only possible by help of a further inferential form, active in the argument so constructed, which might equally claim in its turn to be exhibited as major premise, and so on to infinity. Are we not falling into this error when we say that a surviving idea, one of several alternatives, is fact because it survives? Surely it is fact not because it survives, but because of the special reasons for which it survives. Why should we not appeal to the *fundamentum divisionis*, and endeavour to show that all possible values of the predicate in question are set down as alternatives? Thus the last alternative is fact, because it is the only form of the predicate which is any longer in question, and the reasons which exclude the other, combined with those which make such a predicate necessary at all, are positive proof of this last alternative as fact.

γ. This brings us to the third point of view under which Mr. Bradley regards disjunction. I presume that the type of disjunctive inference which he mentions on page 513, but there treats as spurious, is the type to which the above observations would guide us.

If $b$, $c$, and $d$ are the alternative predicates ascribed to a subject A, then in disjunction of the type now in question, the rejection of $b$ and $c$ is a result of the operation of $d$. In other words, $d$ is not accepted because it survives, but it survives because, in process of being accepted, it rejects the others. It certainly seems to me that this argument, which, I admit to Mr. Bradley, is not an argument from the mere fact of survival, nevertheless is the only warrantable form of disjunction. I do not understand why Mr. Bradley should say that this is not genuine disjunction, because, among other reasons, the rejected alternatives were never possible. Of course, whatever is not actual, we may say in a purist sense, was never possible. But these alternatives were thought possible until the actuality of $d$ was brought to light, and I do not know in what other sense alternatives could be called possible. If we start from the disjunction " a given " or " any given triangle is either isosceles, equilateral, or scalene," we must assume $a$ triangle as subject if we mean to apply the disjunctive inference, though it is true that, construed of triangle as such, the universal judgment has no bias towards one kind more than another. Thus, though we select $a$ triangle as subject, we are not to suppose ourselves to take it as more than *given qua* triangle. We do *not* yet take it as determinately known. That its place in the classification may appear to us the moment it catches our eye, is a fault of the simplicity of my illustration, and is not inherent in the nature of the case. If we take a large triangle with two sides all but equal, we shall then have to measure before we know of what kind it is. If the triangle which we take as subject is really scalene, then the rejection of the alternatives isosceles and equilateral will be owing to the fact of its being scalene, which we have a right to imagine, for the sake of illustration, as dawning on us gradually by examination of the given triangle in the light of those opposite ideal contents. But before the determination is thus effected the three alternatives are surely as possible as anything can be. And a fourth alternative is excluded by the systematic *fundamentum divisionis* based on the number of a triangle's sides.

This disjunction, as I have said, Mr. Bradley considers spurious, the essence of its argument not being *tollendo ponere.* It seems to me that the mere argument *tollendo ponere* is always a formal or second-class argument, and that if disjunction cannot get to deeper, more material ground, it is worth little. I mean that in the wake of any first-class proof you can always have others which simply take its form as justified, and argue from it by subsumption. Certain matters known in certain ways have a right to be arranged in a reciprocally exclusive system. The disjunctive arguments are a result of this reciprocal exclusiveness. But the real basis of proof is not in the result, only in its justification. "You tell me," a pupil may say to his teacher, "that a triangle must be either isosceles, equilateral, or scalene, and that of these strange names the two first are not true of the figure before me ; therefore I conclude that the last is so." This would be a genuine disjunctive argument according to Mr. Bradley, as I understand him ; but to my mind it would miss the whole material guarantee of the conclusion, which is in the perception of a principle, and of its application. The conclusion as the supposed pupil draws it, is certain on the premises, but is, I think, purely subsumptive. *It* does not establish the major; the major is taken or given, and if it were not, the conclusion would not follow.

I do not say that even a motived disjunction is final. But I thoroughly agree with Mr. Bradley's remarks on pages 516, 517, to the effect that we should at least face the possibility that some truths may be final; that, in other words, the impotence or ignorance to which we saw above that all exclusion of predication was reducible, may in some cases be a final and irremediable impotence, in which case we should no longer have the right to call it ignorance, or to wish it were remediable. The old crux at this point is to *distinguish* such final necessity of knowledge from genuine remediable ignorance, and out of this I must confess I do not see my way. The position is this. The existence of ignorance is not a matter of dispute; the existence of final necessity as regards any judgment in human knowledge is a matter of dispute; and we have no means of distinguishing the one from the other. For, since Lotze assented to what is in effect Mill's view, that the test of conceivability is only of temporary value, and operative solely as summing up our intellectual state at any time, I think that the impossibility of a practical distinction must be taken as admitted. I therefore think that Mr. Bradley underrates the force of

the theoretical argument for the possibility of the modification of all judgments and every judgment.   The real
reason why such a possibility has no weight is answered
by himself in another place.   It is that, as we have
seen,[1] nothing can come of nothing, and an unmotived
abstract possibility applying equally to all knowledge
applies effectively to none.   To none, that is, while it
is *held as knowledge;* for then its systematic form
shelters its material content under the ægis of the whole,
and ensures that it shall reappear in whatever transformations the whole may undergo.   But as against
isolated, abstracted truths, truths of science taken as rules
of thumb and matters of fact, as against these dead twigs
of knowledge, the sceptical censure has full force.   At
any moment they may be broken off, and all that
attaches to them may vanish with them.   They are not
kept alive by a connection with the whole, and they
may never grow again.   Or, to drop metaphor, I mean
that the moment we lose sight of processes and begin to
plume ourselves on net results, we fall into danger of
fixing what is unessential in a conception as its characteristic, and therefore meeting with a horrible collision
when modifications come, and the essentials, though pre-
served, are transformed, while our unessentials, on which
we had set our hearts, turn out to have been a mere
confusion.   Against the principle that the gravity of any
portion of matter is constant, and independent of the

---

[1] See p. 249 and " Principles of Logic," p. 520.

shape of objects, I have known it maintained, and by high scientific authority, that this was not so, because weight varies with distance from the earth's centre (weight, at least, as tested by a spring balance), and also that shape makes a difference to it, because it affects the distance of part of the object from the earth's centre. Now, I should have expected that in no scientific mind would the principle that gravity is a constant property of matter, for a moment appear to be controverted by such facts as these. Gravity must be construed as including variation of weight. But to minds which thought they had been told that *weight* was constant, I can imagine a certain surprise being caused by the demonstration that it varied under varying conditions without anything being added to or taken from the matter weighed. I think, therefore, that in treating any truth as necessary, we should be careful to indicate rather that *the body of knowledge must have a corresponding function to that which the truth in question represents*, than that any abstract shape in which it may be familiar to us, with its customary bearings and applications, is beyond criticism. Such a caution applies very strongly to the doctrine of cause and effect, a doctrine which we cannot exactly do without, but which has wrought much havoc by being taken for infallible in any form of it that came to hand.

I must make a protest on another point of the discussion on pages 516, 517. I do not think it fair to say,

" You can not assert that its opposite (the opposite of a character believed to be true of a subject) is possible, until you are able mentally to represent that opposite." If " mentally represent "="imagine " (*vorstellen*) I object to this.　One may have very good grounds for thinking there must be an opposite without being able to picture it in the mind—nay, without being able to remove a contradiction which forbids any consistent intellectual grasp of the alleged opposite.　I firmly believe that in the Indian sword-trick there is an opposite, not only possible but true, to the simple rendering invisible the boy who is supposed to be killed.　But under the conditions of the incident as told to me, *i.e.* as taking place in a paved courtyard with spectators all round, or on a ship's deck with a similar audience, I am totally barred by contradictions from imagining any such opposite.

I do not know whether Mr. Bradley had in his mind some remarks of Lotze[1] in the logic.　In my judgment the passage to which I allude is too favourable to the view which Mr. Bradley adopts.　But it is noticeable that Lotze finds himself compelled to modify his meaning so as to admit suggestions which we can conceive as *possible* objects of perception ; *i.e.* the nature of which seems to us consistent with their being imaginable, if, so to speak, we could get at them to imagine them.　He instances invisibly small atoms.　Thus, if we are to lay stress on mental representation, we must limit the

---

[1] " Logik," sect. 277.

requirement of it to the degree and mode in which the nature of the case may make it possible. Can we mentally represent the soul?

But there is great weight to my mind in Mill's contention that the attempt to imagine (or better, I should say, to conceive) is only a test of the then state of our knowledge (a view which Lotze appears to accept), and that we should not go to such a psychological test, but to the actual evidence, or, as I should say, to our system of knowledge itself, if we wish to know whether an opposite to a given predicate is possible.

# CHAPTER VI.

## SUBSUMPTION AND THE ANALYSIS OF INFERENCE.

I NOW propose to offer some remarks upon Mr. Bradley's treatment of Inference. I expressly disclaim the intention of giving an account of his views. I only mean to mention what I disagree with, and as much more as is necessary to make that intelligible. However, it is but fair to say that I regard his main contention, consisting, I take it, in his view of the place of subsumption in inference, as made out; that of all censures of the traditional syllogism with which I am acquainted, his alone shows an apprehension of the characters which form its strength, and which any new view must preserve; and that my own criticism only aims at helping to analyze and marshal the abundant material which he furnishes.

It will conduce to clearness if I state at once the general purpose of the following remarks. It is to vindicate the old maxim to which I have alluded before, that only he has knowledge who can give the reason for what he affirms. I cannot, as at present advised, attach any importance to your telling me that you have made an intellectual experiment, and you find you cannot help believing this or that. I am no better off even if you give me your data, for I do not know how you may have used them. What I want to be told is the ground on which you have gone ; the elements in the content before your mind and the *modus operandi* of ✓ your mind upon them, which together have caused your intellect to determine that it must think thus and cannot think otherwise. I want, in short, to distinguish true reasoning from calculation (which of course I accept as *a* form of reasoning) from conjecture and from the operation of instinct ; even from acquired instinct, such as the skill of a pianist or of a good shot. In the past, we have generally relied on Subsumption as the guardian of this frontier. If we are to be deprived of Subsumption, as I am convinced that we must be, we should be doubly careful with our new account of Inference.

I begin, then, by asking, " What is subsumption ? " It was perhaps unfortunate for the future of Logic that Aristotle saw, so clearly as he did, the dependence of what has since been called extension on connections of content. Fascinated by the details of the quantity of judgments, but regarding quantity as only an aspect of necessity, he never dreamed that his successors would represent quantity as the essence of argument, nor that he himself was favouring such a conception by his long and careful analysis of the subsumptive syllogism. It was because he was so thoroughly aware that argument had more in it than subsumption under a rule, that he never spoke so narrowly as to rouse the challenge, " Has argument no more in it than the relation of all to some or to one ? "   On the other hand, I should imagine it to be doubtful (I do not speak as an expert in Aristotelian logic) whether he himself clearly distinguished the perception of necessary connection *from* its consequence in universality, though he explicitly distinguished these two sides *in* scientific predication.  It is doubtful, I should think, if he ever asked himself whether subsumptive reasoning was always involved in necessary demonstration.  Some passages in the Analytics seem to show that he had fully and fairly made this separation, but I cannot think that it was always present to him in his logical writings.

In face, however, of the recent growth of Formal Logic, issuing in the Quantification of the Predicate and in the Equational view of reasoning, the above question could not but be asked, and Mr. Bradley is not the first to ask it.  But he is, so far as I am aware, the first to meet it with a reasonable answer, and to point out at once the strength and the weakness of subsumption.

The essence of subsumption is that it only works within the category of subject and attribute.  It is, therefore, in a special sense an argument from what is given.  Not merely that, like all arguments, it needs premises, but more than this ; for in subsumption the subject and predicate of the conclusion need have no scientific or systematic relation with each other, or with the unity which brings them together. The nature of a concrete subject is beyond our powers of construction; we cannot see why a certain priest should have had a neighbouring nobleman for his first penitent,[1] nor why that nobleman should have been a murderer. In each case, the presence of the two attributes in the same subject is simply given, and we have to take it as it is given.

I do not mean that subsumption consists in inclusion within a class. Subsumption, like other kinds of argument, deals primarily with connections of attributes. But the connection it deals with is not rational. It depends on the given nature of a more or less concrete subject, in which attributes are conjoined, and from their conjunction in which we argue to their conjunction with each other. I had better at once clear away an obvious difficulty in this assertion. All triangles have their three angles = two right angles, ABC is a triangle ; Therefore, etc. Is not this a subsumption, and yet a rational, nay, a demonstrable, connection of content? The answer is that where you have a necessary con-

[1] I cannot resist telling from memory a story which may be found somewhere in Thackeray, and which excellently illustrates the compulsory but accidental power of subsumption. The abbé: "Ah, ladies ! what stories an old priest could tell. Do you know my first penitent was a murderer." The principal nobleman of the neighbourhood enters the room. "Ah, Monsieur l'abbé ! Ladies, I was the abbé's first penitent, and I promise you my confession astonished him." The conclusion may be imagined.

T

nection of attributes, you can *a fortiori* have a subsumption, but that the subsumption as such neither requires nor incorporates in itself, as ground of inference, such a connection of attributes. If the attributes are together as differences in a set of subjects taken as identical, that is enough to justify subsumption, and it represents nothing more. This is not to say that the arguments which we practically use in the form " All,—" " Therefore, this,—" are merely subsumptive in their nature ; no doubt in many of them the subsumptive form is an inadequate rendering of what we mean.

But within the category of subject and attribute the traditional syllogism may be said to represent the true course of thought. The major premise really contributes to the argument ; it lays down a rule with a mark, and whatever has the mark is inferred to come under the rule.

2. This being the essence of subsumption, is subsumption, as thus defined, necessary to all argument? Up to this point I have been, I believe, in substantial agreement with Mr. Bradley. I now begin, though but slightly in the first instance, to diverge from his view. Under the present head I admit his main contention, but subjoin two trivial reservations, and anticipate another more serious one.

I admit that in inferences of Mr. Bradley's favourite type, drawn frequently from series in space or time, it is non-natural to construct a major premise, and put it at the head of the argument. Instances are: " A is to the right of B, B is to the right of C, therefore A is to the right of C." " A is prior to B [in time], B to C, therefore A to C." For the first of these the author constructs, as a *reductio ad absurdum* of the subsumptive theory, the portentous major premise, " A body is to the right of that, which that, which it is to the right of, is to the right of."[1] It is true, as contended by the author here, that we do not, in such an argument, employ any such premise; it is also true, as contended by him later,[2] that if we did construct such a premise, and wrote it as a major, we should be doing no good, because we should have to repeat in the minor all that such a major contains;[3] and the minor would suffice by itself to carry · the conclusion. We should have to repeat in the minor that A is to the right of B, which is to the right of C, and this is really the *process which proves the major premise.* Of course you cannot say as a syllogism, " B is to the right of C, A to the right of B ∴ A to the right of C." This omits in the major the relation of A to B, and we get four terms.

The doctrine which Mr. Bradley founds on his rejection of the syllogism is briefly and roughly this:[4] Every inference is a process of construction, followed by a result in the shape of a perception. Logical demonstration is the union of a construction and an

---

<sup></sup>[1] " Principles of Logic," p. 227.    [2] p. 475.
[3] *Cf.* Hegel, " Wiss. der Logik," ii. p. 151.
[4] *Cf.* " Principles of Logic," p. 235.

intuition, or perception. More generally[1] inference
is *an ideal experiment* upon something which is given
followed by an ascription of the result of this process to
the original datum. And in this experiment construction may have its place taken by other operations of
the nature of analysis.[2] But as Synthesis (construction)
and analysis are ultimately (and rightly) pronounced
to be identical,[3] the substitution does not gravely affect
the theory.

The only general or "formal" laws which control
the process of construction are laid down at a point where
the author is still allowing it to be assumed that every
inference has at least three terms. This view is modified
at a later stage of the work to admit of inference whose
centre is not explicit, but subsequently again remodified
in the direction of showing that, implicit or explicit, a
centre can be found in every inference. Therefore I
take it that the laws of construction laid down in considering three-term inferences hold good for all inference
as such. And these laws are : (*a*) Conditions as to the
genus or category within which the terms employed in
inference must be related, for the construction must
have unity, and to secure this must be made about an
identical point ; and (β) this postulate itself, that the two
premises must contain an identical point, with its consequence that one premise at least must be universal.
All this seems to me true and clear.

<hr>

[1] p. 396.          [2] p. 412.          [3] p. 430.

I spoke, however, of two trifling reservations.  They are these : There are two kindred ways in which subsumption still haunts us outside the category of subject and attribute.[1]

In the first place, the process of interpretation, whether applied to the symbols of language, or to other perceptions—*e.g.* to actual figures in space like the diagrams of Euclid—is one of subsumption.  In looking at the figure of the first proposition of Euclid, I have to recognize two circles and a triangle, and to equip these particular figures in their present position with the complex of attributes which I have in my mind as permanent premises about circles and triangles.  At every moment in the course of an intellectual experiment we are subsuming passive or irrelevant details[2] under the thought which is active and essential.  And thus, not only is subsumption the instrument of construction at every point, but the main inference itself, being separable into an active principle and a passive detail, assumes the aspect of a subsumptive relation in the moment in which the mind perceives it.  If the principle will carry one passive matter it will carry another ; even if its application is unique, we per-

---

[1] I am forced to neglect many of Mr. Bradley's most interesting subtleties, if I would not comment on him in a book longer than his own. Ultimately, he suggests, it would not be impossible to bring all inference within the category of subject and attribute.  Everything which is in any way conjoined can be taken as related within some subject.

[2] " Principles of Logic," p. 473.

force conceive of its being so as *per accidens;* and the potential universality of every principle strikes us as soon as we detect that there is a principle before us.

And the second reservation follows from this. Every inference which has once been made by experiment may be made again by subsumption. Though ·the major premise mentioned above [1] sounds ridiculous, yet it is not impossible to employ it; and in working by rule of thumb, *i.e.* under directions which have no ground for us but authority, we always employ such a major. "Multiply the second and third together, and divide by the first." I proceed to do so; and my inference that the result is the answer rests on my knowledge that I have conformed to a rule which I do not understand. At the very least, in a case like that of p. 275, we know that we may substitute any names of points in space for the letters which are employed in this instance. And if we apply a principle, not because we see it to be true in the case before us, but as a rule which covers every case that has certain marks, then we are subsuming. I am inclined to think that much common inference is really of this kind, and might be called "second-class inference;" even reaching a stage of degradation in which we know little more than that we have heard sounds which we are accustomed to hear, and in which we let pass a suggested inference because we are accustomed to let it pass. I therefore think that

[1] See p. 275.

in appealing to practice on the use of major premises Mr. Bradley invokes not only a good, but also a bad logical habit. The absence of a major premise often means, not that we employ construction, but that we infer without consideration, *i.e.* by subsumption under a form of series without criticism of its significance. We subsume under a principle of which we fancy ourselves to be reminded, but which we do not call to mind. I may indicate as a case of spurious subsumption or secondary inference, the appearance made by scientific truth in a law-court, where it counts as a mere matter of fact, and has to be taken on the evidence of witnesses. Consequently any applications of such truth made by judge and jury, are subsumptive of the matter which has interest for them under certain marks supplied by authority in rules furnished *ab extra*. Science taken on authority ceases to be science.

The more serious reservation which I have to anticipate here, and which I shall recur to, is that indicated by Mr. Bradley himself on page 479, and based on the other side of the fact which lay at the root of the two former reservations. As every inference contains irrelevant matter, so it contains an active principle. It is possible, as Mr. Bradley points out in the place to which I allude, to extract this principle and state it explicitly. It does not then become a major premise, but, nevertheless, it serves to distinguish what is relevant from what is irrelevant in the argument, and to exhibit the systematic ground that has compelled our assent. So far as I follow Mr. Bradley, I cannot agree with him that in logic the exhibition of the principle on which an argument rests can be a mere counsel of perfection to be disregarded at pleasure. When an argument is laid before us of which the principle is not thus exhibited, we are simply presented with an enigma. We are told, "Here are the data; here is my answer: *Nexus* or *Ground* I have none to show you." The Construction? Does not that give the *nexus?* On this head I shall have more to say. No doubt what Mr. Bradley calls the construction ought to give the nexus; but if it is a process apart from the perception or intuition, I do not see how it can do so, or how it can be more than a purely accidental aid, by way of suggestion, to the attainment of the ultimate intuition or perception. What we want, it seems to me, is an adequate and articulated statement of the Intuition itself.

In answer to the questions, then, "Is Subsumption the essence of all argument? and, further, is it indispensable to all argument?" I should first thoroughly agree with Mr. Bradley that subsumption is not the essence of all argument; both because subsumption cannot be employed outside the category of subject and attribute, and because in the syllogism itself the function which subsumes does not derive its own warrant from subsumption. If this were not so, we should fall into a progress to infinity, for the principle of any given syllogism would have to be taken out and stated as the major premise of a prior syllogism, in which the whole content of the given argument would appear as minor premise and conclusion.[1] The active principle of a syllogism is simply an apprehension by the intellect of a particular systematic connection, that of subject and attribute.

But, secondly, I should point out that subsumption, though not the essence of argument, is essentially connected with argument, and is constantly emerging. The process of interpretation, subsidiary to all inference and all construction, is subsumptive. Any argument whatever may be taken as a "second-class" argument in a subsumptive sense. As it may then be said to drop into the category of subject and attribute, this does not conflict with the above restriction of subsumptive inference to that category. These second-class subsumptive arguments are far more common than we are apt to suppose, comprising all that we think or calculate under direction, and because of authority; and much that we infer owing to habit.

And finally, though not a major premise, yet an explicit exhibition of ground and principle is indis-

---

[1] We may take the common argument, "Every man is mortal ; Socrates is a man, therefore Socrates is mortal." If we wish to justify the form or principle of this inference by subsumption, we must appeal to some such principle as "any rule which has a mark is true of what has the mark," and proceed, "'Every man is mortal' is a rule which has a mark," "Therefore," etc. ; and then we have to find a warrant for *this* subsumption.

pensable to every inference which claims to be called rational. It may be that such an analysis does not change the intellectual function, but only gives it self-consciousness. I am contending, however, for no ultimate or elaborate analysis, but merely for such a statement as will tell us beyond question what the course of the inference before us really is. Inference so nearly unconscious as to be without assignable ground, cannot possibly be considered *qua* inference in logic, simply because we cannot get at it or say what it is. In such a case the application of analysis really changes the inference altogether, because it alters the ground presented to the intellect. I do not deny that we may comment on "unconscious inference" in Logic or in Psychology ; but if the ground of argument is not merely dim and unnamed, but wholly undistinguishable, then I think the inferential character has really vanished, we have left the sphere of thought, and arrived at that of habit or instinct. "Unconscious Inference," if not a contradiction in terms, must mean inference the ground of which we cannot readily name. The characteristics of this growingly irrational habit are not to be transferred to the statement in black and white of the course of intellectual apprehension. By so doing we omit, instead of dragging to light, the essential element (always dimly present) of ground or reason, and give the lie to the actual fact of our own intellectual procedure. In contending for an explicit statement of ground as essential to inference, I am thus only submitting to a necessity of scientific treatment. I know very well that the ground or process is often too dim to be put down in black and white; but this does not give the right to represent an inference in black and white without a ground at all. Say, if you like, that many inferences cannot be represented on paper; I will agree to this. But do not represent an inference on paper, and in doing so, omit, because you cannot represent *it*, the element which constitutes its essence as inference. The right course is plain. In logic we must treat of typical inferences. We must explain and describe as best we can, how, by the shading off of thought into feeling, many inferences cannot be brought under these types without giving their details a degree of definition which in actual use they do not possess. We may speak of an "implicit centre" if we bear in mind that what is implied is somehow indicated to the intellect in inferences, *not* merely detected subsequently by the logician's microscope. We must not allow the gradations of consciousness in inference to betray us into erecting so general a type of argument that it omits all the characters that distinguish thought from feeling.[1]

---

[1] Closely allied to the question of unconscious inference is that of the connection between proof and discovery. I am quite unable to see how, in essence, the two processes can be separable. Unproved discovery is discovery of what? Not of a fact or truth, for *ex hypothesi* it is not known to be fact or truth. It is plain that the gradations are merely from sugges-

3. Before leaving this question of the necessity of subsumption in inference, I will refer again very briefly to Aristotle. I trust that I am not one of those whose interest in the views of an ancient author centres on denying the originality of a modern one. I say expressly that if we needed, as I think we did, the modern writer to show us what there is in Aristotle, then, though Aristotle might claim priority, *our* debt to the modern is not diminished thereby.

It may be—I can hardly form an opinion—that Aristotle thought the subsumptive syllogism the universal type of argument. Subsumption, however, does not express his view of the connection which is established by, and which justifies, inference. As I have pointed out above, his faith in the syllogism was due rather to an unattainable ideal of the relation between subject and attribute, than to the treatment of all argument as a mere combination of the given, by help of marks. His opinion might be non-natural, or even wrong if, as I think probable, he really contemplated that the middle term or ground should always be such as could be extracted and stated for purposes of reason-

tion and conjecture to reasonable hypothesis and then proof. And if discovery is to be identified with suggestion or guesswork, then discovery is *not inference ;* unless we regard (as we ought) the *ground* of suggestion or guess as conferring a certain probability however slight. Then, *as supported by this ground*, the discovery is inference, but is thus, obviously, also the lowest grade of proof, and, apart from the element of proof in it, is not discovery at all.

ing as the condition of a rule. But as to the act of Intuition or intellectual Perception which forms, as Mr. Bradley rightly maintains, the essence of Inference, I do not think that Aristotle is wanting in clearness; nor do I think that any one who had made the best use of the Posterior Analytics ought to have had much to learn, *in this particular respect*, from "Principles of Logic." And I am inclined to insist on this point, because I think that in one way Mr. Bradley has gone beyond what is necessary; I mean in the demand for a construction, and in the use of the term "experiment."

Aristotle's view seems to me to be simple, and to be sufficient. You obtain, he says in effect, scientific knowledge, when you come to be aware that a certain principle is present, and forms the connection of content which is before you. It does not matter, in his eyes, how you come to be aware of such a principle. It may be suggested to you by a comparison of hundreds of instances; or if you are lucky and wise, a single instance may give you the required connection. According to the familiar passage,[1] which I paraphrase freely, if you had the good luck to be standing on the moon when the earth came between it and the sun, then, supposing you had your wits about you, you could hardly fail to learn the cause of the eclipse; though, strictly speaking, the knowledge would be got by you *out of* your sight of the earth's disc, and your seeing the

---

[1] Anal. post. II., p. 90, a. 24. Compare I. p. 87, b. 39.

disc would not be the same thing as your learning the cause of the eclipse. And so in the earlier passage (see note) Aristotle has said, using precisely the same illustration, that, being on the moon, you would nevertheless not *see* the *cause*, but would no doubt find it out if you saw the eclipse often under such conditions. And when you thus find out a cause, your act of sight is accompanied by a judgment (*νοεῖν*, I think, always means to apprehend *rationally, i.e.* in my sense of the word, to judge), that the connection is universal. It might be thought that to insist thus on the judgment or intuition, is to neglect a mark of inference on which Mr. Bradley insists, "that an inference is *made*, not merely given or seen." I shall recur to this point when I attempt to show that construction is not really an element in inference.

I conclude these few words about Aristotle by recalling the well-known definition of the syllogism as "discourse in which certain things being given, something else different from them necessarily follows from their existence." There is nothing here about subsumption ; nothing that conflicts with Mr. Bradley's account of inference in general or, at all events, of three-term inference.

May we not suppose that Aristotle's chief demand was that you should always say on what ground you go, whether this was really a given rule, or a principle perceived *de novo* in the act of inference? I may subjoin that the apodeictic definition seemed to him the equivalent of a syllogism, and of course in this there could be no question of subsumption.

4. I now pass on to the positive part of Mr. Bradley's account of Inference, which I have 'stated in a few words on p. 276, and need not repeat in detail. The criticism which I wish to urge amounts to this, that "Construction," "Preparation," "Experiment," the phrases by which Mr. Bradley indicates the first step in inference, do not express an element or phase in the inference as such, but only inchoate and imperfect stages of the final intuition itself, usually encumbered with false starts and attempts which have ultimately to be discarded as irrelevant.[1]

I may state my view as follows. I understand that as a step of Inference,[2] Construction corresponds to Experiment or Preparation,[3] and all these processes are resolvable into either Synthesis or Analysis or both. Upon this previous step or stage Intuition or Perception follows as a result. Now it appears to me that Synthesis and Analysis are beyond a doubt characteristics of the Intuitional judgment or perception itself. I do not think that the chapter on the Final Essence of Reasoning which explains that synthesis and analysis are

---

[1] *Cf.* "Principles of Logic," p. 235. "In the first place a process, and in the second place a result." I suppose the process is separate and comes first in time, *cf.* p. 452. "The preparation which precedes the final intuition."

[2] See pp. 397, 398.          [3] *Cf.* p. 412.

different sides of a single operation, and actually shows conclusions got by their means, can leave any hesitation on this point. But if so, what becomes of the distinction between the preparatory process and the final Intuition? It seems to me that this distinction must be rejected, or at least thoroughly modified, and that we are driven back upon the Aristotelian view, that the perception of necessity is the inference, and that you may get it as you best can. "But," Mr. Bradley may rejoin, "the process of getting at it, *plus* the final perception, *is* the Inference." I reply, "Not so, if you mean the historical or actual process of getting at it. That is psychological and accidental. My mistakes, the guesses I make and reject, do not enter into the final inference. The inference is the true or ideal process by which I get at the intuition, *and by which I had a right to get at it.* This is relevant from beginning to end, and all its steps are elements which are taken up into the final intuition. If, as is possible, we have begun with a tentative construction, we have in finally inferring to go back upon it and reject much as irrelevant. *And all that is relevant has itself been made by the intuition in its progress.*"

I will try to illustrate my point by commenting on Mr. Bradley's salient expressions for the prior stage of inference, "Construction," "Experiment," "Preparation." I think that the ordinary meaning of these words, more especially of "Experiment," is misleading, and that Mr. Bradley may mislead even if not misled.

Construction is popularly, no doubt, distinguished from proof, and experiment from observation ; as if construction were separable from proof, and experiment from observation.  This impression, which is in strictness wholly false, is confirmed by the existence of tentative construction and random experiment.  We may make a mistake in a construction and have to go back and begin over again.  The first construction was then tentative.  We may combine certain elements without a *reasonable* purpose (for even a child in playing with gunpowder has some desire to see what will happen, and so *some* purpose); if not, what is done could not be called experiment, but would count as mere accident.  Such dealing with things might be called comparatively random experiment.  Absolutely random experiment, like absolutely tentative construction, is a contradiction in terms ; we cannot experiment without at least wanting to see what $a$ and $b$ will do if put together, or construct without knowing what lines we are to draw.

But the purpose of a construction or experiment may be vague or erroneous compared with the true purpose which emerges when we come to appeal to it in our proof.  Therefore construction and experiment respectively have a fictitious existence apart from proof and observation.  We can imagine ourselves drawing lines or combining elements for no definite purpose, but merely to see what will happen, and we forget that no

U

line or element is of use to an argument which does not represent a step in the proof or a feature in the observation required. Construction and experiment are logically simultaneous with proof and observation, not prior to them. The priority of constructions in Euclid is of merely educational convenience, and would be quite impossible if the proofs had not been made beforehand by a mathematician who stands to the reader as teacher to learner. We are directed to draw such and such a line not in general to see what will happen, but because we already know (or our teacher already knows) of a matter in the proof which needs to be pictured in such a way. You cannot begin your construction till you know your line of proof. It may be said, "The *data* or premises of inference supply you with the rule for putting them together; that is at least the beginning of your construction." I answer that *if*, as in the cases given in many logic books, the proof is transparent from the beginning of the whole process, then no doubt you are safe in putting the *data* together as they are given, and the doing so is the initial step of the intuition itself. But if there is a complicated matter to use, some of which may be irrelevant, your constructions remain tentative until you have hit off the construction that brings you to a proof; it is only this construction that enters into the Intuition, while what you have drawn tentatively does not enter into this construction.

The same is true of experiment. The only essential

of experiment is definite observation ; *i.e.* observation under thoroughly known conditions. The fact that we interfere to produce the conditions of observation does not in itself distinguish the perception so gained from any other perception. Chance may send me a fly on the leaf of a Sundew, and may furnish me with neater instances than I could have devised of typhoid fever pursuing all the ins and outs of a certain milk supply. One may even hear the exclamation, "There is a beautiful experiment, and without the trouble of making it."

The phrase "ideal experiment" appears to me to have first struck Mr. Bradley as an explanation of the peculiarity of "supposal," in the passage which deals with the significance of the hypothetical judgment.[1] And this is quite consistent with the part subsequently assigned to "ideal experiment" in inference, for it is in the hypothetical judgment that inference according to Mr. Bradley, first definitely emerges. I wish to examine the idea conveyed by this comparison of inference, or of a stage in inference, to experiment. Supposal is experiment, as I understand, because, (i.) It is an operation upon the real, (ii.) is not yet judgment, but preparatory to judgment, (iii.) is voluntary, made for a purpose.

I take it that these are the main grounds on which Mr. Bradley subsequently designates the first process of

---

[1] "Principles of Logic," pp. 85–6.

inference, or at times inference as such (for experiment may be taken to include the perception subsequent on it), as "ideal experiment."

In my opinion, "ideal experiment" is a contradiction in terms; and the difference which makes experiment distinguishable from observation or judgment does not exist if you transfer experiment to the medium of thought; being, in fact, merely the difference between construction or operation in the medium of thought, and construction or operation in the medium of the material world.   Experiment (i.) is no doubt popularly taken as involving modification of reality.   But *in this sense* it means especially and distinctively modification of material things by actual mechanical operation.   When this is excluded by the term "ideal" the differentia of experiment is gone.   It is quite true that we do find experiment spoken of as a peculiar method of science, because of the pre-eminent accuracy and plasticity of the observations which it furnishes.   But in this sense it amounts to a species of observation only, and it would be well perhaps if logical text-books made this fact clearer.[1]   "Instance" is a term which renders the essence of the matter, and omits the unessential differences which we connect with "experiment" and "observation."   Ideal experiment is simply observation, apprehension, intuition.   The essence of the *comparison*

---

[1] Professor Jevons, quoting Herschel, "Principles of Science," p. 400, is perfectly clear on this point.

between inference and experiment is gone when we add "ideal" to the latter.

And (ii.) with the mechanical operation on material things disappears the *preparatory* character. It is a confusion to compare the initial effort of judgment, the awakening synthetic intuition itself, with the mechanical contrivance which in an experiment precedes the perception of a result. For in experiment you have the mechanical interference *and* the gradual genesis of the synthetic perception *as well.* This intellectual preparation is as needful where we have arranged a contrivance to facilitate it, as where we are said to rely on purely ideal isolation. For all isolation, it cannot be too often repeated, is ideal, and ideal only ; experiment simply helps ideal isolation by the introduction of known in place of unknown elements. We must not compare the first step of inference with the mechanical preparations that facilitate observation, for those mechanical preparations do not correspond to this first intellectual step, but require it in addition and subsequently to them. We may if we like compare the awakening and growing perception which is inference, with the intellectual apprehension of conditions which guides the perception in an experiment ; but then we are simply comparing inference with inference ; the term "ideal" ceases to indicate a distinction between the two things compared ; and the illustration which I understand to be implied by comparing the first step in inference to experiment which is *preparatory* (while incipient judgment is *not*), and which is *not ideal* (while incipient judgment *is*), becomes an admitted confusion.

And (iii.) the differentia consisting in "special purpose" and voluntariness is owing to the same error. All thought demands will and moral purpose, but is guided in addition by rational or intellectual necessity. *Moral* purpose cannot *guide* thought, and, if it attempts to do so, becomes caprice. Thus, assuming the general will and desire to attain truth, we are as a rule in thinking not conscious of a specific moral initiative. We are guided by necessity, and cannot think just as we please. But as we descend into the province of mere fancy, or mere rhetoric, special purpose, which is here caprice, becomes somewhat emancipated from rational necessity, and emerges as a guide of thought. We may choose how we will illustrate a familiar doctrine or a favourite idea. Such choice is *pro tanto* irrational; it is only possible by defect of rational necessity. Now, all operation on the external world of course involves choice, initiative. No doubt in arranging an experiment we have postulates of knowledge to conform to, but our particular acts are freely initiated by the will as a means to the intellectual perception which we aim at. It is this free initiation, which is in itself irrational and of a nature opposed to that of intellectual insight, that forms the ground of comparison between supposal and experiment. Capricious supposal is possible, but is at the opposite intellectual pole to complete or rational thought. And yet it is the element of caprice in supposal which alone enables it to be compared, as "thinking for a special purpose," with the arrangements of experiment. It is obvious that we ought not to erect such a character as this into the differentia of universal judgments and of inference.

In short, if you take common experiment in the sense of the definite perception which it renders possible, then it is wholly ideal, is not preparatory to judgment, and is not for any special purpose except to think as intellectual necessity compels. If you take common experiment to be operation on nature, then it is not ideal, *is* preparatory and specially initiated, but in this sense can have no parallel in the sphere of true thought and only finds a counterpart in the irrational element of caprice which prevails in fancy, rhetoric, or in exposition *de haut en bas*.[1] You cannot combine the predicates preparatory and ideal. As you begin to suppose you begin to judge, and in reaching your supposition you reach the result *pari passu*.

Thus, as Construction in an Inference is merely an accidental aid to proof, so ideal Experiment in Inference

---

[1] The comparison of supposal with experiment has more meaning than the comparison of inference with experiment, because the arbitrary character which is a point in the comparison has the result that you need not believe your supposal to be true. As bearing upon the classification of judgments the point is dealt with in chap. i. *supra*, where it is discussed how far judgments imply the existence of their subjects.

is merely a feature of synthetic intuition ; neither construction nor ideal experiment are possible or significant
except as the initial stages of the systematic perception
or insight itself.   It makes, therefore, to my mind, no
difference whether you construct or experiment actually
and materially or not.   For, however much you may
construct or experiment materially, you must also
construct and experiment ideally as well.   And therefore I differ from Mr. Bradley's view as expressed on
page 238, from which I quote as follows :—" A is ten miles
north of B, B is ten miles east of C, D is ten miles north
of C ; what is the relation of A to D ?   If I draw the
figure on a piece of paper that relation is not inferred ;
but if I draw the lines in my head, in that case I reason.
In either case we employ demonstration, but only in the
latter do we demonstrate logically."   In the same way,
on page 236 he contrasts ideal preparation with outward
preparation or experiment.

Surely this distinction is quite groundless.   I may
make a futile construction in my head, or I may draw a
relevant one on paper.   I may surely get an inference
even by " following " a printed figure which is furnished
to me.   " Ah ! " it may be replied, " then you mean that
you reconstruct ideally on the pattern of the given
figure ; in that case you do construct in your head."   Of
course I do ; and I therefore maintain that whether the
lines are drawn on paper for me or by me or not at all
makes no possible difference, nor is it even necessary

that I should get the required inference if I do put the lines together in my sensuous imagination.  To under-stand their connection I must more or less represent them, but I may quite well represent them without understanding their connection.  In *both* cases, it appears to me, *if* there is demonstration *of a connection*, it is logical demonstration, and if not, it is not logical.  In the one case there is an additional element, an external aid to definite representation, which in the other case we dispense with.  But in both cases the inference consists in the intuition which sees how the lines *must* go (the mere drawing them results from this and does not give it), and therefore how A must be related to D.

A confusion, as I think it, is possible at this point ; and I mention it because it illustrates the distinction upon which I desire to insist.  I also incline to suspect that it has affected Mr. Bradley's view.  His distinction *might* be interpreted thus : " Draw the figure on paper, and you can then get your result by simple measure-ment, which is not inference.  But draw it in the mind, and measure in the mind, and such measurement is inference, because it follows from properties imputed to a content by an intellectual act."  I admit the second clause of this distinction ; I deny the first.  You can *not* obtain your conclusion, as the result of the *data* before you, by actual drawing *plus* simple measurement. The simple measurement is valueless for inference except as flowing from known properties of the figure.

You can get no conclusion by simple measurement of distances in a geometrical diagram. In elementary cases this distinction is obscured. But it is always there. Suppose a question arises as to a projected building, "Will a wall A B seriously obstruct an ancient light L ?" It is an obvious experiment to put up a hoarding where the projected wall would stand ; and then it becomes possible to see directly what amount of light would be cut off by the wall. Nevertheless, a conclusion thus obtained cannot be justifiably attached to the original datum, the projected wall A B, without our bearing in mind that the wall has been represented by a hoarding, and allowing for any error which might conceivably arise from this substitution. And thus, formally, the conclusion as applicable to the projected wall is got by inference—by inference from the attributes in virtue of which the hoarding does duty for the wall. The actual experiment does not dispense with the ideal nexus.

Now make the case stronger. We may say, "We will build the wall A B, and let them come upon us for damages if the light is enough obstructed to make it worth their while." Here we are on the border line between the sequence of inference and the sequence of fact. As a matter of curiosity, we may still regard what we are doing as an experiment for the sake of inference, as an experiment to try whether the projected wall A B will interfere seriously with the light

L. But also, at the same time, we are acting so as to initiate a sequence of fact ; for the wall we are going to build will subject us to legal liability for any obstruction which it may cause, whether it corresponds to the originally projected wall A B or not. Thus we have here, in one and the same case, the illustration of inference which gives a result about the datum, and also of direct perception which gives a result only about the new state of things which our act brings to pass. From the ideal point of view of our curiosity, if we take the built wall $a\,\beta$ as typical of the original designed wall A B, the perception or result, "$a\,\beta$ is a serious obstruction," may be attached as an inference or conclusion to the original datum A B in the form, "A B, our projected wall, was such as to be a serious obstruction." But from the actual point of view of our legal position, this original datum has become a matter of indifference, and the actual resulting liability depends on the wall which has been built, and not on its correspondence with that which was projected. Thus we have here a direct judgment founded on a new state of the facts, and not applicable as a conclusion to any former datum or premise. The judgment of degree of obstruction caused by the built wall in this instance answers to the judgment which would be obtained by measuring distances on a diagram in Euclid. In both cases you gain a simple fact, but you cannot refer it beyond the case in which you have obtained it. It is not a conclusion of inference except in the sense in which all measurement or estimation is so.

Now, applying this distinction to Mr. Bradley's view in the passage quoted above from page 238, I say that if you build *the* wall, or draw *the* figure, and ascribe a conclusion read off from them to the datum, by correspondence with which the building or drawing is *the* wall or *the* figure, then your conclusion is got at by a complex synthetic judgment, merely aided by a visible or tangible illustration. There is nothing in such a case to contrast or to compare with supposal and inference, for the virtue of the conclusion in it depends on supposal and inference, and the process is ideal from beginning to end. The operation on Nature which it involves does not enter into its ideal character, which subsists along with and in addition to that operation. But if, after describing a certain datum, you proceed to build *a* wall or draw *a* group of lines, and then by simple inspection or measurement establish relations observable in reference to that wall or that group of lines—if this is all, then the back of the inference is broken ; the result of the process *is* a simple fact, but is not capable of being ascribed to the original datum ; for the building or drawing is itself taken as a fact and not as typical of the datum.

Here, then, Mr. Bradley's distinction does apply. Drawing lines on paper in this sense does exclude inference ; not because the lines are drawn on paper, but because they are not used as an aid to supposal or ideal connection. And it is therefore possible to make a contrast or comparison, and say that inference consists in, or at least requires, doing in the mind what in the instance before us is done in brick or on paper. Only this comparison is not the comparison which the tenour of the passage and Mr. Bradley's habitual identification of supposal and inference with ideal experiment, appear to me to require. It is not a comparison between two modes of obtaining a result about certain data, or a *result*—as implying a starting-point and process—at all. We must not say, "*the* figure." What we draw is *a* figure. The relations which we may find in such *a* figure are not predicable of the original data. One event, the building or drawing, happens first ; another event, the inspection or measurement, happens afterwards. The second gives a result with reference to the first, but not related to any attributes typified or embodied in the first. When Mr. Bradley writes, "If I draw the figure on a piece of paper, the relation is not inferred," I had thought that he meant, "The relation is got, but not by inference." But he ought to mean, and perhaps does mean, that the relation, *as a relation between the terms set out in the data*, is not got at all. But then what becomes of the comparison between supposal or ideal experiment, and experiment which is not ideal ? The fact is, that all experiment is ideal.

Now the mere sequence of events, which is not experiment and does not "demonstrate" anything about anything in particular (for the supposed measurement does not issue necessarily from any known attributes of the figure), is the only term of comparison which has the characteristics that Mr. Bradley's identification requires. In the mere sequence of events you may make a thing, and then look at it. Superficially, in rational construction and experiment you seem to make a thing and then look at it. And therefore Mr. Bradley transfers the relations of the mere sequence of events to rational construction and experiment. But I have tried to show, by looking at the same set of occurrences both as an experiment and as a mere sequence of events, that in true construction and experiment you do not make a thing and then look at *it;* but you look all through at your data, and only in looking at them, help your mind's eye by any device which will embody them visibly or tangibly. Therefore the basis of identification between the actual and the ideal process is wanting, and can only be supplied by a confusion. We confuse the comparison between an operation of thought and an operation on Nature with the comparison between an operation of mere thought and an operation of thought identically the same when facilitated by suggestions drawn directly from perception, it may be by help of operation on Nature. We thus transfer to an activity of judgment characteristics which can only belong to isolated and successive acts of will, and so supposal is not illustrated by experiment, for in experiment things are not combined as in supposal but only to assist in supposing. Judgment is the essence of both processes, and it is idle to explain a thing by itself. The comparison is fascinating because it seems to adduce a simple, almost a spatial analogy, for an act of thought ; but the simplicity of the analogy is really obtained by confusing an act which does what supposal does, by means of supposal, with an act which has indeed no supposal in it, but then cannot obtain a result analogous to that which supposal obtains. The former is, to recur to our instance, the case in which we regard building our wall as a somewhat hazardous experiment, which will show us what kind and degree of obstruction makes one liable in damages. The latter is illustrated by the fact that the wall, when built, will have its legal conse- quences, whether we are curious to know them or not, and whether we consider it as proving something about degrees of obstruction or not.

In short, the difference between logical demonstra- tion and any demonstration which is not logical is not the difference between showing in imagination or con- ception and showing to perception, but between showing a definite nexus and showing an isolated, *i.e.* indefinite fact. Mr. Bradley opposes the use of " demonstrate " in the anatomical lecture-room to the logical use. I regret that I cannot speak with certainty of the technical usage to which he appeals ; so that I can only say this. *If* the demonstrator says, " The nerve x, as you see, starts from A, ramifies at B, and supplies C, and therefore is affected by both D and F, and controls G," he is demonstrating logically, though every step may appeal to perception. Demonstration, or showing, only ceases to be logical when it ceases to aim, by whatever means, at evoking in the intellect an ideal nexus of attributes.

I should think the demonstrator must often demonstrate logically, though in difficult dissection it may no doubt be a sufficient achievement to get a nerve or other part clearly separated and hold it up to view. But in virtue of the distinctness of the resulting perception and the skill and knowledge which have gone to the separating activity, the resulting perception, even when this is all, will generally have much of the significance of true logical showing. It is understood that what you are displaying is the true natural or normal structure of the part, or else of course an abnormal growth, which is to be noted and considered. Now, here you are at least striving after a connection, an establishment of general knowledge about structure as such. And you can be right or wrong; every physical severance that you effect implies a judgment. And therefore what you are attempting corresponds in its degree to the logical demonstration which displays the true connection of parts in a geometrical diagram; and not to a mere measurement which issues from no normal or typical relation of the figure.

Thus I cannot consent to treat Ideality as the differentia which separates inference or any step in it from other processes comparable with it.

The idea of such comparable processes is only obtained by including inference and ideality in them ; and apart from these characteristics the processes in question (" construction," " experiment," " demonstration," as performed by a " demonstrator ") are not comparable with inference, and do not illustrate any of its properties. I doubt, indeed, whether, in this sense, such processes really exist, and I have attempted to explain how they come to be spoken of as existing.

" Preparation " has something of the same ambiguity which I noted in Construction and Experiment. Preparation, which, if I may use the phrase, is truly preparatory, takes place according to general rules not determined at all closely by the nature of the particular details which are to be shown. Thus I may be pretty safe in grinding a piece of bone very thin and mounting it in balsam *before* looking at it with the microscope. Such preparation *is* a detached process previous to inspection or intuition, but is not a parallel to anything that could enter into Inference, for the reason assigned above, that in Inference the whole process is throughout relevant to the particular result, and such preparation is not. Or, if we like, we may call it relevant to the first rough perception which tells me that this object must at least be made transparent, and parallel to such an element of inference as the decision that a certain problem must be dealt with mathematically. This is a judgment and a beginning of inference, not a prior and separable process ; it goes to determine the shape of the ultimate conclusion.

Another kind of Preparation, indeed—say, displaying a difficult fibre with the needle under the lens—is a good parallel for what goes on in Inference ; for in this process, as we saw to be the case with construction, the arrangement of material and the discovery of that which is made visible go hand in hand, and the former is guided at every step by the progressive revelations of the latter. If, indeed, the active interference stops before all is seen, and gives place to mere inspection through the lens, then the preparation is *pro tanto* of the former class, for it has then been merely tentative as regards the final result of inspection. However, the needle may at any moment have to be applied again, just as we may at any moment have to go back on our construction. And the illustration I have used makes the matter especially clear, for in one important respect, the adjustment of the high-power lens, which enables us to do consciously and with extreme difficulty what common seeing does easily and unconsciously—in this respect intuition and perception are here accompanied to the very end by the external facilitating activity of construction, experiment, or preparation.

5. The unity which I thus claim for the inferential

intuition leads me to differ from Mr. Bradley on a further point.   Mr. Bradley says that the number of terms in inference is not limited to three, but that you may use as many as you can ; that, in short, the limit is psychological, not logical.   It is not easy to be sure what "one" term is any more than to be sure what " one " idea is. But I think that every step in the construction is a conclusion, and that for every conclusion, as for the final perception, we think of some content having unity as the ground.

Mr. Bradley's geographical instance above[1] alluded to is, no doubt, very neat from his point of view. By apparently deferring any attempt to draw a conclusion till C D is in position, the construction avoids the rather awkward determination of the length of the diagonal from A to C.   But none the less the determinate position of C *is* a conclusion, although, as we mean to cancel the element which makes it hard to reduce to figures, we take this conclusion in the form which keeps separate the element to be cancelled and the element to be retained.   C is ten miles south, and then ten west of A ; by taking D ten miles north of C, we destroy, for D, the ten miles south of A, and the ten miles west remain. This rather proves the unity of the whole process, and the fact that every step in the construction, *as it is finally*

---

[1] p. 296.

*taken up into the proof*, is dictated by the nature of the final Inference, which the author, nevertheless, speaks of as subsequent to the construction. The " three terms " of an inference are, in the last resort, simply the data, their principle of unity, and the special application of that principle which a given interest dictates. The several data of Mr. Bradley's conundrums do not correspond to the terms of an inference as such.

I draw in my own mind confirmation of the above remarks from the excellent chapters of Mr. Bradley's work [1] which deal with synthesis and analysis. Here, it seems to me, we have the entire process of Inference represented as one, and its elements, synthesis and analysis, drop into their proper place as complementary aspects of the same operation. I am aware that the analysis which appears as elimination in the final intuition may not be one with the analysis which accompanies or replaces synthesis in the middle operation, which is, as a rule, constructive. At the same time, when we have learnt that analysis and synthesis are always correlative to each other, and that they appear both in the middle and in the final operation, and when we have examined the schemes of synthesis and analysis respectively, as given on page 433, it is hard to resist the conclusion that the division into construction and intuition, together with the importance attached to such phrases as preparation and ideal experiment, might

---

[1] " Principles of Logic," book iii., part i., chaps. iv. and vi.

be got rid of, and an account of inference given which would be clearer *ab initio*, if the author were to start again from the point reached in these chapters.

The whole matter seems to me to hinge on what the author calls (page 237) "the selective action." This, to my great surprise, he there denies to be of the essence of inference;[1] and I judge from the context that he says so because elimination may be dispensed with in the final act of intuition. Surely this is no reason. Selection is not a question of quantity, but of intention ; and if sometimes, in an extreme case, I *choose* to take my whole construction as my conclusion, it is little better than an equivocation to say that I do not *select.* The essence of the matter is purpose in accepting and the power to reject. And in this choice or "selective connection," it seems to me that we have the ultimate nature of inference and unity of synthesis and analysis. In fact, if the final intuition need not be a selection, still the construction or preparation must. "The dropping of part" (of the sensuous mass), Mr. Bradley says on page 437, "is the forced selection of the part which remains." Exactly ; and the selection of part is the enforced dropping of the part which is left.

Synthesis and analysis seem to me to mean ultimately that you select one thing because you want it,

---

[1] Indeed, I doubt if this statement is reconcilable with the context in which (p. 330) I find the phrase "selective perception of one connection of attributes throughout our whole subject-matter." I should naturally read this latter passage as indicating an essential of inference.

and reject another because you do not.  The names are, therefore, after all, names of formal aspects of almost any operation which deals with things or thoughts.  The essence or root of the matter is in the particular reason which makes the intellectual apprehension take this and leave that.  Such a reason can only be found, I imagine, in the perception of a principle or nexus which combines differences in an identity.  Wherever we apprehend such a principle in its differences as controlling and dominating them, we have the esssentials of inference. I mean, for instance, when we see that under a given formula and with certain values assigned to the terms of the formula a curve must be drawn in a certain way.[1]

6. Finally, it may be said, as I anticipated above, that to reduce inference to a perception of principle

---

[1] In the account of Synthesis and Analysis, as elsewhere, I find a certain difficulty in Mr. Bradley's reliance on unexplained spatial metaphors. Analysis is distinguished from Synthesis by "not travelling beyond the area which is given it at the beginning." "Analysis is the internal synthesis of a datum." "The whole precedes, and is followed by its internal relations." I suppose the distinction is to be practically interpreted by the author's instances, in which analysis starts from a datum represented by a single name, synthesis from two names.  Then analysis is to keep within the meaning of the word which indicates its datum, while synthesis is to find a whole which the two or more data may be "within." But suppose the single datum offered to analysis has the character of a whole in space, and our analysis deepens our conception of it, and reveals new functions and powers in it, have we then gone "beyond its area" or not?  In examining a crystal, or an embryo, or a common plant-cell, we should be apt to give ground for such a question.  The point is, however, of no practical importance, as Mr. Bradley agrees with me, that even if a function may be analytic or synthetic *par excellence*, the two characters imply each other.

contradicts an important attribute of inference on which Mr. Bradley insists—that inference is *made*, not merely *seen ;* that it is a process, is something which *we do* to the data.   I admit the attribute, but venture to allege a confusion in Mr. Bradley's account of it.   "Made" may mean "new-made," or simply "not given."   I believe that to require inference to be new-made is a confusion of psychology with logic, such as is involved in making familiarity the distinguishing mark of analytic judg- ments and novelty of synthetic.   In that case a judg- ment by the act of being made must become analytic ; and so an inference, if the same test were followed, by the act of being made would cease to .be an inference. In other words, only discovery would be inference, and proof would not.   This, as I have shown above, is an untenable distinction, and if carried out would extinguish inference altogether.   In our ordinary somewhat care- less way of distinguishing we should have ill-supported conjecture left as the only inference, and proof excluded. It is mere carelessness to make inference co-extensive with a fresh combination of data, and thereby to assign a purely psychological differentia which no familiar proof can possess.   A proof which is thoroughly familiar, and the whole course of which is transparently in the mind, surely does not thereby cease to be an inference. It is *made* in the sense of including a felt intellectual act, an effort by which the unity of differences is realized ; and I will not deny that in every proof—at least in every intricate proof—there may be psychologically a certain to and fro of the mind's eye within the steady insight which tracks out the essential nexus. But it is not essential to inference to be new-made, *i.e.* to be discovery; and it is my conviction that in so far as it remains discovery, and does not attain to proof, in so far as it falls short of the character which a familiar Euclidean proof has for a geometrician, just so far it fails to be inference at all.

Do I accuse Mr. Bradley of such a confusion as this? I have no alternative but to express my suspicion that he does make this confusion. I found the allegation partly on the antecedence attributed to experiment, construction, or preparation, as compared with the step of intuition, partly on the extreme emphasis with which the attribute of being *made*, not merely *seen*, is claimed for inference. There are two things in question, as I believe. One is the tentative synthesis or experiment, which is open to error and irrelevancy, and represents the first effort to realize and understand the combination of data which, *when understood, will* form the premises of proof. And there is the ultimate and successful act itself, the true synthesis which is no doubt built up by degrees, and usually with error and irrelevancy, but which cannot fairly have imputed to it, *qua* proof, the errors which were made before we reached it, as if these were a prior stage of itself. When complete, such an intellectual act is one; it takes up into itself all relevant steps, which are simply rudimentary judgments, early forms of the intuition itself, but it cannot have imputed to it any tentative processes which do not ultimately turn out to be relevant elements in the proof. The effort of tentative realization is not essential to inference, though the effort of continuous realization is. Thus, while I agree that inference is not *merely seen*, if this involves passivity of the percipient (which relatively, though not absolutely, it does), I do accept the challenge involved in the comparison, in so far that I would much rather compare inference to a single act of conscious vision than to two separate acts, the one antecedent to the other, of which the first is voluntary, like an operation on external nature, and only the second controlled by natural necessity.   If four roads meet, and we know some marks which distinguish the right one, but not yet seeing them are left to caprice to go first down which we will, none of this arbitrary character can be imputed to the final perception when we have got the right road.   The process of trying all the roads drops out of the nexus altogether ; the inference does not begin till we become aware of the marks on the right road, unless we insist on the slight disjunctive inference, which, for our present purpose, is no more than every ascertained error furnishes, in proving that it at least is not the truth.   Going down the wrong roads is the tentative experiment which is really free and prior ; seeing the marks of the right one is the inferential judgment conditioned *in fact* by our having come along the right road (a felicitous experiment), but drawing its evidence *not* from this chance, but from rational necessity, and therefore not *made* except as being *thought*.

Before I conclude these observations, it may be convenient that I should point out more definitely how I regard the problem of stating inference in logical form, if we are to abandon the major premise. We must then demand, I think, *either* an explicit declaration of the active principle which is present in the argument, as suggested by Mr. Bradley, *or* at least a careful statement of the construction employed, so as to exhibit the actual argument which is in fact taken as carrying the conclusion.

7. I have always understood the Syllogism, as considered in logical theory, to be an analysis of inference, itself subsequent to the inference, and bound to exhibit the actual nexus of reasoning which we are to take as having been employed. This function was discharged by the premises, whose form, together with the conventional position of the middle term, displayed the actual conclusion drawn as issuing from a certain specified reason. But in Mr. Bradley's instances of proof, I do not find the same analysis, or any substitute for it. I take a case from page 246. "A is due north-west of C because B is five miles south of A, and again, the same distance west of C." This is more like a conundrum

than an inference. If an inference of any complexity were stated thus, no one could be sure what the inference really was. For here is the point: you may make sure that the construction can produce the right answer, and we may try it and find that it does. But, for all that, such a statement does not tell us what inference is actually used. It furnishes data, not premises. The statement of an example in Colenso's arithmetic is not a statement of premises but of data. Data are the materials of proof; premises are its analysis. Here, for instance, by stating the number five miles you lead one to consider whether it would be different if the distance were ten miles. The real point is that the north-west line makes half a right angle with the meridian and also with the parallel of latitude, and therefore is the diagonal of a square erected on either. It is essential to point out that C A halves the angle between the parallel and the meridian, and therefore falls on the north-west line, if you are to explain how "five miles" can have to do with making any line go north-west. If in a more complex problem we did not envisage the matter in some such general way, but were guided, *e.g.* by the general look of some construction that we might light upon, our conclusion would be, in proportion as the ground was inexactly thought, more of a guess and less of an inference. Any one who thinks that a "construction" cannot deceive the judgment should read De Morgan's " Budget of Paradoxes."

More especially I wish to point out that many of Mr. Bradley's inferences are taken from what I may describe as the reading of a series, especially in the case of inferences from position in space and priority in time. So, too, he speaks of arithmetical calculation as "the movement of an ideal experiment which gives a judgment we had not got before." Now, the reading of a series is a process that may be carried on at the most various levels of reflection, and often drops without detection to a scarcely conscious activity. In calculation itself how much is done by "rule of thumb;" from the schoolboy who multiplies the second and third together and divides by the first, but sometimes vitiates his inference by a wrong arrangement of terms, to the computer who carries out lengthy calculations, the bearing of which he does not in the least understand! But in stating the nature of an inference, the precise degree in which we know the nature of the series which we employ is, of course, essential to the inference, for the nature of the series is the very core of the inference itself. I have not thought it worth while to allege that the position of the observer must be constant for "A to right of B, B to right of C," etc. But if we were making such an inference in a series whose nature was less familiar, we should have to begin by carefully establishing the character of the series, as one in which every term might safely be taken to indicate an advance upon the last in a constant direction. We should then probably read the series by rule of thumb, *i.e.* by accepting each conclusion as following from the mere observance of the form of the series.

Perhaps it may not be time wasted to insist upon the very different levels of inference which are compatible with arguing from a series, by help of a somewhat detailed example. I select for the purpose a process of measurement, perfectly simple, but such as might cost a moment's reflection to any one to whom it was unfamiliar, viz. the process of reading a measurement with a vernier. The vernier in the case I propose to consider is a movable rule nine inches long, and divided into ten parts of $\frac{9}{10}$ in. each. It is used by applying it to a larger scale divided into inches. Suppose now that you have measured an object with the larger scale, and find it to be between one foot and thirteen inches long, and you wish to measure the fraction of an inch, by which it exceeds one foot, more accurately. To do this you apply the zero point of the vernier to the point on the larger scale between one foot and thirteen inches, which the object reaches (the increasing numbers on the vernier being in the same direction as those on the larger scale), and then you look up the two scales for the point at which a division-mark on one is opposite a division-mark on the other. The number attached to that division-mark on the vernier will be the number of tenths of an inch by which the object which is being measured exceeds one foot. If this excess, for instance, is $\frac{4}{10}$ in., the vernier will have its mark 4 opposite to mark 16 on the larger scale, which is divided into inches. The reason is that the vernier has each of its divisions exactly $\frac{1}{10}$ in. shorter than a division of the inch-scale (being $\frac{9}{10}$ in. against 1 in.), and therefore any given number of tenths of an inch, *plus* the same number of divisions of the vernier, will make up a length of as many inches. Thus, obviously four divisions of the vernier (being $\frac{9}{10}$ in. each) *plus* $\frac{4}{10}$ in. = 4 in., or 4 in. *minus* four divisions of the vernier = $\frac{4}{10}$ in., which is therefore the measurement of the interval between the lower end (zero point) of the vernier and the next mark below on the inch scale, *i.e.* of the excess length of the object to be measured above that next mark below.

How far is it necessary to understand this simple process in order to carry out a measurement by it? The instance is of course purely illustrative, for as a matter of fact, no doubt every one who has ever used a vernier understands its principle. But theoretically, and to illustrate what might happen with more intricate processes, we may fairly suppose a child or workman, who has never seen the instrument before, to be merely instructed, " Put the mark o of the smaller scale at the end of the length to be measured ; look along the two scales till you find marks on each in the same straight line, and read off the number which belongs to that mark on the smaller scale." We need not even suppose that such an agent knows what the answer will indicate. To measure by help of such an instruction as this is clearly a subsumptive act; it is what I have called above a second-class inference. We do not understand the principle of the series which we employ, but we conclude from a rule with a condition, that what has the condition comes under the rule; here, that the number at the coincident marks is the number we are to record. I may add, as an illustration of the hazard of this inference, that if the vernier is loose instead of sliding on the larger scale, any one who knew nothing of it might apply it upside down, *i.e.* with the zero in the right place, but with the numbers running the wrong way; and then it would read the interval between the end of the object and the next *higher* division on the inch scale. I do not say that this error is practically possible, but it is an illustration of the consequences which are quite conceivable if we do not distinguish reading a series by rule of thumb (secondary inference), from the inference which can only be gained by a sound understanding of the principle on which the series depends. One cannot be said to use a primary or first-class argument in the instance I gave, unless one has observed the relation of one division of the vernier to one of the large scale, and the consequent equality of any number of divisions of vernier *plus* the same number of tenths of an inch to the same number of divisions of the larger scale. Unless this principle is consciously active in our inference, and is seen to be independent of the particular numbers employed, but dependent on the ratio between the two scales, our reading, however warranted by custom, is theoretically a hazardous conjecture. Our workman may even have got hold of two scales which have not the relation needed by his instructions, but some other; but he will be none the wiser and will take his readings quite contentedly.

This is the point of view the neglect of which I fear if we come to state inferences by simply throwing down the data and saying, "Put them together and you will find such and such a conclusion to result." I am not desiderating an antecedent criterion of the Validity of Inference. Mr. Bradley urges as a cardinal point of his view, that no such criterion is possible, and that in attempting to furnish an exhaustive list of forms which inference must take, traditional logic blunders as hopelessly as the ethics which claims to guide moral action. I fully agree with Mr. Bradley on both these heads, and have always believed that Kant's proof of the impossibility of a criterion of truth applies no less to Inference. Nevertheless, I persist in contending that we have no Inference which logic can consider, if our statement exhibits no emphatic answer to the question "Why?" I know that inference has in fact many degrees of consciousness, and I especially insist that all judgment involves inference, and therefore am not at all disposed to confine inference *in fact* to judgment which issues from a distinct and separate reason. But in taking instances of inference for logic it seems to me that we must make our reasons explicit, simply because otherwise we do not know what inference in particular we are talking about. The reason *is* the inference; and the premises if they are to be analyses of Inference must exhibit the reason. From such data as Mr. Bradley gives we cannot tell whether the argument is second-class and subsumptive, or first-class and constructive, or of a class in which nothing but subsumption is possible.

Do I, then, deny logic the right to represent the actual fact of inference, which, as I admit, sometimes has a very confused and all but latent ground ?  Not at all ; but I say that in speaking of such an inference, we must, if we mean to know what it is, *analyze* it first, though we may *describe* it as dim or indistinct afterwards. There is no appropriateness in trying to understand an obscure mental process obscurely.  If a friend says, in a picture gallery, " That picture is a Veronese," of course, apart from special knowledge, I have absolutely no clue to the ground of inference.  But if I want to make a logical instance of it, I must not treat it as an inference without a ground, but must cross-examine my friend, and elicit what I can of the reasons for the assertion, must assign them as the ground, but must add, "Of course cross-examination has made them more distinct ; what actually operated was perhaps little more than a feeling, or at best a very indistinct apprehension, of these peculiarities as characteristic of Paul Veronese."

Y

I believe that Mr. Bradley's observations on pages 479, 480, in which he admits that it is well to extract the active principle of every inference, if only we do not call it a major premise, place him in substantial agreement with me on this point.  But I cannot concede that such a process is optional, as he seems to think.  Only in as far as there is an apprehended source of necessity is there, to my mind, an inference at all ; and in as far as we fail to represent this in black and white when we state our premises, so far does the inferential character of the inference escape our analysis.

# CONCLUSION.

## THE IMMEDIATE PREMISE.

I WILL end with a word on the foundations of knowledge arising out of the instance of the vernier.

Too much, to my mind, has been said of late years about the immediate necessity of the ultimate judgments on which knowledge rests, and about the final dependence of science on the trained perception of the individual. I have expressed my dissent from this doctrine near the beginning of these remarks, and wish to insist upon it at their close. Trained perception is of course essential to science. And, though loaded with inference, yet such perception becomes so rapid and so sure, that to insist upon its inferential character seems pedantic. But there is much exaggeration and confusion upon this subject.

The trained eye *is* more accurate than the untrained eye ; but not to a degree which so much as tends to account for the value of scientific observation as compared with ordinary looking. In very precise measurement, *e.g.* with a micrometer, the coincidence of two visible marks is the ultimate fact of perception. No doubt the trained observer will establish a coincidence more exactly, or will estimate a small discrepancy far more precisely, than most untrained observers can. But this advantage is not the measure, is not in most cases an appreciable part of the measure, of the greater precision of his observation compared with that of the layman, *if the layman were left to describe his own observation.* If, on the contrary, the layman merely looks where he is told, and notes the coincidence of marks which a man of science tells him to note, and the observation is recorded and interpreted by the latter, then it is (barring a sheer blunder on the layman's part, to which, as I have shown, he is very liable if left to himself), in its main elements of significance, a scientific observation ; although the trained eye has not been employed. These elements consist in the knowledge to which the perception is relative. It is this that confers on the observation not only its import but also its precision.

As for the import, that is acknowledged, and I need not enlarge on it. A measurement, ultimately the perception that two marks coincide, is valuable of course solely by what it proves.

But that the *accuracy* of the perception depends on knowledge and on systematic relations is a less familiar. fact, and is worth insisting on, for it strikes at the root of the belief in immediate knowledge. It is only for convenience, and not from necessity (though convenience and necessity in these matters run into each other), that the more delicate instruments are usually made so that none but highly skilled observers can use them with effect. Every additional facility is an additional complication in the fabric of an instrument, and increases both cost and the hazard of inaccuracy. Thus, as a rule, very accurate instruments require highly skilled observers. But the accuracy of a result does not arise *directly* out of the observer's skill, but indirectly, because a skilled observer is able to use a very accurate instrument. The accuracy of the result, like its import, really depends on knowledge, and, if an instrument is used, *on the knowledge embodied in the instrument.* A great observer no doubt has this knowledge as a rule himself in its intellectual form, as well as embodied in his instrument, and therefore can control his instruments and allow for special or unexpected errors as no common man could, and *his* perception is a first-class inference. Whereas to an amateur or beginner the perception is a *second-class* inference ; *i.e.* he obtains it by subsumption under the rules given him by some handbook, or possibly by the instrument maker, for the use of his instrument. Thus the true man of science has an advantage, only not chiefly from his trained eye, but from his systematic knowledge. It is this that guarantees a perception, in itself often no harder than to read the time on the great dial of the Victoria clock tower, to be a measurement of the extremest attainable delicacy. We cannot get at the microscopic or telescopic world with the naked hand or eye. The perception " Such and such is the pattern on the envelope of this Pleurosigma," comes to us mediated by a most intricate system of embodied inference which alone warrants our faith in the simple interpretation of the image that has been so extraordinarily transformed. It was only to be expected, that, as has happened of late years, doubt should be cast on some portion of such a scheme of inference, and the laws of light should be invoked to show that all had not been seen which was believed to have been seen.

Or, to put the case otherwise, if we count the *mere* sense perception as the immediate judgment, then all that makes its accuracy may be treated as part of its import. That these micrometer divisions just include that fibre, we see ; that this fact measures the width of the fibre we infer, from knowledge or from authority. The mere immediate judgment, thus interpreted, would approach, as we were more strict in excluding knowledge external to it, more nearly to the mute sensation, and would lose all the determinants which make it a foundation of science. All accurate perception is mediate in virtue of the knowledge which guarantees its accuracy ; only the dim and indefinite feeling approaches immediacy.

It has always appeared to me that the element of

knowledge incorporated in our instruments of measurement and observation has met with insufficient recognition from logical theory, and that this neglect has
avenged itself in the doctrine of immediate perception.
What right have I to take a variously coloured band
several inches in apparent length as a representation of
the light admitted by a slit which I can hardly see?
If we concede that in using the very best reasoning
machine, we must ourselves *make* the conclusion, *i.e.*
read it off *as* a conclusion—and this is Mr. Bradley's
opinion, in which I agree—then I think that a spectro-
scope, or a fine compound microscope with all sorts of
illuminating devices, or even a first-rate chronometer,
is perhaps as truly a reasoning machine as any logical
apparatus that has been devised. The operations of
such an instrument are less typical and general than
those of the reasoning or calculating engine, but they
are more original, more plastic, more responsive to the
peculiarities of special material. The logical machine
can get a conclusion from any set of typical premises within the category of subject and attribute;
but it cannot take a ray of unknown composition that
looks homogeneous, and lay out its components before
the eye, so that their respective places, to any one
furnished with a scheme of the spectrum, even indicate
their names. In this comparison I am glad to say that
I am far from depreciating the work of the late
Professor Jevons; for if his name is peculiarly identified

with his ingenious logical machine, it is no less true that he has called special attention to the principles by help of which our instruments furnish us with exact measurements.[1]    Thus when Wundt concludes his treatment of physical measurements by observing that in all of them the ultimate limit of precision is given by the power of the eye, aided by optical devices, to measure a spatial interval, he means much less than he seems to mean.    Under the head of "optical devices" we must include every process of inference by which an accessible ocular perception can be taken in lieu of an inaccessible one.    Of course many principles besides optical principles are concerned in such substitutions.    When we read the fraction of a revolution from the graduated head of a micrometer screw, and infer that the screw has advanced by that fraction of the distance which a whole revolution would advance it ; we are really, I should suppose, relying on the uniformity with which, as we know by practice, such screws are habitually cut.    Theoretically, indeed, this does not impugn Wundt's statement, which may be taken as a truism.    Of course all measurement must involve sense-perception ; and of course where no perception can be obtained, we can no longer substitute the accessible observation for the inaccessible one.    But the implication which is introduced by speaking of the optical contrivances as if they were mere accessories to

---

[1] " Principles of Science," p. 282, ff.

sight, is absolutely false. Science does not rest on abnormal acuteness of perception, but on inferences drawn from perfectly normal perception. The power of vision for science is not in the least proportioned to its actual immediate penetration ; the structure of inference into which it enters is the main thing, and the acuteness of the observer's eye, though useful, is a subordinate element.

So it is with our immediate perceptions in the province of time and space. It is interesting to speculate about a natural small unit of time, such as the pendulum swing of the leg, by which, it may be, we habitually form for ourselves our lax personal ideas of duration. But men have always, with a strangely though justly reliant faith, adopted as the measure of time such processes as they conjectured or inferred to be uniform ; the changes which made the day, the lunation, and the year ; the flow of sand or of water, or the oscillation of a pendulum. Much might be said about the early history of the time-perception ; animal life is enough to show that many things which we now do in obedience to the measure of time would be done quite adequately without any such measure under the mere stimulus of appropriate conditions. Seed-time and harvest might be rightly employed, and the night be used for sleep, and the day for labour, without raising the question whether the recurrent intervals were of uniform duration. But my present point is merely that neither now nor in primitive times do men expect perception to estimate duration. The perception of duration is of interest for psychology, but has no place, and never had one, in practice. All that perception does is to compare the phases of the change which we wish to measure, with the phases (*not* directly with the duration) of the change which we select as a standard. The uniformity of our standard itself rests on inference, and inference alone.[1]

"Ah, yes!" I shall be told, "Time is a peculiar case, because its parts are successive ; but what about space ? Surely measurement of lengths in space is carried out by comparison with a fixed and constant standard, and without dependence upon postulates drawn from science ?" To illustrate the theoretical error of such a view, I transcribe Mr. Lockyer's account of the measurement of a base line for the triangulations of the British Ordnance Survey. "In the first instance, a base line was measured on one of the smoothest spots that could be found. One of those chosen was on the sandy shore on the east side of Lough Foyle, in Ireland ; the length of this line was measured with most consummate care by means of bars of metal, the length of which at a given temperature was exactly known, and was, at the time of observation, corrected for expansion or contraction due to variations of temperature. The bars were not placed close together, and the

_________________________

[1] *Cf.* Locke, "Essay," 2, 14, 16.

intervals between them were measured by means of microscopes. The base line by these means was measured to within a small fraction of an inch." The corrections mentioned may be simple ; yet, as it is only science that enabled them to be made, so it is only science that guarantees their adequacy.

Thus I hold that the immediate or unproved premise of proof is not merely unattainable in practice, but a contradiction in theory. Knowledge is not like a house built on a foundation which is previously laid, and is able to remain after the house has fallen ; it is more like a planetary system with no relation to anything outside itself, and determined in the motion and position of every element by the conjoint influence of the whole. I cannot think that we have a right to neglect these truths because they are so obvious, and were formulated more than two thousand years ago. They may have been too tediously reiterated without special constructive interpretation, and the positive qualities given in normal human perception may have been too much ignored. Thus we are right to welcome Lotze's account of "first universals," by which we are shown how entirely knowledge is dependent on what might be called the given generalities of sense. I only contend that the moment we begin to speak about precision we have quantity, when we have quantity we have a unit, where we have a unit we have a standard, and where we have a standard we become dependent upon a system of knowledge which endows this standard with all that constitutes its precision. And of course in higher forms of knowledge than quantity, in causation, for instance, or in teleology, we find our sense-perception still more obviously transfigured in the making, by a significance beyond itself.

We must not confuse psychological and logical necessity. It is true that every judgment is made because we cannot help making it ; but this is not the logical reason for making the judgment, only a psychological description of the effect which that reason produces. Therefore, to say that the ultimate basis of knowledge is in the necessity which attends each individual judgment, is to make a psychological fact into a logical ground. The logical reason which compels us in any judgment to judge so and not otherwise must be not a general and formal, but a special and individual necessity, relative to the individual judgment in question and to no other, and can only be found in the systematic relations of knowledge which at the moment form the totality of the intellect's world. If I have read Mr. Bradley right, he joins a thorough understanding of the ideal of knowledge[1] to a peculiar impatience of something, I do not quite know what, in the ordinary doctrine of relativity. I seem to remember a furious note[2] in

---

[1] A former work of Mr. Bradley's, " The Presuppositions of History," gives the best account known to me of the process by which *all* the parts of a whole can be criticised and adjusted *on the basis of each other.*

[2] " Ethical Studies," p. 61.

" Ethical Studies " which asks the common believer in the Relativity of Knowledge, whether he had a father, and how he reconciles his answer with his doctrine. I never quite saw the point of the question, but have always imagined that it must be in some distinction between fact and inference. In spite of Mr. Bradley's absolute judgment that all the past is for us an ideal construction, I seem to myself to be haunted by a similar distinction in " Principles of Logic ; " and I simply cannot understand what it does there, or in any European philosophy.

THE END.

PRINTED BY WILLIAM CLOWES AND SONS, LIMITED, LONDON AND BECCLES.